"This book must be regarded as prescribed therapy for every Business and IT leader that is struggling to climb the steep global sourcing learning curve."

—**Michiel Boreel**, *Vice President of Strategy, Sogeti*

"Outsourcing of information technology and business processes is now an established, and rapidly growing, practice. Yet, it is very difficult to do successfully. Based on work by the authors and their colleagues in 600 organizations throughout the world, Willcocks and Lacity present a comprehensive overview of the many types of outsourcing as they are practiced today. More important, they provide extremely insightful guidelines for the effective management of outsourcing. For anyone involved with outsourcing, this book is a 'must read'."

—**Jack Rockart**, *Senior Lecturer, Emeritus, MIT Sloan School of Management, Cambridge, MA*

"An excellent strategic view, coupled with the tactical prescription for successful global sourcing. Their research is the necessary combination of both rigor and relevance . . . bridging from the academic to the practitioner."

—**Ray Hoving**, *Ray Hoving Associates, past president of the Society of Information Management and CIO for Air Products and Chemicals*

"Much has been written about outsourcing over recent years, not all of it complimentary. But then, being polite doesn't seem to make good copy, disaster stories do. Again, most stories are anecdotal, supporting the writer's predetermined view on Outsourcing, opinions are generally polarised in favour, or against. So it is refreshing to see the subject attracting impartial academic scrutiny, based on research over a period of 17 years. The important lesson that emerges is that generally as the process matures, the early, perhaps disappointing experiences turn into activities that bring out the best in cost savings and also a partnership and sharing of skills between the two sides. This book will be an invaluable read for those thinking of outsourcing for the first time. Also required reading for those whose experiences of such an activity initially fall short of requirements."

—**Lord Renwick**, *President, The European Information Society Group*

Technology, Work and Globalization Series

Knowledge Processes in Globally Distributed Contexts   Julia Kotlarsky, Paul C. Van Fenema and Ilan Oslan

Global Sourcing of Business and IT services   Leslie P. Willcocks and Mary C. Lacity

Global Sourcing of Business and IT Services

Leslie P. Willcocks
and
Mary C. Lacity

palgrave
macmillan

First published in 2006 by
PALGRAVE MACMILLAN
Houndmills, Basingstoke, Hampshire RG21 6XS and
175 Fifth Avenue, New York, N.Y. 10010
Companies and representatives throughout the world.

PALGRAVE MACMILLAN is the global academic imprint of the Palgrave
Macmillan division of St. Martin's Press, LLC and of Palgrave Macmillan Ltd.
Macmillan® is a registered trademark in the United States, United Kingdom
and other countries. Palgrave is a registered trademark in the European
Union and other countries.

ISBN-13: 978–0–230–00659–1
ISBN-10: 0–230–00659–0

This book is printed on paper suitable for recycling and made from fully
managed and sustained forest sources.

A catalogue record for this book is available from the British Library.

A catalog record for this book is available from the Library of Congress.

10 9 8 7 6 5 4 3 2 1
15 14 13 12 11 10 09 08 07 06

Printed in China

CONTENTS

LIST OF TABLES

LIST OF FIGURES

ACKNOWLEDGMENTS

First and foremost, we sincerely thank the 1000 plus executives who participated in our research during the past 17 years. Without them this just would not have been possible. Due to the sensitive nature of outsourcing, many participants requested anonymity and cannot be individually acknowledged. Participants who did not request anonymity are acknowledged in the appropriate places throughout this book. We offer special thanks to David Andrews, founder and CEO of Xchanging, whose support will become evident while reading Chapters 6 through 8. We also appreciate the insights from senior executives at companies highlighted in this book, including ABZ Insurance, BAE Systems, Commonwealth Bank Australia, DuPont, Lloyd's of London, Siennax, and many others.

We also wish to acknowledge the supportive research environments from our respective institutions. We both found Templeton College, University of Oxford a special place to work and offer grateful thanks to all the staff and colleagues there who made research and study such a pleasure. Leslie is grateful to all colleagues at Warwick University and London School of Economics for their tolerance and support over the years. Mary thanks Vice Chancellor Nasser Arshadi at the University of Missouri-St. Louis because his Office of Research provided or facilitated three research grants to support Mary's work. She also thanks her colleagues in the IS department at UMSL, including Marius Janson, Kailash Joshi, Dinesh Mirchandani, Rajiv Sabherwal, Vicki Sauter, Ashok Subramanian, Joseph Rottman, and Dena Will.

Obviously research work of this scope over such a long period is not just a two-person effort. Several colleagues who became friends made significant contributions and published with us in the earlier period, in particular Rudy Hirschheim, Wendy Currie, and Guy Fitzgerald. Latterly we have thoroughly enjoyed researching, digesting, and writing with Thomas Kern, Joseph Rottman, Eric van Heck, Sara Cullen, Peter Seddon, and John Hindle. They provide intelligence, inspiration, and hard work in equal measure and have been a joy to be with. Amongst all these David Feeny stands out as the person we owe most to. His insight and wisdom have been guiding lights.

We would like to thank our circles of family and friends for their forbearance and humour. Mary thanks her parents, Dr and Mrs. Paul Lacity, and her three sisters: Karen Longo, Diane Iudica, and Julie Owings. She thanks her closest friends, Jerry Pancio, Michael McDevitt, Beth Nazemi, and Val Graeser. Finally, to her son, Michael Christopher – to whom this book is dedicated.

As a further testimony to value of global sourcing, we would like to acknowledge the contribution of our global publishing team. Stephen Rutt, our Palgrave publishing director in the UK, has been a great facilitator. Alexandra Dawe, also in the UK, unfailingly made things happen as assistant editor. Vidhya Jayaprakash was was our wonderful copy editor from Chennai, India. She also coordinated the typesetting and art-work with other partners from Newgen Imaging Systems based in India. Paul Fielding of Fielding Design designed the cover design. The book was printed in Asia by Macmillan Production. Thus, the production tasks of this book were assigned to various people based on three continents, with many of us coordinating work exclusively through information technology. Our experience has been that global sourcing is both effective and efficient.

Technology is all too often positioned as the welcome driver of globalization. The popular press neatly packages technology's influence on globalization with snappy sound bites, such as "any work that can be digitized, will be globally sourced." Cover stories report Indians doing US tax returns, Moroccans developing software for the French, Filipinos answering UK customer service calls, and the Chinese doing everything for everybody. Most glossy cover stories assume that all globalization is progressive, seamless, intractable, and leads to unmitigated good. But what we are experiencing in the twenty-first century in terms of the interrelationships between technology, work and globalization is both profound and highly complex.

We launched this series to provide policy makers, workers, managers, academics, and students with a deeper understanding of the complex inter-links and influences between technological developments, including in information and communication technologies, work organizations and patterns of globalization. The mission of this series is to disseminate rich knowledge based on deep research about relevant issues surrounding the globalization of work that is spawned by technology. To us, substantial research on globalization considers multiple perspectives and levels of analyses. We seek to publish research based on in-depth study of developments in technology, work and globalization and their impacts on and relationships with individuals, organizations, industries, and countries. We welcome perspectives from business, economics, sociology, public policy, cultural studies, law, and other disciplines that contemplate both larger trends and micro-developments from Asian, African and Latin American, as well as North American and European viewpoints.

The first book in the series represents only a beginning. *Global Sourcing of Business and IT Services* is based on over 1000 interviews with clients, suppliers, and advisors and fifteen years of study. The specific focus is on developments in outsourcing, offshoring, and mixed sourcing practices from client and supplier perspectives in a globalizing world. We found many organizations struggling. We also found other practitioners adeptly creating global sourcing networks that are agile, effective, and cost efficient. But they did so only after a tremendous amount of trial-and-error and close attention to details. All our participant organizations acted in a context of fast moving technology, rapid development of supply side offerings, and ever changing economic conditions. In this inaugural edition to the series, we seek to help others understand and apply the rich experiences, practices and lessons shared by our research participants.

Leslie P. Willcocks
Mary C. Lacity
April 2006

Notes on Co-authors

We have had the privilege to work with some of the world's leading experts on global sourcing of business and IT services. We thank them whole-heartedly for their contributions to this work.

Sara Cullen gained her PhD at the University of Melbourne, Australia in the field of outsourcing. She was formerly a national partner at Deloitte Touche Tohmatsu (Australia). She has a leading profile in Asia-Pacific and is one of the region's most experienced outsourcing practitioners. She has consulted to 85 private and public sector organizations in 110 outsourcing projects with contract values up to AU$1.5 billion a year. She has designed innovative partnering arrangements, franchise-type agreements, shared risk/reward structures, and incentive programs, in addition to traditional fee-for-service arrangements. She is a widely published, internationally recognized author having written 19 publications, conducted seven reviews for government, been featured in more than 40 articles, presented at over 100 major conferences, and conducted research with Oxford, Warwick, and Melbourne Universities since 1994. Sara may be emailed at scullen@ cullengroup.com.au.

David Feeny is a Fellow of Templeton College, University of Oxford, and Director of the Oxford Institute of Information Management (OXIIM). David's teaching and research interests center on the connections between strategy, organization and information technology. He has worked with large organizations in many different sectors and parts of the world, and is a regular contributor to the University's Oxford Executive Education programs. Research topics in recent years have included the role of the CIO, IT sourcing strategy, IS capabilities to be retained in-house, the role of the CEO in the information age, e-business opportunity, business process outsourcing. His work has won international recognition, and has been published in leading academic journals as well as general management journals such as *Harvard Business Review, MIT Sloan Management Review, McKinsey Quarterly*. In the recent book *What's the Big Idea* (Davenport and Prusak, HBS Press) he is identified as one of today's 200 leading management thinkers. David is a Fellow of the Royal Society for

Arts, Manufactures and Commerce. He holds an MA from Oxford University and an MBA from Harvard Business School. He was Vice President of Templeton College from 1995–99, and is currently an Advisory Board Member of two new venture companies. Before returning to Oxford in 1984 he was for many years a senior marketing manager with IBM. David may be emailed at David.Feeny@templeton.ox.ac.uk.

Dr Eric van Heck holds the Chair of Information Management and Markets at RSM Erasmus University, where he is conducting research and is teaching on the strategic and operational use of information technologies for companies and markets. He is best known for his work on how companies can create value with online auctions. He has coauthored or co-edited 12 books such as *Making Markets* (Harvard Business School Press, 2002) and *Smart Business Networks* (Springer, 2005). His articles were published in *California Management Review, Communications of the ACM, Decision Support Systems, Electronic Markets, European Management Journal, Harvard Business Review, International Journal of Electronic Commerce, Journal of Information Technology, Information Systems Research*, and *WirtschaftsInformatik*. He is a member of the Erasmus Research Institute of Management. He is currently member of the editorial board of *Electronic Commerce Research*, the *Journal of Information Technology*, and the *European Journal of Information Systems*. In 2003, he was honoured with a honorary fellowship from the Athens University of Economics and Business for his exceptional contribution to the international academic community. He received both his MSc and PhD from Wageningen University. Eric may be emailed at evanheck@rsm.nl.

Dr John Hindle is Head of Global Marketing for Accenture HR Services, and a founding partner of Knowledge Capital Partners. John has an extensive international business background, with over 25 years' experience as a senior executive and adviser to companies in both the United States and Europe. Prior to his business career, Dr Hindle was a university teacher, researcher, and administrator. John holds appointment as Adjunct Professor of Human and Organizational Development at Vanderbilt University, and publishes widely in trade, popular, and academic media. John may be emailed john.hindle@vanderbilt.edu.

Thomas Kern is Managing Director and Chief Information Officer of KERN Global Language Services (www.e-kern.com). He has an international reputation for his work on Information Systems Outsourcing, Application Service Provision, and Relationship Management. He holds a MSc (Econ.) from the London School of Economics and Political Science and a DPhil in Management Information Systems from Christ Church, University of Oxford. He was Assistant Professor at Rotterdam School of Management, European Editor of the *Journal of Information Technology*, a Lloyds of London Tercentenary Foundation Business Scholar and partner and director of InSync Limited, Strategic Management Consultancy in the UK. He has coauthored two books *NetSourcing – Renting Business Applications and Services over a Network* (2002) published by Financial Times, Prentice Hall and *The Relationship Advantage – Technology, Outsourcing and Management* (2001) published by Oxford University Press. In addition he has published over 25 reviewed papers in the *European Journal of Information Systems, European Journal of Management, Journal of Information Systems, Journal of Global Information Management, Journal of Strategic Information Systems, Journal of Information Technology, Journal of Management Information Systems, California Management Review* and *MISQ Executive*. Thomas may be emailed at Thomas.Kern@e-Kern.com.

Dr Joseph Rottman is an Assistant Professor of Information Systems at the University of Missouri-St. Louis. He earned his Doctor of Science in Information Management from Washington University. He has conducted research and spoken internationally on global sourcing, innovation diffusion, and public sector IT. Dr Rottman presented a keynote address at the Michael Corbett Conference on Outsourcing in Bangalore India. He has conducted case studies in over 40 firms. His research is being published and presented to senior executives worldwide, including the Advanced Practices Council of the Society for Information Management, the World Outsourcing Summit in India, and in publication outlets such as *MIS Quarterly Executive, The Journal of Information Technology*, and *Information and Management*. Joe can be emailed at Rottman@umsl.edu.

Dr Peter B. Seddon is an Associate Professor in the Department of Information Systems at the University of Melbourne, Australia. His teaching and research focus on helping people and organizations gain greater benefits from their use of information technology. His major publications have been in the areas of evaluating information systems success, packaged enterprise application software, IT outsourcing, and accounting information systems. Peter has recently been appointed as a Senior Editor for *MIS Quarterly*. Peter may be emailed at p.seddon@unimelb.edu.au.

CHAPTER 1

Transforming back offices through outsourcing

Approaches and lessons

Mary Lacity and Leslie Willcocks

Introduction

Senior executives are bombarded with messages to source business services globally. Global outsourcing is prescribed for everything from back office services like information technology development, human resource trans-actions, and indirect procurement to core services such as innovation, research and development, marketing, and customer care. While the vision of global sourcing networks that are agile, effective, and cost efficient is certainly achievable, it requires an immense amount of detailed manage-ment to make it work. That is the message from over 17 years of research.

Since 1989, we and our coauthors represented here (Sara Cullen, David Feeny, Eric van Heck, John Hindle, Thomas Kern, Joseph Rottman, and Peter Seddon) have studied the best, worst, and emerging IT and back office sourcing practices in over 600 large and small organizations worldwide. We have defined outsourcing as the handing over of assets, resources, activities and/or people to third party management to achieve agreed performance outcomes. This can be distinguished from the buying-in of external resources to work under in-house management, and in-house sourcing where internal management and operational resources are used almost exclusively. We have done in-depth case studies based on inter-views with now thousands of senior executives, line managers, supplier account managers, business users, and outsourcing advisors in the United States, United Kingdom, Australia, Europe, and Japan. We have surveyed over 400 senior executives in the United States, United Kingdom, and Europe. Our client profile is representative of the overall outsourcing market. Outsourcing clients are primarily North American companies (60 %) followed by European companies (22 %) and Asian/ Pacific companies (18 %).[1] One key feature of our body of research is that we measured actual outcomes compared to expected outcomes in our case studies and surveys. This enables us to draw conclusions as to the practices associated with success and failure and to analyze results over time. Overall we found:

Outsourcing can deliver on its promises, but it takes a tremendous amount of detailed management on both the client and supplier sides to realize expected benefits. This book provides in-depth insights into the detailed practices that lead to success.

Piecemeal outsourcing frequently yields piecemeal results – slightly lower costs or better service. But transformational outsourcing can lead to transformational results – significantly lower costs, better services, and increased revenues. This book provides in-depth case studies on global companies that have successfully transformed IT, human resources, indirect procurement, and other back office functions through outsourcing. Of course organizations may pursue other approaches to transform their back offices. Let us look at the main options.

Approaches to back office transformations

Back office functions such as human resources, information technology, indirect procurement, finance, and accounting are often perceived as costing too much, providing too little, and responding too slowly. Dysfunctional back offices often occur because large companies grow through mergers and acquisitions, dragging along and neglecting the back office stepchildren. This neglect results in over-staffed, idiosyncratic, duplicate, and incompatible back offices across business units. Brave senior executives are not satisfied with incremental improvements to a few processes. They want organizational reformation and cultural revolution in back office functions.

The goal of a back office transformation is to radically reduce costs, improve service, and even to increase revenues. The practices to achieve these results normally include centralization, standardization, re-orientation of staff, technology enablement, and process redesign. In considering which back office change approach is best suited to an organization, senior executives should consider the resources and skills needed to implement these new practices, such as upfront investment in technology and physical facilities, proven management capability, and effective and strongly motivated staff. Furthermore, they should consider which approach is politically feasible with the stakeholders, including senior management, business unit directors, process directors, process staff, and of course, the large body of users.

We have identified six approaches to improving dramatically back office functions. Two are fairly typical: do-it-yourself or hire management consultants; four entail various approaches to outsourcing: netsourcing, fee-for-service outsourcing, joint ventures, and enterprise partnerships. Each provides different levels of benefits (see Table 1.1) and some approaches are more suited for certain types of activities (see Table 1.2).[2] The four outsourcing models are fully explored throughout this book, but all the models are briefly introduced below.

Table 1.1 Benefits of back office transformation approaches

Benefits	Do-it-your self	Hire management consultants	Outsourcing			
			Netsourcing	Fee-for-service	Joint ventures	Enterprise partnerships
Ability to realize all cost benefits internally	X					
Ability to sell approach to internal organization	X	X				
Ability to control in-house	X					
Ability to infuse external energy and capabilities		X		X	X	X
Ability of outsiders to bypass political resistance				X	X	X
Provides clear indication that management is committed to transformation	X	X	X	X	X	
Ability to scale solution	X	X	X			
Achieve one-time savings upfront				X	X	X
Guaranteed cost and service improvements for 5 years on baseline services				X	X	X
Guaranteed cost-plus pricing on new services						X
Potential for upfront investment by supplier					X	X
Joint Board of Directors					X	X
Service Review Board and Technology Review Board promote client participation and oversight						X
Revenue generation and sharing					X	X

Table 1.2 Suitability of various outsourcing models

Model	Resource ownership (Infrastructure and people)	Resource management	Client/ supplier relationship	Typical location of supplier staff	Typical client/ supplier contract	Activities most suited for this model
Management Consultants	Supplier	Client	One-to-one	Supplier staff on client site	Time and Materials	Core or non-core capabilities; Customized products and services; Uncertain business or technical requirements
Fee for Service Outsourcing	Supplier	Supplier	One-to-one or One-to-some	Mixed (some supplier staff on client site, some staff centralized at supplier site)	Highly customized contract defining costs and service levels for that particular client	Non-core capabilities; Customized products or services; Stable business and technical requirements
Netsourcing	Supplier	Varies	One-to-many	Supplier staff not on client site	Generic contract specifying rental costs and very minimal service guarantees	Non-core capabilities; Standard products or services; Stable business and technical requirements
Joint ventures	Venture	Supplier investor	One-to-one: Client is both investor and first major customer	Mixed (some supplier staff on client site, some staff centralized at venture)	Highly customized for operations delivery; broadly defined for revenue sharing	client non-core, supplier core capabilities; Significant market for venture's product and services Frequently used to access offshore resources
Enterprise partnerships	Partnership	Client and supplier	One-to-one	Mixed (some supplier staff on client site, some staff centralized at venture)	Broadly defined for revenue sharing, customized after partnership is formed	Client non-core, supplier core capabilities; Significant market for venture's product and services Used for large scale transformation of large back offices

Do-it-yourself. This approach scores high on retaining control and keeping the value of the transformation within the company. But to succeed, it requires both funding and appropriate skills, which may be lacking. It is also the option most likely to encounter internal resistance if senior management does not give a clear signal of its importance. When other internal efforts are more important, management may not provide this signal.

Hire management consultants. This approach has three major benefits over doing it yourself. One, it brings in external energy. Two, management gives a clear signal of commitment to major change by bringing in outsiders. Three, that commitment reduces political resistance. But this approach does have several major risks. The two most significant ones are potential cost escalation and lack of sustainability because the consultants have no long-term commitments. The result can be a lessened sense of accountability and a lack of alignment between the parties. Furthermore, expertise and knowledge leave when the consultants leave.

Netsourcing. Netsourcing is more about using outsourcing to *build* back offices rather than to *transform* existing ones. In the netsourcing model, the client pays a fee to the supplier in exchange for a product or service delivered over the Internet or other networks. This model may be more familiar to readers under the name "application service provision (ASP)." We ceased to use the term ASP after an extensive study of the space we conducted in 2001. We found a significant amount of complex service offerings beyond the initial one-to-many model, and renamed the space "netsourcing" to capture the complexity (see Chapter 10 for a full discussion of netsourcing).

Netsourcing is primarily used by small organizations to build back office capabilities that would be too expensive to develop in-house, such as accessing supply chain management or enterprise resource planning packages. But we have studied one organization, ABZ Insurance, that used netsourcing to transform both its back and front offices. Their story is explored in detail in Chapter 10. Unlike ABZ Insurance, most large organizations use this approach to seek cost reductions on targeted activities rather than for radical back office transformation. But netsourcing is frequently involved in the following three approaches as a delivery platform.

Fee-for-service outsourcing. With fee-for-service outsourcing, the client signs a contract that specifies the fees it will pay suppliers to perform services. This is the most common approach, and is primarily used to seek cost reductions on back office services. Service improvements may or may not be specified. Detailed examples are explored in Chapters 3, 5 and 8.

This approach has the benefit of bringing in an outsider. It almost always offers one-time savings and on-going cost and service improvements. However, the long-term relationship can be a difficult one. Once the contract is signed, there is a built-in lack of alignment of incentives and a crucial movement of power to the supplier. This asymmetric power shift can lead to premium pricing of add-ons, lower levels of attention as time goes on, and deterioration of the relationship into an "us-versus-them" mentality.

In our early studies of IT outsourcing, we found that clients often had naive expectations about this model. For example, many clients expected to save 25 percent on IT costs by signing ten-year, fixed-price contracts for a set of baseline services. Many clients subsequently re-negotiated, terminated, or switched suppliers mid-stream. For example, our survey found that among those respondents who had prematurely terminated an outsourcing contract, 51 percent switched suppliers, 34 percent brought the function back in-house, and the remainder eventually reinstated their initial suppliers due to prohibitively high switching costs.[3]

But the good news is that the lessons for assessing which activities to outsource, evaluating suppliers, and negotiating exchange-based contracts are well proven by over 15 years of research. The model continues to be the dominant form.

Joint venture. As Tables 1.1 and 1.2 suggest, a joint venture solves some of the relationship problems through a shared Board of Directors and sharing of profits. However, power asymmetries still exist and most of the joint ventures we studied do not guarantee sustained improvement. Instead, they rely on nebulous notions of partnership, which can lead to real discomfort between the partners – especially if costs escalate.

In the past, joint ventures between clients and suppliers often failed to attract external clients and the relationships were redefined as exchange-based. Examples include Delta Airlines and AT&T, and (part of) Xerox and EDS (see also Chapters 6 and 7). Problems arose among several such deals because the parties thought they could sell homegrown client assets and capabilities to external clients. But the reality of delivering daily services devoured resources, and client assets and capabilities turned out to be too idiosyncratic for commercial delivery in highly competitive markets like enterprise resource planning (ERP).

In the offshore outsourcing space, joint ventures have been the preferred vehicle for large organizations to create safely a large offshore facility without the risks and hassles of a fully owned captive center. Joint ventures allow US investors access to local expertise for leasing offices, creating infrastructure, and hiring locals. Client investors, such as MasterCard, CSC, Perot Systems, and TRW chose this model over a captive model because they wanted to sacrifice some control in exchange for the supplier bearing some of the risk. For example, MasterCard created a joint venture with Chennai-based Mpower Software Services called MPACT, which had 250 employees performing IT work for MasterCard in 2005.[3] In addition to servicing MasterCard, MPACT has done work for Capital One, Household, Comdata, MagTek, Nedbank, and Alliance Data among others. Offshore models are more fully explored in Chapter 9.

Enterprise partnership. With an enterprise partnership, the client and supplier create a jointly owned enterprise that both services the client investor as well as seeks external customers. However, enterprise partnerships are different from joint ventures. The first difference is the primary purpose for joining together. With an enterprise partnership model the main focus is delivering cost savings and better services to the client investor. The client's back office is not world-class, so it seeks a supplier to help transform the function through better management, better IT systems, and better processes. External sales are merely a bonus. In a joint venture, on the other hand, the primary purpose is revenue generation through sales to third parties. Essentially, the client views its function as world-class and believes it can gain more revenues by selling to competitors than keeping the advantage to itself. It seeks a supplier to help with commercialization. In our experience, however, the venture often becomes so preoccupied with providing service to the client investor that it has no resources for external sales. In instances where clients truly had a competitive offering, a spin-off has been a more successful vehicle for creating a venture.

The enterprise partnership model has yielded significant back office transformations in organizations such as BAE Systems formerly British Aerospace and Lloyd's of London. Indeed, we have devoted three chapters to the use of this model to transform HR (Chapter 6), procurement (Chapter 7), and insurance policy and claims administration (Chapter 8).

The first enterprise partnership we examine is between BAE and Xchanging for the transformation of BAE's human resource function. The enterprise partnership is called Xchanging HR Services (XHRS). Becoming the venture's first customer, BAE signed a ten-year contract worth £250 million and transferred 430 HR employees to the enterprise. By 2005, BAE had already received the following benefits:

- Cost savings on baseline services
- Service improvement in many service areas
- New web-based technology capabilities rolled out to over 40,000 users in BAE
- A new state-of-the art shared service center was built and occupied
- Retained BAE managers now focus on more strategic activities
- Transferred BAE staff have been retrained to make them more service focused
- Obtained new business, including a £500,000-deal with Spirit Group for HR services in 2005
- Partnership has earned numerous nominations and awards including UK's National Outsourcing Association (2004) and BAE's HR Excellence Award (2005)

The second enterprise partnership we present in Chapter 7 is also with BAE and Xchanging. But this time, Xchanging tackled BAE's indirect procurement. The enterprise partnership is called XPS. Again, BAE was the venture's first customer. BAE initially signed a £800 million, ten-year contract but subsequently added £490 million to the deal during the first three years. Xchanging transformed BAE's indirect procurement and reduced prices for BAE by 12 percent overall. Furthermore, Xchanging improved the procurement service, including user desktop ordering from a newly developed sourcing web portal. By 2005, XPS's business was booming, with XPS controlling US$6 billion worth of procurement spend for BAE and nine other customers.

The third enterprise partnership we present is between Lloyd's of London and Xchanging. This partnership, called XIS, has radically transformed the London insurance market back office (see Chapter 8).

Size of the global business and IT outsourcing market

Despite the challenges with the four back office transformation approaches that entail outsourcing, the global IT and business process outsourcing markets consistently grew during the 17 years we have been studying it.

When we began research in this area in 1989, the IT outsourcing (ITO) market was quite small, only an estimated US$3 billion market. During the 1990s, the global ITO market swelled to what is today a US$200 billion market, as more organizations outsource their hardware, software, and IT staff. The offshore ITO market (primarily India and China) will represent about 25 percent of the global ITO market at US$56 billion by 2008, according to WR Hambrecht. But other research firms such as McKinsey and NASSCOM predict that India alone could grab US$142 billion of the ITO market by 2009. Such figures for ITO (and Business Process Outsourcing – BPO below) are difficult to arrive at accurately, and often turn out to be over-estimates, but do indicate the possibilities.[4]

The BPO market is about three quarters the size of the ITO market but certainly growing rapidly. McKinsey estimates the global BPO market will be US$140 billion by 2008, of which US$17 billion will be outsourced to India. Gartner has even bigger estimates, estimating the size of the global BPO market to be US$173 billion by 2006, of which US$24 billion would be outsourced offshore.[5] It is important to note that BPO deals include a lot of IT. For example, most human resource outsourcing entails the HR IT systems and infrastructure.

Table 1.3 Size of various ITO and BPO markets

Outsourcing market	In-depth coverage Chapter nos.	Global outsourcing size estimates in US$ billion
Information Technology outsourcing	2, 3, 5	$200
Human Resource outsourcing[1]	3, 4, 6	$30 to 50
Indirect Procurement outsourcing[2]	2, 7	$7 to 10
Financial Services outsourcing[3]	2, 8	$15
Offshore IT outsourcing[4]	9	$50
Netsourcing[5]	10	$4

Notes: 1 McIlvaine, A. (2004), "HR's Influential: BPO Pioneer James Madden," *Human Resource Executive Magazine,* April 19.
2 Davies, C. (2004), "The pitfalls of supplier bashing," *Supply Chain Europe,* March, Vol. 13, 12, pp. 46–47.
3 NASSCOM McKinsey Study
4 Op. cit. www.ebstrategy.com
5 John Harney estimates that the ASP market has not only recovered since the dot.com burst, but that it is thriving with 1500 suppliers in a market that will be $20 billion by 2006. See Harney, J. (2005), "The new world of ASPs," *Cutter Consortium,* Vol. 5, 9.

Table 1.3 presents the best estimates we found for various outsourcing markets. We study six of these markets in detail in this book: information technology outsourcing (ITO), human resource outsourcing (HRO), indirect procurement outsourcing, financial services outsourcing, offshore outsourcing of IT work, and netsourcing. Our own estimates of trends in client behavior and in the outsourcing marketplace are presented in detail in Chapter 11 of this book.

The outsourcing learning curve

Most of our research participants found they needed to conquer a significant learning curve before they realized expected benefits from outsourcing. It took most organizations a few tries to get outsourcing to work (see also Chapter 2 on this). Thus, we are not surprised that one DiamondCluster study found that 78 percent of executives had terminated at least one outsourcing contract. Our own survey of US and UK CIOs found that 32 percent had cancelled at least one IT outsourcing contract.[6] But clients were quite capable of learning from mistakes, and subsequent outsourcing relationships were frequently successful. Figure 1.1 illustrates the typical client learning curve for outsourcing. During Phase I, senior executives we interviewed became aware of an outsourcing market

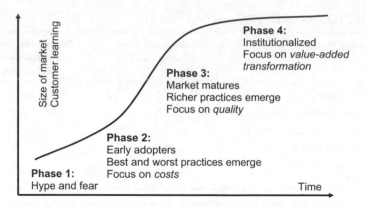

Figure 1.1 Outsourcing learning curve

through marketing hype ("you'll save 60 percent off your costs") or irrational propaganda ("you'll lose all your internal capabilities and intellectual property"). Senior executives quickly learn about potential benefits, costs, and risks by talking to peers, consultants, and reading research. Most senior executives initially engaged in outsourcing (Phase II) to seek lower costs. *During the pilot testing, senior executives learn about the immense amount of in-house management required to effectively work with suppliers and to achieve real cost savings.* As learning accumulated, some senior executives moved to Phase III when they exploited outsourcing for quality as well as cost reasons. One phrase we heard over and over again from participants was, *"we went for the price, we stayed for the quality."*

More mature adopters in Phase IV use outsourcing to strategically enable corporate strategies, such as increasing business agility, bringing products to market faster and cheaper, financing new product development, accessing new markets, or creating new business. From our research, these strategic initiatives often evolved over time. For example, a large US Financial Services firm uses global sourcing of IT and back office functions primarily to enable strategic agility. It has captive centers in Manila and Mumbai, and various joint ventures and fee-for-service relationships with 14 Indian suppliers. During the refinancing boom, the company was able to beat competitors by quickly meeting the immense surge in demand for IT and business process services. As the refinancing boom burst, the company was able to immediately scale back resources. But it took them *15 years* to develop this well-oiled global network.

While at an aggregate level the learning curve suggests a sequential progression and at the micro level, learning is iterative and concurrent.

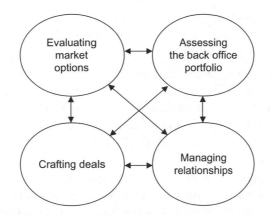

Figure 1.2 Learning and feedback in effective sourcing

Clients continually learn how to assess better their own service portfolio, evaluate suppliers' capabilities, craft contracts, and manage supplier relationships. Even within the same client–supplier relationship, clients frequently revisit the scope of the deal and re-craft contracts several times. This iterative learning process is reflected in Figure 1.2.

In the next sections, the most important client lessons for managing these four processes are described.

Assessing the back office portfolio

Lesson 1: Treat back offices as a portfolio of capabilities. Sound sourcing strategies begin with the assumption that back offices should be treated as a portfolio of activities and capabilities. Some of these activities must be kept in-house to ensure current and future business advantage and flexibility, while others may be safely outsourced. This portfolio perspective is empirically supported by our research findings that selective outsourcing decisions had a higher relative frequency of success than total outsourcing decisions.[7] We defined the scope of sourcing options as:

Total outsourcing:[8] *the decision to transfer the equivalent of more than 80 percent of the function's operating budget for assets, leases, staff, and management responsibility to external providers.*

Total in-house sourcing: *the decision to retain the management and provision of more than 80 percent of the function's operating budget internally after evaluating the services market.*

Selective outsourcing: *the decision to source selected functions from external provider(s) while still providing between 20 and 80 percent of the function's operating budget internally.*

Selective outsourcing decisions have been generally successful with a 77 percent success.[9] This couples with selective outsourcing also being the most common sourcing practice.[10] With selective outsourcing, organizations select the most capable and efficient source – a practice some participants referred to as "best-of-breed" sourcing. The most commonly outsourced functions in IT were mainframe data centers, software development and support services, telecommunications/networks, and support of existing systems. The most commonly outsourced functions in human resources were payroll, benefits administration, and employee training and education.[11] In most cases, suppliers were judged to have an ability to deliver these products and services less expensively than internal managers. The ability to focus in-house resources on higher-value work also justified selective outsourcing.

In general, total-outsourcing decisions achieved their expectations less frequently than selective outsourcing decisions or total in-house decisions. With total outsourcing, only 11 of 19 companies we studied achieved expectations. An example of some total outsourcing success was the South Australian Government's economic development package with EDS. The supplier (EDS) exceeded yearly targets for delivering US$200 million in economic development during the nine-year contract. However, other aspects of the deal were less successful and resulted in moves towards multi-sourcing in 2005.[12]

Participants frequently encountered one or more of the following problems with total outsourcing:

- excess fees for services beyond the contract due to increase in user demand
- excess fees for services participants assumed were in the contract
- hidden costs
- fixed-prices that were mis-matched with market prices two to three years into the contract
- inability to adapt the contract to even minor changes in business or technology without triggering additional costs
- lack of innovation from the supplier
- deteriorating service in the face of patchy supplier staffing of the contract

Exclusive sourcing by an internal department was 76 percent successful.[13] These companies were able to transform their back offices with the "do- it-yourself" approach. We found, however, that such success stems from a potential threat of outsourcing. *Only through the threat of competition did internal managers have the power to overcome organizational resistance to change, to implement cost reduction tactics used by suppliers, and to temper realistic service level expectations against available resources.* Once empowered through the threat of competition, internal managers often had cost advantages over suppliers (such as no marketing expense, no need to generate a profit). In addition, they often had service advantages, such as idiosyncratic knowledge of business applications.

Given that back offices should be treated as a portfolio, the next issue is how to assess the parts of the portfolio to outsource or keep in-house. While common wisdom tells us to keep core capabilities in-house and to outsource non-core capabilities, the distinction is not very useful. More thorough assessment tools are needed to identify exactly what is core and non-core. The following two lessons therefore explore the frameworks used to make core/non-core assessments.

Lesson 2: Identify core capabilities to keep in-house. There are many frameworks based on theories to help managers assess core capabilities to keep in-house. Indeed, we have devoted all of Chapter 3 to this topic. In this section, we introduce three frameworks. *The most important point here is that different frameworks will lead managers to different conclusions, thus as much thought should be put into the selection of the framework as to the actual portfolio assessment.*

The most popular portfolio assessment frameworks are based on theories such as resource dependency theory, agency theory, auction theory, game theory, institutional theory, and, by far the two dominant theories: transaction cost economics (TCE) and the resource-based view (RBV). In many ways, TCE is the ideal theoretical foundation because it specifically addresses make-or-buy decisions based on generic attributes of assets and describes appropriate ways to govern client–supplier relationships. For example, transaction cost economics posits that transactions with high asset specificity (essentially customization), high uncertainty, and/or frequent occurrence are best managed internally, while the rest should be more efficiently outsourced.[14] Indeed, a number of outsourcing empirical studies have found that asset specificity has been a significant factor to consider in make/buy decisions.[15] The RBV has been the second most widely applied theory to the outsourcing context.[16] RBV suggests that managers keep valuable, rare, non-imitable, and non-substitutable strategic assets in-house,[17] while potentially outsourcing the rest. Both TCE and RBV are valuable perspectives because they guide managers to treat the entire business functions as a portfolio of transactions/capabilities – some of which must be kept in-house while some may be outsourced.

The most direct assessment of IT as a portfolio was the Core Capabilities Model, first developed by Feeny and Willcocks.[18] This is the model we have since updated and generalized beyond IT to include other business functions in Chapter 3. We define four broad categories which clients must keep in-house, even if they intend to outsource nearly all of the business function:

- Governing
- Eliciting and delivering business requirements
- Ensuring technical ability and architecture
- Managing external suppliers

Table 1.4 summarizes the activities to be kept in-house by these different perspectives. To illustrate how these three different assessment perspectives might yield different prescriptions, consider the example of an ERP implementation in a global manufacturing company. Based on the

Table 1.4 Different portfolio assessment perspectives: what core activities should be kept in-house?

Transaction cost economics	Resource-based view	Core capabilities model
High asset specificity: The physical or human assets are non-redeployable for alternative uses or users. The activities are so idiosyncratic and customized that keeping them in-house is less costly than outsourcing.	*Valuable:* the resource can be used to exploit strategic opportunities or ward off threats	*Governance:* strategy, mission, and coordination
High uncertainty: Activities cannot be clearly defined for effective third-party contracting. Threat of supplier opportunism is high unless client incurs excessive transaction costs.	*Rare:* Few competitors have the resource	*Business requirements:* understanding business needs as they relate to the service function (IT, HR, etc), and relationship building among management, users, and the service function
High Frequency: Transactions that occur frequently *and* are highly asset-specific are less costly if kept in-house.	*Non-imitable:* It is difficult or costly for competitors to imitate the resource *Non-substitutable:* The resource has no immediate equivalents	*Ensure technical ability:* The architecture operation may be outsourced, but the client maintains control over architecture design *External supplier management:* Clients must make informed buying decisions, monitor and facilitate contacts, and seek added-value opportunities from suppliers

resource based view, the ERP project would not likely pass any of the core capability tests as ERP systems are widely used by competitors, thus outsourcing would be prescribed. But transaction cost economics suggests doing the implementation in-house if

1. The ERP system had to be highly customized to meet a specific business context (high asset specificity) or
2. The client's unique requirements could not be fully articulated in a sound contract (high uncertainty)

The Core Capabilities Model would suggest a mixed sourcing solution. This model would guide managers to insource parts of the ERP project associated with governing the project, articulating business requirements, and managing the political terrain among users. But their model would suggest outsourcing certain aspects of the project, such as programming, testing, and systems integration to access market scale and expertise.

Lesson 3: Best source non-core capabilities. Once core capabilities are identified, it does not automatically mean that the remaining non-core capabilities should be outsourced. We found that clients who considered additional business, economic, and technical factors of non-core capabilities were most frequently happy with their sourcing decisions.[19]

From a business perspective, some capabilities, which are non-core today, could become core in the future. Outsourcing this non-core function now may impede strategic exploitation in the future. For example, one of our case studies outsourced their web site design and hosting in 1995, which initially served as a marketing tool. As the web became increasingly important to their strategy, including online sales and customer service, the client found their outsourcing relationship impeded the strategic exploitation of the web. It subsequently terminated the supplier at a significant switching cost and brought the function back in-house. From an economic perspective, some non-core activities can be more efficiently kept in-house. For example, several of our case study participants were willing to outsource their large data centers but could not find suppliers who could do it cheaper.

From a technical perspective, some non-core capabilities are highly integrated with other core activities. This makes outsourcing extremely difficult. For example, one case study participant outsourced factory automation but found the supplier could not adapt to the rapid redirections from the sales department, let alone manage the supply chain implications. The system was eventually brought back in-house after paying a significant early termination fee. Assuming non-core capabilities pass these litmus tests, the client must

still evaluate the market options to further validate an outsourcing model
and to identify viable suppliers, as discussed in the next section.

Evaluating market options

An important and ongoing sourcing process is to keep abreast of market
options, even if the organization is exclusively insourcing at present. The
following section introduces three lessons to help executives use the right
evaluation process to find the right supplier. These lessons will be fully
expanded in Chapters 2 and 4.

Lesson 4: Assess twelve supplier capabilities. Clients have thousands of
suppliers from which to choose. Some clients prefer large global suppliers
like Accenture, IBM, EDS, and Wipro because of their reputation, scale, and
scope. Other clients prefer niche suppliers for specific domain expertise or
local suppliers for extra control and attention. In making these choices, *we
found that many clients make one major mistake when assessing suppliers:
they tend to assess suppliers' resources such as physical facilities, technology,
and workforce composition, rather than supplier capabilities to effectively
manage and deploy these resources for the client's benefit.* For example,
many senior executives ask for evidence of excellent supplier employees.
This assessment does not distinguish suppliers because all credible suppliers
have excellent people. Instead, senior executives need to ask about the supplier's behavior management capability – how does the supplier motivate and
manage people to deliver service through a customer-focused culture?

A better way to assess the myriad of suppliers is to consider the
12 supplier capabilities model created by Feeny, Lacity, and Willcocks
(see Figure 1.3). This model will be thoroughly explored in Chapter 4, but
is introduced below.

The 12 capabilities establish the basis for three supplier competencies:

- **Relationship Competency:** the ability to create aligned incentives
  between client and supplier
- **Delivery Competency:** the ability to deliver daily operations while
  still generating a good supplier margin
- **Transformation Competency:** the ability to meaningfully transform the client's operations to decrease costs and improve service.

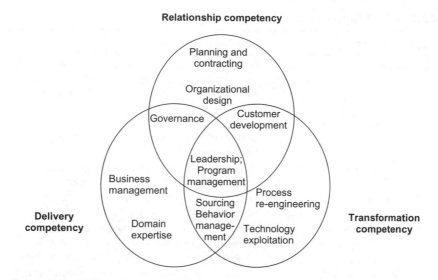

Figure 1.3 12 Supplier capabilities

High-level definitions of the 12 capabilities are found in Table 1.5. Although a detailed explanation of the capabilities is found in Chapter 4, an example will illustrate how the model can be used to compare suppliers. Consider the *leadership capability, defined as the capability to identify, communicate, and deliver the balance of delivery, transformation, and relationship activities to achieve present and future success for both client and provider*. After completing 76 case studies of client–supplier relationships in IT outsourcing, we found that the main differentiator between success and failure was the individuals who were leaders of the supplier (and client) account teams.[20] Leaders must operate more as the CEOs of the relationships, rather than as traditional account managers. Supplier leaders must also have significant clout within their parent organization to mobilize resources on behalf of their clients. For example, one US client was initially thrilled when the supplier hired a high-powered managing director specifically to serve as account leader. However, this outside hire was ineffective in gaining resources and attention at supplier headquarters because no one knew him. The point is that the supplier leader must not only be an excellent "CEO" of the relationship, but must have significant clout within his/her own organization.

To summarize, senior executives cannot merely assess supplier resources and hope to achieve high performance. Instead, senior executives must assess suppliers based on 12 specific capabilities (see Table 1.5).

Table 1.5 12 Supplier capabilities defined

Supplier capability	Definition
1. Leadership	The capability to identify, communicate, and deliver the balance of delivery, transformation, and relationship activities to achieve present and future success for both client and provider
2. Planning and contracting	The capability to develop and contract for business plans which deliver "win/win" results for client and supplier over time
3. Organizational design	The capability to design and implement organizational arrangements to realize plans and contracts
4. Governance	The capability to define, track, assess, and fix performance
5. Customer development	The capability to transition users of an internally provided service to customers who make informed decisions about service levels, functionality, and costs
6. Process improvement	The capability to design and implement changes to service processes to meet improvement targets
7. Technology exploitation	The capability to swiftly and effectively deploy technology in support of critical service improvement targets
8. Program management	The capability to prioritize, coordinate, ready the organization, and deliver across a series of inter-related projects
9. Sourcing	The capability to access whatever resources are required to deliver service targets
10. Behavior management	The capability to motivate and manage people to deliver service with a "front office" mindset
11. Domain expertise	The capability to apply and retain sufficient professional knowledge of the process domain to meet user requirements
12. Business management	The capability to consistently deliver against both client service level agreements and suppliers' own required business plans

Lesson 5: To be sure that outsourcing would be a better approach than do-it-yourself, compare request-for-proposals to internal bids. During the last 15 years, organizations that invited both internal and external bids had a higher relative frequency of success than organizations that merely compared a few external bids to current performance.[21] We believe that this was because formal external supplier bids were often based on efficient managerial practices that could be replicated by internal managers.[22] The question was, "If my managers could transform the back office, why haven't they done so?"

In some cases, internal managers could not implement cost reduction tactics because the internal politics often resisted cost reduction tactics such as consolidating departments, reducing headcount, and standardizing processes and technology. This, we saw, was the major impediment to the do-it-yourself transformational approach.

In the IT space, for example, business unit managers in two divisions at a US food manufacturer did not want to consolidate their data centers into the corporate data center. One data center Director stated, "[The two divisions] didn't want to come to corporate IS in the first place. They didn't want to close their data centers, a control thing, 'my car is faster than your car' thing." Senior executives at this company felt that IT costs had become too expensive and decided to outsource its data centers. The data center Director lobbied to submit an internal bid. Once granted permission, he prepared an internal bid that beat an external bid on cost. Within three years, he cut costs by 45 percent by consolidating and standardizing. But the legitimate threat of outsourcing was the catalyst for change.

In other cases, internal managers were not motivated to improve costs, particularly if the legacy of insourcing had created an environment of complacency. For example, the unionized employees at a US telecommunications company maintained inefficient work practices to protect their jobs. It was not until the union was threatened with losing the job site through outsourcing that union representatives acquiesced and improved efficiency. One of the union representatives expressed the following view: "When you are in the frying pan, you get creative."

Internal bids, however, might be infeasible in some circumstances. For example, rather than use its own capital to invest in much needed IT renewal, DuPont wanted a supplier(s) to make the investment upfront in exchange for variable fees based on usage. Clearly an internal bid team could not compete with the US$4 billion deal DuPont subsequently signed with CSC and Accenture.

Lesson 6: Involve multiple stakeholders in sourcing decisions. Concerning *who* should be making these assessments, our case study and survey data both suggest that multiple stakeholders need to be involved. In our survey data, 68 percent of respondents had at least two stakeholders driving the decision, most frequently the back office manager and lawyers or the back office manager and senior executives.

Successful sourcing decisions require a mix of political power and domain knowledge.[23] Political power helps to enforce the larger business perspective – such as the need for organization-wide cost cuts – as well as the "muscle" to implement such business initiatives. Domain knowledge on back office services, service levels, measures of performance, rates of service growth, and price/performance improvements are needed to develop requests-for-proposals, evaluate supplier bids, and negotiate and manage sound contracts.

Crafting deals

Assuming an appropriate sourcing model and viable supplier has been identified, the parties must still negotiate a contract. The two most important proven practices for crafting contracts are discussed below:

Lesson 7: Detail fee-for-service contracts, including responsibilities of both parties and mechanisms of change. Of the outsourcing models found in Table 1.2, the fee-for-service model is still the most common model. But our data reveals there are several types of fee-for-service contracts:

Standard contracts: the client signed the supplier's standard, off-the-shelf contract. This is primarily restricted to the netsourcing space.

Detailed contracts: the contract included special contractual clauses for service scope, service levels, measures of performance, and penalties for non-performance.

Loose contracts: the contract did not provide comprehensive performance measures or contingencies but specified that the suppliers perform "whatever the client was doing in the baseline year" for the duration of the contract at 10 to 30 percent less than the client's baseline budget.

Mixed contracts: For the first few years of the contract, requirements were fully specified, connoting a "detailed" contract. However, participants could not define requirements in the long run, and subsequent requirements were only loosely defined, connoting a "loose" contract.

Detailed contracts achieved expectations with greater relative frequency than other types of contracts (75% of detailed contracts were successful). These organizations understood their own functions very well, and could therefore define their precise requirements in a contract. They also spent significant time negotiating the details of contracts (up to 18 months in some cases), often with the help of outside experts. For example, the Financial Manager at a US bank spent three months negotiating the data center contract, assisted by the VP of IS, internal attorneys, and two hired experts:

> And that's when [the VP of IS] and I and the attorneys sat down everyday for three solid months of drafting up the agreement, negotiating the terms, conditions, and services. (Financial Manager, US Bank)

From our survey, clients included the following clauses in their detailed contracts:

- costs (100%),
- confidentiality (95%),
- service level agreements (88%),
- early termination (84%),
- liability and indemnity (82%),
- change contingency (65%), and
- supplier non-performance penalty (62%).

Increasingly, contracts also include responsibility matrices, which outline the responsibilities for both clients and suppliers. This innovation recognizes that suppliers sometimes missed service levels because of their clients. For example, in one of our cases, the supplier did not connect new client employees to the network within the contractual time limit because the client systematically failed to properly authorize new accounts.

No matter how detailed contracts become, changes in requirements will occur. Many detailed contracts now have mechanisms of change, including:

- planned contract realignment points to adapt the contract every few years,
- contingency prices for fluctuation in volume of demand,
- negotiated price and service level improvements over time,
- external benchmarking of best-of-breed suppliers to reset prices and service levels.

In contrast to the success of the detailed contract, all seven of the loose contracts we studied were disasters in terms of costs and services. Two of these companies, actually terminated their outsourcing contracts early and rebuilt their internal departments. Another company threatened to sue the supplier. Senior executives in these companies had signed flimsy contracts under the rhetoric of a "strategic alliance." However, the essential elements of a strategic alliance were absent from these deals. There were no shared risks, no shared rewards, and no synergies from complementary competencies nor any other of the critical success factors identified by researchers. Instead, these loose contracts created conflicting goals. Specifically, the clients were motivated to demand as many services as possible for the fixed-fee price by arguing, "You are our partners." Supplier account managers countered that their fixed-fee price only included services outlined in the contract. The additional services triggered supplier costs, which were passed to the client in terms of excess fees. Because the clients failed to fully specify baseline services in the contract, the clients were charged excess fees for items they assumed were included in the fixed-price.

Six of the eleven "mixed" contracts we studied achieved expectations. The contracts contained either shared risks and rewards or significant performance incentives. A Dutch electronics company spun-off of the IT department to a wholly owned subsidiary. Because the newly formed company's only source of revenue was the electronics company, they were highly motivated to satisfy their only client's needs.

Lesson 8: Keep contracts short enough to retain relevancy and control, but long enough for suppliers to generate a profit margin. From the client perspective, there is clear evidence that short-term contracts have higher frequencies of success than long-term contracts. From 85 case studies we studied, 87 percent of outsourcing decisions with contracts of three years or less were successful, compared to a 38 percent success rate for contracts eight years or longer.

Short-term contracts involved less uncertainty, motivated supplier performance, allowed participants to recover from mistakes quicker, and helped to ensure that participants were getting a fair market price. Another reason for the success of short-term contracts is that participants only outsourced for the duration in which requirements were stable, thus participants could articulate adequately their cost and service needs. Some participants noted that short-term contracts motivated supplier performance because suppliers realized clients could opt to switch suppliers when the contract expired. As the IS director of a UK aviation authority commented, "It's no surprise to me that the closer we get towards contract renewal, it's amazing what service we can get."

In contrast, long-term contracts have remained troublesome, with failure to achieve cost savings as the primary reason. Few total outsourcing mega-deals reach maturity without a major stumbling block. Conflicts are increasingly being resolved through contract re-negotiations.

The suppliers, however, have a clear preference for long-term relationships to recoup excessive transition and investment costs. Returning to DuPont's ten-year deal, the transition activities lasted over 18 months as the contract was operationalized in 22 countries to a population of nearly 100,000 users. The transition also included massive investments by one supplier in IT infrastructure, which the supplier could only recoup in a long-term deal. Clearly, the client's incentives for short-term deals must be balanced with the supplier's incentives for long-term deals.

Managing external suppliers

For all the sourcing models, there is an inherent adversarial nature in the contracts in that a dollar out of the client's pocket is a dollar in the supplier's pocket. (This is even typically true for joint ventures because the client investor is also the venture's primary or even sole paying customer.) If the client followed best practices up to the point of signing the contract, they should be sufficiently protected from the devastatingly negative consequences experienced in the early days. If the supplier negotiated a favorable deal, they should be able to deliver on the contract and still earn a profit margin. But even under the most favorable circumstances, relationship management is difficult:

> Really our challenge is relationship management ... I know I certainly haven't found the answer yet, but not too many other people have found the answer either. (Client of a Au$600 million contract)

Lesson 9: Put core client capabilities in place to protect the client interests as well as to foster supplier success. In addition to informed buying, these capabilities, which are more fully explored in Chapter 3, include contract facilitation, contract monitoring, and supplier development.

Contract facilitation is the capability to provide a vital liaison role between the supplier and the client's user and business communities to ensure supplier success. In our experience, both users and suppliers place high value on effective contract facilitators. The role arises for a variety of reasons:

- business users want one-stop shopping
- the suppliers need the buffer to foster realistic user expectations
- multiple suppliers need coordinating

- it enables easier monitoring of usage and service
- user demand must be managed to prevent excess charges

Contract monitoring is the capability to ensure that the supplier delivers on the contract. As organizations exploit the burgeoning external market for outsourced services, contract monitoring becomes a core capability. While the contract facilitator is working to "make things happen" on a day-to-day basis, the contract monitor is ensuring that the business position is protected at all times. Effective contract monitoring involves holding suppliers to account against both existing service contracts and the developing performance standards of the services market. It enables the production of a "report card" for each supplier that highlights their achievement against external benchmarks and the standards in the contract.

Supplier development is the capability beyond the legal requirements of a contract to explore increasing ways the clients and suppliers can engage in win-win activities. The single most threatening aspect of outsourcing is the substantial switching costs. Changing suppliers is expensive and difficult. Hence it is in the client's interest to maximize the contribution of existing suppliers, and also, when outsourcing, to guard against what we call the "mid-contract sag." A supplier may be meeting the contract after two or more years, but none of the much talked-about added value of outsourcing materializes. As the contract manager in a major US bank commented after his firm consolidated and outsourced its data centers,

> Sure, the suppliers deliver the contract, but to the letter. They've incurred only one penalty in more than two years. But trying to get them to identify the added value we both talked about at the beginning, let alone deliver it, is very difficult. They've had changes in management staff, so they are driven by what is written down rather than by some of our initial understandings.

In supplier development, clients look beyond existing contractual arrangements to explore the long-term potential for suppliers to create the "win-win" situations in which the supplier increases their revenues by providing services that increase business benefits. A major retail multinational has many ways to achieve this, including an annual formal meeting. An executive from the multinational stated:

> It's in both our interests to keep these things going and we formally, with our biggest suppliers, have a meeting once a year and these are done at very senior levels in both organizations. There are certain

things we force on our suppliers, like understanding our business and growing the business together ... and that works very well.

Lesson 10: Embrace the dynamics of the relationship. Even with these capabilities in place, client and supplier relationships will sometimes be troublesome, but the parties still have a good relationship overall. Rather than seek to extinguish such troubles, the best relationships embrace the dynamics of these quite complex interactions.[24]

We identified four common types of client–supplier interactions: adversarial, tentative, cooperative, and collaborative. These are based on the extent of goal alignment for the task at hand:

- **Tentative interactions** occur when goal alignments are unknown, such as during the bidding process. At such times, each side tends to exaggerate their strengths and hide their weaknesses.
- **Adversarial interactions** occur when goals are conflicting, such as interpreting which party should pay for something ambiguously stated in the contract.
- **Cooperative interactions** occur when goals are complementary, such as the client wants the service and the supplier wants the payment.
- **Collaborative interactions** occur when both sides have shared goals, such as educating the user community on what they can expect from the contract.

By attending to the expectations and goals of many outsourcing stakeholders, apparent anomalies in relationships are understood. Why, for example, do client contract managers and supplier account managers *collaborate* to mediate user expectations and then feel perfectly comfortable *fighting* over a monthly bill? Quite simply, the dynamics of stakeholder relationships vary with the task.

We do, however, note one caveat about stereotyping interactions. While generalizations are an effective tool for summarizing common experiences, they ignore the role of individual personalities in the success of client–supplier relationships. In several instances, stakeholder relationships improved when the person was replaced. Client and supplier account managers, in particular, had a high turnover rate in several of the mega deals studied.

The following participant quotes testify to the effectiveness of new faces:

> At the beginning of this contract, we actually had to change both of the contract managers three months into the contract to get a more reasonable basis for the relationship because the two of them over the opening three months had continued the negotiations. They were locking horns day-in-day-out. We had to take both of those individuals out and try to recover that relationship. I think that's been successful. Account Manager, public sector organization.

> I think it's unhealthy in any case to perpetuate the same relationships for too long, because you then know each other so well that you very rarely bring a new perspective onto things, a fresh pair of eyes with a new set of ideas. General Contract Manager, British Aerospace

Thus, relationship management not only requires an understanding of goal alignment, but also a human resource sensitivity as to the individuals who fill these roles.

Another important lesson here is that each side must have similar power so that they can achieve equitable outcomes. The aims of each party should be fairness, not domination or exploitation. Again, this common playing field can only occur if the client has successfully executed the assessment, supplier evaluation, and contracting processes.

Other sources for client learning

This chapter has demonstrated that clients have learned many lessons about evaluating their back office portfolios, evaluating market options, crafting contracts, and managing suppliers. The learning has served to significantly improve outsourcing transactions since 1989. While this book intends to disseminate these lessons, we recognize that novice clients may need richer learning experiences, thus we offer the following lessons.

Lesson 11: Consider incremental outsourcing to develop experience with outsourcing. Just as you cannot learn to drive from reading a manual, you cannot learn to successfully outsource merely by reading a book.

We found that the best way to accumulate learning is through incremental outsourcing, in which clients adopt this outsourcing strategy precisely to develop an in-house knowledge about outsourcing. With incremental outsourcing, organizations outsourced a small and discrete part of their activities, such as third-party maintenance or shared processing services. The experience gained from this first incremental approach was then fed back into further outsourcing. In two cases, a petrochemical company and an electric utility, organizations found themselves ultimately engaging in total outsourcing.

One US Fortune 500 biotechnology company took a very systematic approach when entering the offshore outsourcing market for the first time. It chose 17 pilot projects that were mostly small in size, required frequent delivery of milestones, and gave pieces of the same project to two suppliers. For example, the company decided that before they would commit to one supplier for a Peoplesoft to SAP conversion, they would have two of the large Indian suppliers do small pieces of the conversion. The company experienced much better project leadership from one of the suppliers in terms of onsite coordination, project status reporting, technical fit, and superior daily communications. The company selected this supplier to complete the entire conversion. When the company went live with SAP, the Indian supplier was granted an ongoing maintenance contract for seven FTEs.

Lesson 12: Hire help. Another very important factor in client learning is the widespread use of key outsourcing consultants and outsourcing legal firms. We are witnessing an institutional isomorphic effect[25] where outside experts seed client organizations with similar standards and methods.

In the ever-expanding BPO market for human resources, Equaterra is the consulting company frequently hired to help clients create RFPs (request for proposals), assess suppliers, and negotiate contracts. In the more established IT outsourcing space, Technology Partners International[26] and the Everest Group have been the prime consulting companies, and Shaw Pittman has been a major legal council. These are just examples. The overall effect of such external constituents is the dissemination of best practices. In particular, mega-deal contracts are now templated, with all the client costs, service levels, performance measures, mechanisms of change, and other clauses nearly identical. Although each organization participating in the research regards these practices as "competitive secrets," practices are nearly identical across mega-contracts. One can usefully debate the impact of such "best practices" of course – for example does their spread reduce competitive advantage from outsourcing, are best practices suitable for every situation and deal? Are they applied in the right spirit or mechanically?

Post-contract management practices are also becoming increasingly standardized, such as external benchmarking of services, color-coded problem resolution systems, joint supplier/client teams to resolve disputes, and responsibility matrices to clearly define client responsibilities and supplier responsibilities. For example BP, BAE, DuPont, UK Inland Revenue, Government of South Australia use some or all of these practices.

In addition to hiring external experts, clients may also access external expertise through outsourcing interest groups, such as the Sourcing Interest Group. Groups provide an opportunity for both clients and suppliers to share and disseminate data. For example, the Outsourcing World Summit draws over 500 outsourcing clients and suppliers each year and features prominent speakers, panels, Q&A sessions and many opportunities for informal exchanges.

Lessons for suppliers[27]

The suppliers in most of our large ITO case studies (where the deals were worth in excess of US$500 million) were EDS, IBM, CSC, Accenture, or Infosys. These suppliers are among the few organizations that have a significant global presence to service such large deals. We found significant variability in the success of such deals. Given the suppliers are the same, it is logical to assume the differentiating factor is the client. Put simply from the supplier perspective: *good clients make for good relationships*. The ideal client has significant experience with outsourcing the right activities, crafting the right types of contracts, and ensuring supplier success through the previously discussed roles and practices. The following lessons stand out as viable ways to educate, inform, and attract good clients, primarily through superior supplier integrity.

Lesson 13: Educate your client during the earliest possible phase. Increasingly, we advise suppliers to help educate naive clients on the issues discussed in this book. For example, after presenting the core IT capabilities framework to one supplier bidding on a significant US government contract, the supplier went back to the US government agency and told them to reduce the scope of their RFP and to retain more supplier management capability. The agency was quite taken aback with this approach, revised its RFP, and subsequently selected the aforementioned supplier because they trusted them.

Lesson 14: Bridle your public relations staff, unbridle your account managers. Increasingly, we talk to outsourcing shoppers who are shying away from some suppliers because they simply don't believe them. The potential clients complain that the supplier oversells with polished PR and salespeople. Legitimate concerns about possible escalating costs and service lapses are readily dismissed with appeals to their "world class expertise." Client reference lists often include only new clients, where expectations are still high and supplier delivery is still unproven. Clients are not naive; they know that outsourcing relationships will encounter roadblocks and problems. They want to hear stories of past disasters and how the supplier responded to them, what the supplier learned from them. Consider one from our case study of multi-billion dollar company. Senior managers rejected bids from big suppliers and instead signed a ten-year, US$1 billion dollar contract with a small start-up company. The big players sent their slickest salespeople to present. The start-up sent the unpolished, but enthusiastic team of people who would actually be doing the work:

> The early presentations were really quite crap, but they had lots of feeling, lots of passion, lots of drive, lots of enthusiasm. There is a certain pleasure in the naivety ... it's like looking at a Lowry painting, it's still beautiful but is naïve, rather than a Gauguin or something like that. I would hate to lose the touch that's in here for the sake of being slick. (Outsourcing client from large UK Company)

Lesson 15: Submit realistic, open bids. Some suppliers underbid in order to secure the contract. This practice is so common, we have devoted Chapter 5 to its consequences, called "The Winner's Curse." Such a strategy was often fruitful in the past because suppliers knew that the client's needs would change, and opportunities for upsell would more than compensate for the loss on the baseline contract. But clients are increasingly aware of such strategies and intentionally select other suppliers for add-ons to keep a competitive playing field. It serves the supplier far better to offer a realistic bid and to disclose how they can deliver on the bid and still earn a profit. Such disclosure might entail their non-imitiable costs in infrastructure and capabilities due to economonies of scope and scale.

Lesson 16: Propose and price value-added options. Once transition periods are complete, clients generally find that suppliers can deliver on operational objectives of IT contracts. But clients increasingly expect more innovations and opportunities for generating revenues, even if the deals are essentially fee-for-service. Clients express continued dissapointment on this front:

> Yes, the supplier can achieve all the things that were proposed – but where is this famous added-value service? We are not getting anything over and above what any old outsourcer could provide. (IT Services Director, Aerospace Company)

The value-added supplier proposes and prices options which significantly benefit the client. Examples from our case studies include significant cost savings and service improvement by web-enabling human resource management, creating wireless connections for sales force support, and helping clients use online auctions to reduce procurement costs.

Conclusion

Back offices have clearly been neglected in most organizations. There are many ways to transform back offices, including IT functions, and increasingly organizations are looking to various outsourcing suppliers to help reduce costs, streamline processes, and improve services. From the client perspective, the increasing numbers of global suppliers affords them more power to transform back offices. But to harness this market opportunity, clients need to learn how to continually monitor market options, assess the contribution of their service portfolio for current and future business value, decide what type of relationships suit their needs, craft optimal contracts, and successfully manage supplier relationships. The overall message for clients is clear: *all outsourcing requires continual and significant in-house management*.

For suppliers, they must be able to select educated clients with clear goals, and have the ability to execute such deals while still generating a profit. At the end of the day, success is measured by the operational delivery of the contract, ability to fairly adapt to change, and the ability to identify added-value services.

Notes

1. "Global Size of BPO" on http://www.indobase.com/bpo/global-market-of-bpo.html
2. For other research that examined the suitability of different types of outsourcing see Lee, J., Miranda, S., and Kim, Y. (2004), "IT Outsourcing

Strategies: Universalistic, Contingency, and Configurational Explanations of Success," *Information Systems Research*, Vol. 15, 2, pp. 110–131.

3. See http://www.mpowerss.com/mpact.shtml
4. "Offshore Statistics: Dollar Size, Job Loss, and Market Potential," on www.ebstrategy.com
5. "Global Size of BPO" on http://www.indobase.com/bpo/global-market-of-bpo.html
6. The DiamondCluster 2005 study has some weaknesses in research methodology. Our earlier survey is represented in Lacity, M. and Willcocks, L. (2001), *Global IT Outsourcing: Search For Business Advantage*, Wiley, Chichester.
7. A detailed description of the research methodology was published in Lacity, M. and Willcocks, L. (1998), "Practices in Information Technology Outsourcing: Lessons From Experience," *MIS Quarterly*, September, Vol. 22, 3, pp. 363–408.
8. There is a recent study that suggests that large scale IT outsourcing is motivated by managerial self-interest. See Hall, J. and Liedtka, S. (2005), "Financial Performance, CEO Compensation, and Large-Scale Information Technology Outsourcing Decisions," *Journal of Management Information Systems*, Summer, Vol. 22, 1, p. 193.
9. Lacity and Willcocks (2001), op.cit.
10. Other sample surveys on selective IT outsourcing can be found in Apte, U., Sobol, M., Hanaoka, S., Shimada, T., Saarinen, T., Salmela, T., and Vepsalainen, A. (1997), "IS Outsourcing Practices in the USA, Japan, and Finland: A Comparative Study," *Journal of Information Technology*, Vol. 12, 4, December, pp. 289–304; Grover, V., Cheon, M., and Teng, J. (1996), "The Effect of Service Quality and Partnership on the Outsourcing of Information Systems Functions," *Journal of Management Information Systems*, Spring, Vol. 12, 4, pp. 89–116.
11. Lawler, E., Ulrich, D., Fitz-enz, J. and Madden, J. (2004), *Human Resources Business Process Outsourcing*, Jossey-Bass, San Francisco.
12. See Chapter 3 in Lacity and Willcocks (2001) for the full case study of South Australia government. For another successful case of large-scale outsourcing at British Petroleum see Cross, J., Earl, M., and Sampler, J. (1997), "Transformation of the IT Function at British Petroleum," *MIS Quarterly*, December, pp. 401–420. For an overall analysis of success factors, see Hu, Q., Gebelt, M., and Saunders, C. (1997), "Achieving Success in Information Systems Outsourcing," *California Management Review*, Vol. 39, 2, pp. 63–79.

13. Lacity and Willcocks (2001), op. cit. The updated case appears in Lacity, M., Willcocks, L., and Cullen, S. (2007) *Global IT Outsourcing*. Wiley, Chichester.

14. For a more thorough explanation of TCE, please see: Williamson, O. (1991), "Strategizing, Economizing, and Economic Organization," *Strategic Management Journal*, Vol. 12, pp. 75–94; Williamson, O. (1991) "Comparative Economic Organization: The Analysis of Discrete Structural Alternatives," *Administrative Science Quarterly*, Vol. 36, pp. 269–296.

15. Examples of empirical testing of Transaction Cost Theory (TCT) in IT context see Ang, S. and Straub, D. (1998), "Production and Transaction Economies and Information Systems Outsourcing – A Study of the US Banking Industry," *MIS Quarterly*, Vol. 22, 4, 535–552; Lacity, M. and Willcocks, L. (1996), "Interpreting Information Technology Sourcing Decisions From A Transaction Cost Perspective: Findings and Critique," *Accounting, Management and Information Technology*, Vol. 5, 3/4, pp. 203–244; Nam, K., Rajagopalan, S., Rao, H., and Chaudhury, A. (1996), "A Two-level Investigation of Information Systems Outsourcing," *Communications of the ACM*, Vol. 39, 7, July, pp. 36–44; Poppo, L. and Zenger, T. (1998), "Testing Alternative Theories of the Firm: Transaction Cost, Knoweldge-Based, and Measurement Explanations for Make-or-Buy decisions in Information Services," *Strategic Management Journal*, Vol. 19, pp. 853–877.

16. Examples of empirical testing of RBV in IT outsourcing context: Straub, D., Weill, P., and Stewart, K. (2002), "Strategic Control of IT Resources: A Test of Resource-Based Theory in the Context of Selective IT Outsourcing," *Working paper*, Georgia State University and MIT Sloan School of Management; Teng, J., Cheon, M., and Grover, V. (1995), "Decisions to Outsource IT Functions: Testing a Strategy-Theorectic Discrepancy Model," *Decision Sciences*, Vol. 26, 1, pp. 75–103; Dibbern, J. and Heinzl, A. (2002), "Outsourcing of Information Systems in Small and Medium Sized Enterprises: A Test of a Multi-Theoretical Causal Model," in R. Hirschheim, A. Heinzl, and J. Dibbern (eds), *Information Systems Outsourcing in the New Economy*, Springer-Verlag, Berlin, Heidelberg, New York.

17. For a concise explantation of the resource-based view, please see Barney, J. (1991), "Firm Resources and Sustained Competitive Advantage," *Journal of Management*, March , Vol. 17, 1, pp. 99–121.

18. Feeny, D. and Willcocks, L. (1998), "Core IT Capabilities for Exploiting Information Technology," *Sloan Management Review*, Vol. 39, 3, pp. 9–21.
19. Lacity, M., Willcocks, L., and Feeny, D. (1996), "The Value of Selective IT Sourcing," *Sloan Management Review*, Vol. 37, 3, pp. 13–25.
20. Lacity and Willcocks (2001), op.cit.
21. Lacity and Willcocks (2001), op.cit.
22. For a list of practices clients implemented themselves, see Hirschheim, R. and Lacity, M.(2000), "Information Technology Insourcing: Myths and Realities," *Communications of the ACM*, February, pp. 99–107.
23. For for the role of business executives as IT project champions, please see Beath, C. (1996), "The Project Champion," in M. Earl (ed.), *Information Management: The Organizational Dimension*, Oxford University Press, Oxford, pp. 347–358.
24. For another study that examines four types of outsourcing relationships, see Kishore, R., Rao, H., Nam, K., Rajagopalan, S., and Chaudhury, A. (2003), "A Relationship Perspective on IT Outsourcing," *Communications of the ACM*, Vol. 46, 12, pp. 86–92. To better understand the role of trust in IT outsourcing relationships, see Sabherwal, R. (1999), "The Role of Trust in Outsourced IS Development Projects," *Communications of the ACM*, Vol. 42, 2, pp. 80–87.
25. For more information on institutional isomorphism, see DiMaggio, P. and Powell, W. (1991), "The Iron Cage Revisited: Institutional Isomorphism and Collective Rationality in Organizational Fields," in W. Powell and P. DiMaggio (eds), *The New Institutionalism in Organizational Analysis*, The University of Chicago Press, pp. 63–82; Mizruchi, M. and Fein, L. (1999), "The Social Construction of Organizational Knowledge: A Study of Coercive, Mimetic, and Normative Isomorphism," *Administrative Science Quarterly*, December, Vol. 44, 4, pp. 653–683; Ang, S. and Cummings, L. (1997), "Strategic Response to Institutional Influences on IS Outsourcing," *Organization Science*, Vol. 8, 3, pp. 235–256; Jayatilaka, B. (2002), "IT Sourcing: A Dynamic Phenomenon: Forming an Institutional Theory Perspective," in R. Hirschheim, A. Heinzl, and J. Dibbern (eds), *Information Systems Outsourcing in the New Economy*, Springer-Verlag, Berlin, Heidelberg, New York.
26. On November 14, 2005 EquaTerra and TPI announced they signed an agreement to merge the two companies.
27. Surprisingly little research has studied the supplier's perspective in outsourcing. Some excellent exceptions include Levina, N. and Ross,

J. (2003), "From the Vendor's Perspective: Exploring the Value Proposition in IT Outsourcing," *MIS Quarterly*, Vol. 27, 3, pp. 331; Koh, C., Ang, S., and Straub, D. (2004), "IT Outsourcing Success: A Psychological Contract Perspective," *Information Systems Research*, Vol. 15, 4, pp. 356–374.

CHAPTER 2

Managing the sourcing process: A life cycle perspective

Sara Cullen, Peter Seddon, and Leslie Willcocks

Introduction

Outsourcing, whether of IT or business processes, onshore or offshore, continues to raise expectations and pose challenges for private and public sector organizations alike. Time and again, we have found even experienced organizations running into massive problems, suffering from slow organizational learning, and working in a reactive rather than an anticipatory mode.[1] The results are troubling. Here are some recent examples:

- In 2000, UK retailer Sainsbury signed a seven-year US$3.25 billion deal with Accenture to outsource its IT operations. By late 2004, the deal had been renegotiated twice, and Sainsbury had announced a 2004/05 write-off of US$254 million of IT assets, and a further US$218 million write-off of automated depot and supply chain IT. In October of 2005, Sainsbury announced that it was terminating the Accenture relationship and bringing IT back in-house.[2]
- A 2004 report into 182 outsourcing deals found more than a fifth ended prematurely.[3]
- In 2004, JP Morgan and Chase scrapped its US$5 billion contract with IBM two years into a seven-year deal, concluding that much of the work could be better handled in-house.[4]
- Also in 2004, DuPont was reported to have discovered US$150 million in over-charges relating to outsourcing services with its supplier.[5]
- In autumn 2004, the Child Support Agency–EDS outsourcing arrangement was just the latest in a catalog of problem deals in the UK public sector.[6]

The outsourcing process matters because outsourcing keeps changing. While it appears that outsourcing client organizations have a history of outsourcing experiences to draw upon, the problem is change. First generation outsourcing clients often changed what they outsourced and how they outsourced the second and third times around. Each time, they found themselves in a relatively new situation, having to learn anew. Furthermore, if their knowledgeable people had left and not been replaced, organizational learning could not occur until sometimes the fourth or fifth generation deal. What more can client organizations do to mitigate such risks? Our research found that the key is to never lose sight of the fundamentals.

The outsourcing process also matters because of the huge number of details that must be handled. Outsourcing is neither good nor bad in itself. The outcome is determined by how it is managed, before and after the contract has been signed.

For example, in a study of organizations seeking IT cost savings, Willcocks and Fitzgerald (1994) found that management made a 40 percent difference in cost savings achieved.[7] The risk of self-interest and conflict between client and supplier always exists, which is why planning, implementing, and operationalizing the details matters. As the CIO of a major bank that had outsourced its IT in 1997 in a ten-year deal commented, "The major lesson? Getting sufficient **granularity**, in plans, processes and actions, to give us transparency, then control."[8] Similarly, the account executive of a major supplier summed it up in saying, "Outsourcing contracts are agreed in concept but delivered in detail. That's why they can break down; the devil is in the detail."[9]

A decade of in-depth studies demonstrates that outsourcing cannot be contracted for and then not managed. These studies, mainly in the ITO area, have linked numerous factors to outsourcing success, including retaining core IS capabilities, optimizing sourcing options, sourcing selectively, having an intent that supports enterprise strategy (such as cost reduction or business transformation), signing the appropriate type of contract, managing across the lifecycle, managing the relationship, and motivating the supplier by knowing its behaviors and capabilities.[10]

However, successful outsourcing processes have been given surprisingly scant attention in the literature. Lacity and Willcocks (2001: 291–308) describe a six-phase outsourcing process model. However, this work only delineates processes at a high level.[11] The most comprehensive process models in the literature are from Klepper and Jones (1998), Hurley and Costa (2001), and the US General Accounting Office (2001).[12] All three recognize the importance of pre-agreement and post-agreement activities and their complexities. However, their models are based on just a few cases. Specifically, Klepper and Jones (1998) base their model on the experience of "a number" of CIOs and practitioners; Hurley and Costa (2001) base theirs on nine Australian cases provided by suppliers; and the US General Accounting Office (2001) bases its model on seven US corporations, two suppliers, and five academic/professional authorities.

In short, various researchers and practitioners have recognized the importance of the outsourcing process, and a limited number of models have been proposed. But a major gap still exists in the ITO and BPO (business process outsourcing) literature. Furthermore, although many of the individuals we have encountered endorse aspects of their outsourcing approach, none would outsource exactly the same way again. They have since learned ways to get round the problems they faced.

We have taken the hindsight and experiences of 100 cases to develop an outsourcing process model in the form of a lifecycle, with activities within building blocks within phases. The goal is to create a template that defines the fundamental process activities for managing outsourcing together with the evidence of their importance.

The Outsourcing Lifecycle Model

The Outsourcing Lifecycle Model consists of four phases: architect, engage, operate, and regenerate (see Figure 2.1). These phases are composed of nine building blocks (see Figure 2.2). These building blocks contain 54 key activities (see Figure 2.3). The authors deemed an activity as being *key* if "as a result of its presence or absence, a directly attributable, notable benefit or problem arose." Two obvious examples are transitioning staff well, and establishing a baseline for assessing benefits.

This process model was created using information compiled by the first author, who observed and participated in 100 outsourcing cases from 1994–2003 when she was the former partner of a major outsourcing consulting practice. The cases ranged in contract value from Au$200,000 to Au$1.5 billion a year, and they can be categorized as *typical* in that each had aspects that worked and aspects that did not work. The model was then tested on seven additional case studies. (For more detail on the research process and a listing of the 100 organizations studied, see Appendix 2.1.)

In the lifecycle, each phase, and its building blocks, prepares the way for the following phases and building blocks. Likewise the success of each building block depends on the preceding ones, with the last one paving the way for the next-generation sourcing strategy and its lifecycle.

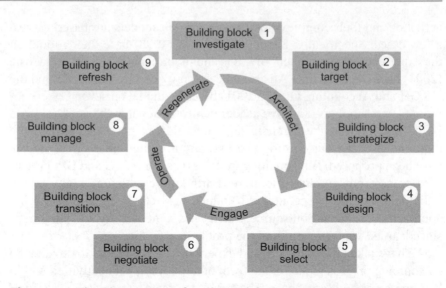

Figure 2.1 The Outsourcing Lifecycle Model: Phases and building blocks

The Architect Phase, where the foundation for outsourcing is laid, consists of the first four building blocks – investigate, target, strategize, and design. At the end of this phase, the organization knows itself well enough to confidently publicize its needs.

The Engage Phase, where one or more suppliers are selected and the deal is negotiated, consists of the fifth and sixth building blocks – select and negotiate.

The goal of both of these pre-contract phases is for the client organization to collect and analyze information so that its decision makers can make rational and informed decisions in the phases when they have the greatest leverage with the prospective suppliers.

The Operate Phase, where the deal is put in place, operationalized, and managed through its term, is comprised of the seventh and eighth building blocks – transition and manage. At this point, the client organization generally faces a monopoly provider. After this point, if the deal is not working, management rarely has economic or political options other than to continue with the supplier. Outsourcing deals can be prohibitively expensive to renegotiate, terminate, and either backsource (bring back in-house), or transfer to another supplier.

It is in this phase that the benefits of the previous work done (or not done!) come home to roost. The Operate Phase either proceeds smoothly as a result of the strategies, processes, documents and relationship management designed in the earlier building blocks, or the phase suffers, due to misinterpretations, ambiguities, disagreements, and disputes. At this

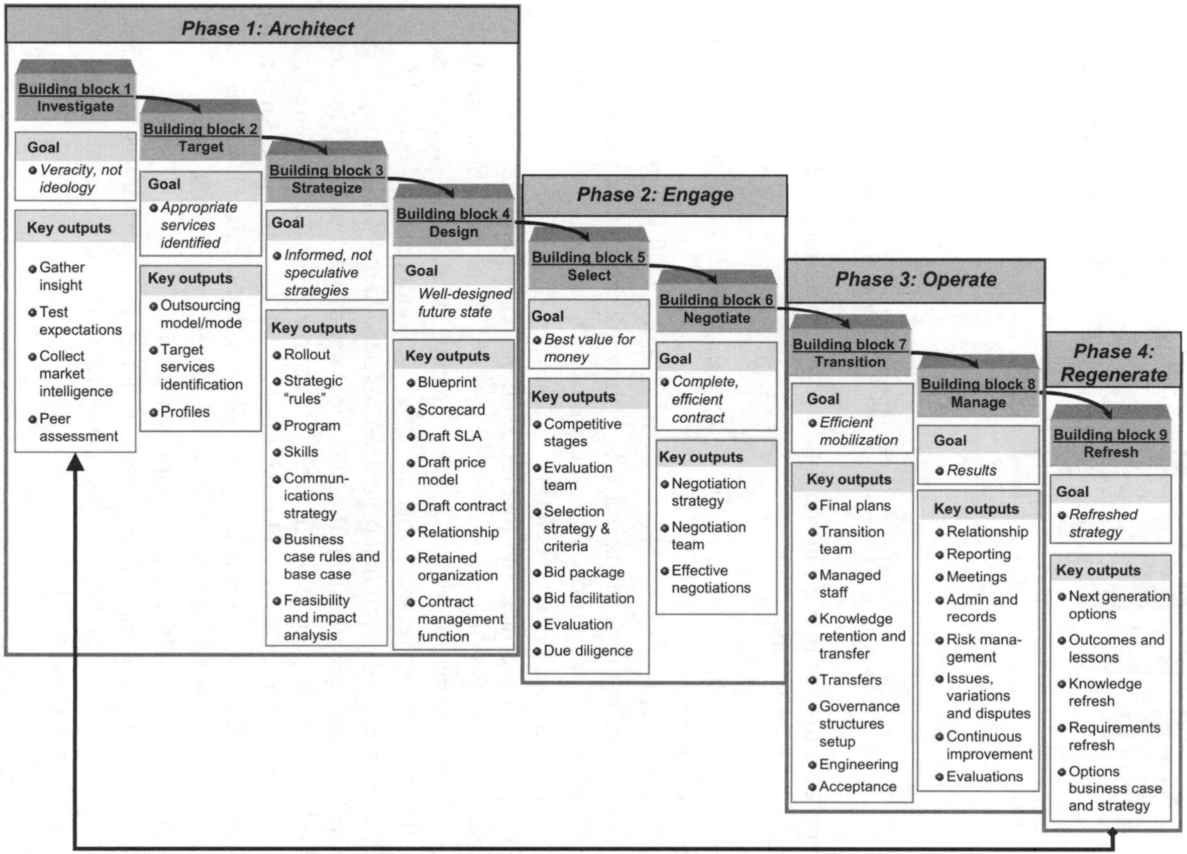

Figure 2.2 The Outsourcing Lifecycle Model: Goals and key outputs

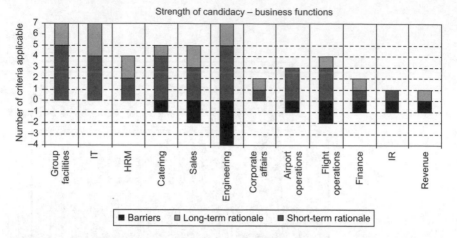

Figure 2.3 Strength of outsourcing candidacy of 12 business functions at an international airline

stage, such problems can only be corrected through huge and tedious remedial efforts.

The Regenerate Phase, where next-generation options are assessed, consists of one building block: refresh. Following this phase, the lifecycle begins anew, returning to the Architect Phase, where the organization prepares for its next-generation deal(s).

We found that organizations that followed the phases and building blocks in this sequence had more success and fewer problems than those that followed other sequences. However, the sequence of activities within each building block could be somewhat more fluid without deleterious results.

Furthermore, we found that organizations needed to "walk through" the lifecycle before embarking on it, to decide what they would need to know and what events or actions would need to take place for the outsourcing to succeed as a multi-generational program. For this reason, in the Architect Phase, organizations essentially need to work backwards from the last building block to the first to understand the entire lifecycle. They then need to execute from the first building block onward.

We now discuss each building block in detail, using examples from the case studies. The numbers on the cases refer to the case numbers in Table 2.3 in Appendix 2.1.

Building Block (BB) 1: Investigate – Discard Myths

Many misconceptions exist about what outsourcing can and cannot do for an organization. In practice each firm, and its circumstances, is different.

In this building block, the primary goal is to replace ideological beliefs with goals appropriate to the organization's circumstances, its industry, and the markets where it procures services. Because outsourcing can be a highly imitative behavior,[13] where organizations attempt to duplicate the imperfectly observed success of others, there is a real need to discard myths and simplistic beliefs. An organization will never know what really made another deal successful, it may not be in the same position (for example, the other client may have been a loss leader for the winning supplier), it may not be in the same market, it may not have the same structure, and it may not even be outsourcing the same mix of activities. The need, then, is to develop acumen about claimed benefits so that management can focus outsourcing on its own goals and characteristics.

As shown in Table 2.1 BB1 has four main activities. The goal of all four is "veracity, not ideology," that is, to understand what can really be achieved and how, rather than make decisions based on ideology.

Case Example: A state agency gains acumen, changes its plans

A state government agency (Case 45) beginning a BPO initiative had formed some preliminary ideas and expectations, but believed it was prudent to investigate further. It investigated two state government agencies like itself, a federal agency, and two private sector companies, studying in particular the service structure and strategy in each case, the sourcing decisions and lessons, and implications for itself. The organization studied public records and contacted key personnel at the firms and suppliers (if the organization had gone ahead with outsourcing).

This investigation helped form, as well as adjust, its previous thinking. Management learned, for example, that market offerings did not have IT systems up to their expectations. So they required the bidders to use its IT system and propose a development process to move to a new system. This approach caused little disruption to operations during transition, and allowed the organization to fully retain all its information during the term of the contract.

Management also found the outsourcing market to be immature and disparate. So it opted for a staged open tender rather than a direct closed tender (invitation only), which had been the original plan.

The winning bid ended up being from an organization it would not have invited.

In its investigation, management also observed the importance of having both a dedicated transition team and a dedicated contract-management team. When these were missing, they saw significant problems. So management identified these team members right away and formed the core lifecycle project team quickly. They also gave all other employees significant professional and personal assistance in making the transition. As a result, this state agency did not suffer the typical staff morale plunge and loss of key personnel that many others experienced.

Most importantly, the investigation taught management the value of the SLA (Service Level Agreement) schedule in the contract and the need to develop KPIs (Key Performance Indicators), which it had not known about. Management invested two months in getting the SLAs and KPIs right for the organization. Both parties credit that with making the deal run smoothly over the entire term of the contract.

Table 2.1 Outsourcing Lifecycle Model: Building blocks and key activities

Building block (BB)	Key activity	Goal
Architect		
BB1: Investigate	1. Gather insight via experts and experienced organizations 2. Determine and test goals/expectations 3. Collect intelligence on market conditions and potential suppliers 4. Investigate similar decisions and peer organizations	Veracity, not ideology
BB2: Target	5. Match goals to appropriate outsourcing model 6. Identify, with objective criteria, suitable services to outsource 7. Prepare the 7 baseline and future state profiles: service, cost, asset, staff, stakeholder, current contracts, and governance	Targeted and defined scope
BB3: Strategize	8. Decide the rollout approach (big bang, phased, piecemeal) 9. Determine key "rules" (e.g. governing docs, # suppliers, asset ownership, risk/reward) 10. Design the detailed end-to-end lifecycle program/projects 11. Identify and source the lifecycle skills 12. Prepare the lifecycle communications strategy 13. Prepare the business case rules and the base case 14. Assess feasibility, risk, and impact to the organization	Informed, holistic strategies
BB4: Design	15. Prepare the commercial and operating blueprint 16. Develop the 4 balanced score metrics – service, financial, relationship and strategic	Well-designed future state

Continued

Table 2.1 Continued

Building block (BB)	Key activity	Goal
	17. Draft the service level agreement – scope, metrics/ incentives, reporting, and governance	
	18. Draft the price framework (fixed, variable, and cost plus items)	
	19. Draft the contract considering the standard 90+ issues	
	20. Design the inter-party relationship (structure, roles, authorities, etc.)	
	21. Design the retained organization (kept functions)	
	22. Design the contract management function (governance)	
Engage BB5: Select	23. Plan and detail the tender stages	Best value
	24. Identify the right evaluation team – breadth and depth	for money,
	25. Determine the right evaluation criteria and strategy for each tender stage	sustainable solution and
	26. Request the right, clear, and comprehensive bid data for each tender stage	provider
	27. Facilitate the best responses (briefings, Q&A, data room, tours, etc.)	
	28. Use interactive evaluation techniques (interviews, site visits, etc.)	
	29. Select supplier based on value for money	
	30. Conduct the 5 due diligences on supplier: company, price, solution, contract, and customer references	
BB6: Negotiate	31. Prepare negotiation strategy and prioritize negotiation items	Complete contract
	32. Conduct effective negotiations	
Operate BB7: Transition	33. Finalize and mobilize all plans (e.g. communications, risk, setup, acceptance)	Efficient and complete
	34. Resource the transition project	mobilization
	35. Manage the impact on staff (retained, transferring, and departing)	
	36. Manage the transfers (staff, asset, 3rd party contracts, work-in-progress, etc.)	
	37. Manage knowledge retention and transfer	
	38. Implement retained organization and contract management	
	39. Engineer workflows, communication channels, authorities, etc.	
	40. Conduct acceptance, closeout and post-implementation review	
BB8: Manage	41. Invest in the relationship (plan, assess, and improve) results	Ongoing results
	42. Meaningful reporting and analyses	
	43. Regular communication and meetings	

Continued

Table 2.1 Continued

Building block (BB)	Key activity	Goal
	44. Diligent documentation and administration	
	45. Manage risks and plan contingencies	
	46. Manage issues, variations, and disputes	
	47. Effect continuous improvement and streamlining	
	48. Evaluate and audit supplier (controls, performance, compliance)	
	49. Evaluate organization both as a customer and contract manager	
Regenerate		
BB9: Refresh	50. Assess next generation options (backsource, retain, handover)	Refreshed strategy and options
	51. Assess contract outcomes and lessons	
	52. Knowledge refreshment (e.g. market, technology, price, metrics)	
	53. Reassess requirements – re-scope, re-bundle and re-design	
	54. Determine the strategy and business case for each option	

Building Block 2: Target the services – identify the right activities to outsource

There are no hard and fast rules about what should and should not be outsourced. Certainly, some types of services have been more popular targets, particularly those with mature markets, predictable demand, predictability of service costs, and well-known performance standards. The goal of this building block is for organizations to identify and then profile those areas where they can actually achieve sought-after benefits.

Case Example: An international airline creates an objective targeting process

As part of the two-year business review process at an international airline (Case 25), all the division chiefs, who reported to the CEO, needed to decide together what to outsource. In lieu of an objective framework, the journey began with each executive telling the others what "could go." Each executive, of course, believed his silo was absolutely core to the business and should not be outsourced. Sometimes their opinion, though, was based solely on, "We've always done it, so it must be core or we wouldn't be doing it."

But when consultants were brought in, the process changed, significantly. The business was mapped into processes (what took place) and silos (where processes took place). The group based its objective criteria on the business benefits sought from outsourcing, in the short and long term, and the apparent barriers that could preclude a service from being outsourced. The final criteria are shown in Table 2.2.

Table 2.2 Benefits and barriers of outsourcing at an international airline

Benefits Sought		
Short-term (within the first year)	**Long-term**	**Barriers**
1. A proven, competitive market exists with positive results in the industry. 2. We can better align supply with demand, particularly where we have a backlog of work or cannot satisfy demand. 3. We can substantially upgrade our services without incurring capital investment. 4. We can gain a cash infusion from selling our assets or transferring our staff. 5. We can reduce costs in areas where our costs are currently above industry standards. 6. We can access staff and skills in short supply.	1. We can focus on strategic work in-house, not day-to-day operations. 2. We can improve our customer focus. 3. We can make positive cultural changes within the airline.	1. The service is core to our airline; we will not outsource it. 2. Customer perceptions of us will be excessively adverse if we outsource the service. 3. Regulatory restrictions or imperatives prevent outsourcing (i.e. chief pilot). 4. We might inadvertently create a monopolistic market for the outsourcer due to the specifity of the assets and/or the knowledge required. 5. We obtain a sustainable competitive advantage by performing this service.

Based on the above criteria, 18 business processes and 12 business functions became the strongest candidates for outsourcing. Figure 2.3 shows the strength of candidacy for the 12 business functions using the three criteria: short-term benefits, long-term benefits, and barriers.[14]

Thus, the benefits and barriers listing allowed the airline to systematically identify target services to outsource, rather than rely on the persuasiveness of individual executives. Having the consultants facilitate the process also helped make it more objective. A clear picture of what to outsource emerged. The to-be-outsourced activities were then prioritized based on benefits, business needs, and risk management.

Building Block 3: Strategize – get prepared

The purpose of this building block is to conduct the planning that enables objective and knowledgeable decisions to be made throughout the remainder of the lifecycle. It is important to get this right. Wrong strategies create pathway inflexibilities that are difficult and expensive to change later. The strategies developed in this building block include:

- **Rollout strategy:** How the outsourcing initiative will be rolled out as a program
- **Organizational "rules of the game" strategy:** The underlying rules to be followed in outsourcing, such as allowing or not allowing in-house bids, conditions for transferring staff, the use of penalties and rewards in the contract, to name but a few
- **Lifecycle strategy:** The detailed program for the outsourcing lifecycle, focusing particularly on building blocks 4 through 7
- **Staffing strategy:** The expertise and people needed to manage and execute the program
- **Communication strategy:** The how, what, when, where, and who to communicate
- **Decision making strategy:** The business case rules for key decisions, as well as the base case for the outsourcing "go/no go" decision
- **Analysis strategy:** The feasibility, risk and impact assessment over the outsourcing initiative

Case example: A telecommunications company's policies and unions mattered

The industrial relations division of this telco (Case 44) had agreed with all the company's unions that they would get to bid on any outsourcing tender, but the outsourcing project team in one division did not know about this agreement. The team only discovered the agreement after it had chosen a preferred supplier. The unions complained, so the entire process had to be put on hold for six months to give the unions time to jointly bid on the work. Their bid was unsuccessful, and the tender was awarded to the original preferred supplier, but the process was much tougher than it should have been.

The outsourcing team in a different division (Case 43) did not have that problem because, as part of its strategy work in planning the outsourcing program, the team identified all the internal stakeholders and studied all the relevant issues. This team knew of the union agreement through its discussions with the industrial relations division. It overcame the bidding issue by agreeing with the unions that all work put out to bid would not cover "core" telco business. Thus, the agreement did not apply.

During strategy development, this same team uncovered other issues early, in time to address them and prevent ill effects on their outsourcing initiative. One issue: They could not use the "clean-break" approach to transferring staff to a supplier. The clean-break approach provides staff with a severance package *and* allows them to accept a position with the outsourcing provider. The company's severance provisions, however, barred staff from working for the winning supplier for two years if the employees took the severance package. Accordingly, the outsourcing team did not make staff transfers a requirement of the tender and informed all the potential bidders of that company policy so that their offers did not depend on their gaining telco staff.

The other telco outsourcing team (Case 44), though, chose to use the clean-break approach because management believed that it was in the provider's best interest to give them full control over hiring *and* it was in the employees' best interest to give them a severance package as well. The winning provider's bid required 70 percent of the workforce to transfer. But, of the 300 people let go, only five transferred to the provider. They were new employees; the severance package offered them little gain.

This mishandling by the outsourcing team delayed the handover by three months. And by then, only a skeleton crew had been assembled. During those three months, neither organization had staff to conduct normal service delivery, so it was essentially abandoned. Furthermore, because the organizational knowledge had walked out the door, normal operations did not resume for another six months. In all, a year passed before the supplier was handling the full scope of work at the agreed key performance levels. This outsourcing team had not delved into the details in its strategy preparation.

Building Block 4: Design – detail the future

This building block wraps up the Architect Phase. Together with the other three building blocks, this phase leads to defining the planned *configuration* of the deal. An outsourcing configuration describes what services will be outsourced, where they are to be provided, for how long, by whom (prime contractor or multiple suppliers), how they will be paid for, who will own which assets, how performance will be monitored, and which governance structures will be put in place.[15] These configuration choices define the "rules for the upcoming game," so they need to be detailed. The intent is to balance the often-competing interests of client and suppliers, while, at the same time, motivating the suppliers to provide the services and quality its client desires.

Building Block 4 results in detailed documents that articulate the future arrangement using commercial language, that is, in language potential providers understand and can bid on. The three main documents are the desired contract terms, the detailed SLAs, and the pricing model for the services. If these key governing documents are prepared in as close to final form as possible, and used as the baseline for the bidding process (in BB5), the client increases the probability of obtaining exactly the services it requires, under the conditions it requires. And by leaving little to chance or opportunism, it gains considerable negotiating leverage and efficiency.

By the end of BB4, management should also have designed the retained organization (the portion of the organization that will remain part of the service delivery chain), the contract-management function that will monitor the relationship, and the desired inter-party relationship. An organization that has defined, at this point and in some detail, not only its contract/supplier management strategy but also these organizational structures immediately gains the superior position over prospective bidders.

The time to decide what needs to be done, and by whom, is before opening bidding, not after the deal has been signed and everyone knows where they will be working. While it is tempting to wait and "make a go of it," delaying organizational decisions is rarely successful. More likely, the organization suffers out-of-control costs, high staff turnover, inadequate supplier monitoring, and poor coordination among the parties.

Case Example: An international airline's handshake agreement costs it plenty

The general manager of an international airline (Case 26) made an agreement with the top executive of a supplier because they had worked together before and trusted each other. The deal was simple enough. The supplier would take over call center operations, its core business, so that the airline could focus on *its* core business. This was to be a *strategic partnership*, so both parties believed they only needed a brief, high-level memorandum of understanding (MOU). The contract and other specifications would be developed over time.

Years later, after both executives had left their companies, an internal audit revealed that (1) there was never a signed contract or a specification, and (2) the supplier had been over-billing for years. Each business unit was being charged a price per call, and simultaneously, the centralized accounts payable section was being charged for full cost recovery (even for such items as toilet paper at the supplier's facility). The over-billing resulted from there being no detailed descriptions of the services included in *price per call* nor the items to be charged as *reimbursable costs*.

The lesson this airline learned, and knowledgeable firms know, is that they should never give suppliers complete discretion over what to charge or how to charge. By and large, most of the case study organizations prepared their SLA (activity #17), price framework (#18) and contract (#19) *before* selecting their supplier so that the deal they want is put to market. In that way, negotiation is constrained to just a few elements, rather than the entire deal.

In nearly all the cases where substantial portions of the deal were negotiated after selecting the supplier, or after the supplier had begun work, significant problems arose.

Building Block 5: Select – choose the best supplier(s)

Building Block 5 begins the Engage Phase. Its eight main activities involve the competitive bidding process, facilitating and evaluating the bids, and conducting discovery and due diligence. Competitive bidding is the most common selection technique, with most organizations using a tender (a request for proposal) to see how the marketplace will respond to its needs. This approach not only pressures suppliers to deliver their best value for money against their peers, but it also gives the client information to evolve and mature its selection decision.

Unfortunately, many organizations start here at BB5. But skipping the Architect Phase and beginning at this Select building block is equivalent to starting to build a house before it is designed, hoping everything will turn out right in the end. The Engage Phase (BB5 and BB6) builds on the Architect Phase. Select is where all organizations should increase their bargaining power by leveraging the competitive tension that naturally occurs in this phase. Once the contract has been awarded, the organization's bargaining power plummets.

Determining which supplier(s) to depend upon for many years is akin to acting as the matchmaker for an arranged marriage. Vigilant selection delivers the best match – if the organization truly knows itself. The best technique for uncovering one's true needs is a multi-stage competitive process, which means marketplace discovery and due diligence should not be confined just to BB5. That is why organizations should walk through the entire lifecycle before they reach this building block.

Our casework shows that appropriate selection depends on:

- The client's knowledge of the market and its players, including standard capabilities and processes, niche competences, geographic reach and differentiation, price ranges, and approaches. To gain all this information, the organization may need to issue an RFI (Request for Information) in BB1.
- The stability of the market's offerings. If the work to be outsourced is characterized by a short lifecycle, the client may need to scan offerings more than once. Again, an RFI is one way to assess market changes.
- The degree of influx of new entrants into the market. New entrants can change price/performance dynamics, competitiveness of the market, and current once-off opportunities. If this is the situation, the organization may need to issue an ROI (Registration of Interest) in BB1 to identify interested parties and their capabilities.
- The number of potential suppliers. If sizeable, the organization may need to create a culling process to, say, evaluate only five bids rather than 20. An ROI in BB1 helps determine market size, and an EOI (Expression of Interest) in BB3 helps create a shortlist for the BB5 tender.
- The degree to which the organization knows what it wants. If requirements are not certain and have not been commercially articulated (via the contract, service level agreement, and pro forma price schedule), then it may need to explore options and alternatives, typically done through an EOI.
- The completeness and competitiveness of preceding bids. If the organization does not receive enough information to make the right decision on solutions, pricing, and providers, it can conduct a post-RFT (Request for Tender) process. This process commonly involves (1) asking for a BAFO (Best and Final Offer), (2) conducting parallel negotiations with two bidders to short-list to one, or (3) extending the clarification period after the bids have been received until all concerns have been ameliorated.

Case Example: A bank approaches the market without understanding its full needs

A bank (Case 27) issued a voluminous EOI in an open tender process before determining its evaluation criteria. After receiving 14 widely varying bids, the evaluation team realized it needed a structured evaluation methodology to select a supplier. The 11-member team therefore convened a methodology workshop to develop the evaluation criteria. By its close, the team realized the voluminous EOI had elicited only 30 percent of the information it needed to select a supplier. To maintain the bank's credibility in the market, rather than short-list to fewer suppliers, the team issued its request for tender (RFT) to all 14 suppliers. Evaluating all RFTs added two months to evaluation and cost an extra Au$200,000 (not to mention the cost to the 14 suppliers). It took only one day to develop the criteria and the evaluation methodology, which would have prevented this excessive cost.

Building Block 6: Negotiate – seal the deal

So much emphasis has been placed on negotiation in outsourcing contracts that an inexperienced person could believe it is the pinnacle of the outsourcing lifecycle, involving the greatest amount of work and the greatest risk of signing a bad contract. If it does become the pinnacle, then something has gone seriously wrong earlier. Organizations place themselves at risk in at least four ways:

1. The organization has not drafted its desired contract and SLA requirements prior to opening the competitive process.
2. Its business case is based on invalid baselines.
3. It has not developed a feasible BATNA (best alternative to a negotiated agreement), so it has no well-thought-out alternative if a supplier radically changes its offer once at the negotiation table. This does happen.
4. It has made itself vulnerable, perhaps by being on a firm, short deadline, thereby giving the supplier the leverage to act opportunistically.

When the Outsourcing Lifecycle Model is followed, negotiation simply involves refining the exact wording of various documents. It should not involve give-and-take negotiations over the intent of the deal because that's when parties win or lose depending upon the particular individuals involved. As one experienced respondent put it to us, "Don't negotiate, calculate."

The contract and SLA should have already been developed (in BB4), the supplier's preferred alternatives declared, the discovery/due diligence by both parties concluded (in BB5), and the preparations for transition completed (novated or assigned licenses, asset inventories and audits, and so on, in BB4). But when prior lifecycle activities have not been thoroughly conducted, there will inevitably be issues that require negotiation.

The key is planning the negotiation in detail, by prioritizing the issues, determining the organization's position on each issue, knowing the individuals involved from both parties, and having BATNAs in hand and reviewed and approved by management beforehand.

Case Example: An international accounting firm's negotiations takes months

After months of discussions, an international accounting firm agreed, in principle, to use the services of an international equipment company. All that was left was to negotiate the details. The supplier's sales team handed over negotiations to the operations team that would be responsible for making the deal work.

The client's outsourcing team had no negotiation strategy – other than go through the supplier's standard contract, line-by-line. Of course, the standard contract did not reflect the prior agreements with the supplier's sales team. Furthermore, the operations team discarded the sales team's agreements as unworkable. As a result, the client was left with a deal bearing little resemblance to the one it expected.

Rather than terminate discussions, which was its first instinct, the client team went back to the sales team with its issues. The provider put a more commercially astute, relationship-oriented operations manager in charge; it brought the sales manager back into the picture, and it conducted a renegotiation around the client's issues. As a result, the deal met, and in some instances, exceeded the client's expectations. But negotiations took months rather than weeks, as originally expected.

The cases that had thorough, but brief, negotiations did a number of things right. One, they prepared the SLA (activity #17), price framework (#18), and contract (#19) before selecting the supplier. Two, they then required the bidders to give exact wording changes to any item they wished to negotiate as part of their bid (#26). Three, these changes (and perhaps additions or deletions) were then clarified during evaluation (#27, #28) and incorporated into the selection (#29). Four, all items to be negotiated were detailed in the negotiation strategy (#31), including the client's estimate of each party's position, the underlying drivers of those positions, potential win/win scenarios, and each party's BATNA.

Contracts worth over Au$10–25 million a year were negotiated in less than two weeks using this approach (Cases 18, 34, 70, 87), whereas Case 72, worth Au$2.7 million a year, took months to negotiate because it did not follow the process. Likewise, Case 100 (worth Au$1.5 million a year) and Case 41 (worth Au$1.8 million a year), also took months, for the same reason.

Building Block 7: Transition – the starting gate

The Operate Phase (BB7 and BB8) starts with transition, which officially begins at contract commencement and ends on a specified date or when both parties sign a transition acceptance form, confirming that all aspects of the arrangement are fully operational. Irrespective of the official start and end dates, the transition actually begins much earlier, and actually ends much later. In fact, if not managed properly, transition may never end. Therefore, all parties need to begin planning the transition as soon as it is reasonable to believe the deal may go ahead.

Just as the Select building block (BB5) is not the beginning of the outsourcing lifecycle, transition is not the first building block for planning its operation. This transition building block should merely execute the plans made earlier. Inevitably, of course, there will be contingencies and adjustments needed when, as one CIO put it, "the rubber hits the road."

Case Example: An insurance company successfully transitions its IT staff

An insurance company (Case 13) wanted most of its 70 IT staff to transfer willingly to the supplier. The contract stated that the transferring staff's employment conditions would be no less than their conditions at the insurance company, and furthermore, they would be with the provider for at least two years. But both parties knew these provisions would not be enough to excite the staff about transferring.

Therefore, the two parties agreed on a plan to win the "hearts and minds" of the staff before announcing the deal. The supplier would make presentations to the staff and conduct site visits at its operations center. Both parties would hold joint formal and informal gatherings. The staff would receive branded merchandise (hats, mouse pads, t-shirts, backpacks, etc.) and be given introductory sessions on the training the supplier would provide them once they became employees. Finally, the insurance company CIO initiated an open door policy so that any staff member could have a one-on-one chat. These activities were so successful that all the staff transferred enthusiastically.

Other cases had similar results using different techniques:

- Offering free financial, career, and personal counseling to affected staff (Case 7)
- Enlisting the staff's help in determining what should be in scope and out of scope, thereby gaining their buy-in to the outsourcing initiative (Case 16)
- Involving staff in supplier selection (Case 49)
- Make staff part of the working group that determined the supplier evaluation criteria (Case 69).

Building Block 8: Manage – get the results

In essence, all previous seven building blocks prepare for this building block: Manage. The game is actually played out in this part of the Operate Phase. This is where the benefits (and problems) of outsourcing appear.

The goal of all nine activities in BB8 is to manage for results. Depending on the extent of the outsourcing, it can require the client to make profound changes in its strategic and operational mechanisms. Basically, client managers must learn to manage outputs, rather than inputs, use negotiation and relationship management in place of direct control, and rely on periodic planning and reviews to take the place of day-to-day oversight of service delivery operations. These changes in management work are significant.

Case Example: A government organization learns how not to manage a provider

A government organization (Case 57) assumed that compliance with the contract was a foregone conclusion, so no oversight of the contract was required. Thus, it handed oversight over to a low-level contract administrator and did not perform any compliance reviews until four years into the five-year contract. At that point, it hired an independent audit firm to evaluate the situation.

After an extensive process, the auditors determined that the supplier was only 40 percent compliant with the contract. Work totaling Au$200,000 a year had not been performed, many KPIs were not being reported, many reports were not being generated, and the list went on. The supplier noted that it had not done the work because the contract required the client to request the work, which it had not done (even though it paid for the work). Furthermore, the client did not follow up on KPIs or request missing reports, did not ask for performance review or planning forums, and so on. The key finding of the audit report was that the client did not install any governance over the contract, so the supplier was allowed almost complete discretion in what it did.

As a result of this audit, and to better manage its next-generation deal, the government organization put in place a seven-person contract-management team, led by a senior contract manager. This contract-management function cost Au$360,000 a year, but it was required to ensure savings of Au$830,000 a year through specific contract-management activities, experienced personnel, and proactive management.

Building Block 9: Refresh – towards next generation

All contracts end, either through early termination or by reaching the natural end of the term. During a contract's life, firms, and markets change, perhaps in ways that render past decisions inappropriate in a current context. For example, the degree of uncertainty may have diminished, market growth may have created more competition, supplier capabilities have likely changed, and information disparities between the parties may have decreased. Thus, all clients should reassess their initial sourcing decision before coming to the end of their contract. All five activities in BB9 involve re-assessing outsourcing options and considering cost-effective strategies for each option. Then the lifecycle begins anew, returning to BB1.

Depending on the decisions made – the work to be re-tendered, back-sourced (brought back in-house), or renegotiated with the incumbent supplier – the lifecycle is repeated, individually for each option chosen. If the outsourcing configuration will differ significantly, the entire lifecycle may need to be repeated. But if only re-tendering the same scope of work with little change to the deal, the organization may be able to begin at BB5 (Select). If backsourcing, BB7 (Transition) may be the appropriate starting point. And if renegotiating the same scope but an improved deal, the organization might begin at BB4 (Design) then skip to BB6 (Negotiate).

Irrespective of the decisions reached as a result of BB9, the five activities in this building block are critical to beginning the next generation. As with all the building blocks, its work depends on the work done in preceding building blocks.

As a guideline, one very large organization began its BB9 work 2.5 years before the end of a ten-year contract. As a result of this work, it successfully switched suppliers and signed a further ten-year deal with the new supplier in 2004. Interestingly, this organization paid out US$12 million to serious bidders to attract them, also signaling that the re-bid would be truly competitive, with the incumbent having no "inside track" advantage.

Case Example: A university finds no baseline for assessing benefits

Toward the end of a five-year contract, the Chancellor of a university (Case 24) directed the contract manager to assess whether or not the benefits sought by outsourcing were actually being achieved. The results of this analysis were critical to the steering committee's planning on future outsourcing.

No documentation, other than the original contract, had been maintained and none of the people involved in the outsourcing negotiations remained with the university. Furthermore, the current stakeholders all had differing opinions about the original objectives: cost savings? permitting the university to focus on its core activities? allow it to broaden its offerings? temporary or eventually backsourcing to the university? The contract manager made a valiant effort, but he could not determine the intended benefits let alone whether or not they had been achieved.

As a substitute, he enumerated actual achievements, and how they had been accomplished – what had worked well:

1. giving the supplier a greater span of control (that is, responsibility for a process or a function not just a task), improved the supplier's performance because the work could be measured by business outcomes via KPIs;
2. using rewards as well as recourse motivated the supplier's behavior;
3. conducting reference checks and using known approaches to supplier integration led to the supplier working well with other suppliers; and
4. locking in explicit accountabilities in the contract reduced finger pointing.

Conclusion: Getting on the optimal, cost-effective path

This chapter has presented a comprehensive process model for client organizations to use when undertaking an outsourcing initiative. It is the most thorough description of the outsourcing process presented in the literature to date. It is also based on detailed understanding of the experiences of 100 case study organizations, so the model is backed by far more empirical evidence than most published research on IT and business process outsourcing. Finally, seven organizations not used to the model have since independently and strongly confirmed the importance of the 54 activities in the model.

In short, outsourcing will be most successful if it is viewed as a strategy with a lifecycle rather than as a one-off transaction. Client organizations can have more successful outcomes and ITO/BPO deals that operate in a cost-effective manner when they proactively manage the entire outsourcing lifecycle.

Figure 2.4 illustrates the crux of outsourcing management, as uncovered in this and other research: outsourcing costs can get way out of control if the program is not well managed. There is a recommended path and a flawed path. The difference is management.

Although organizations initially outsource for a range of reasons, they all generally worry also about reducing costs. Figure 2.4 supports the belief that organizations need to spend and invest in the outsourcing management process to truly save money.

It is worth looking at outsourcing management costs. In re-analyzing three research bases (representing nearly 800 deals) for this paper,[16] we

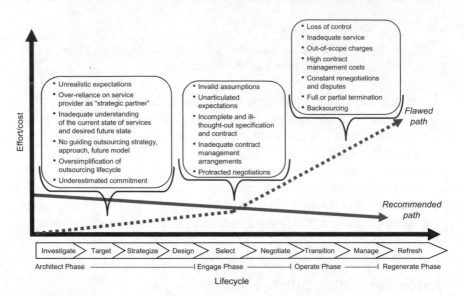

Effort/cost

- Unrealistic expectations
- Over-reliance on service provider as "strategic partner"
- Inadequate understanding of the current state of services and desired future state
- No guiding outsourcing strategy, approach, future model
- Oversimplification of outsourcing lifecycle
- Underestimated commitment

- Invalid assumptions
- Unarticulated expectations
- Incomplete and ill-thought-out specification and contract
- Inadequate contract management arrangements
- Protracted negotiations

- Loss of control
- Inadequate service
- Out-of-scope charges
- High contract management costs
- Constant renegotiations and disputes
- Full or partial termination
- Backsourcing

Flawed path

Recommended path

Investigate > Target > Strategize > Design > Select > Negotiate > Transition > Manage > Refresh >

Architect Phase --------------------------------------I Engage Phase ------------------I Operate Phase -------------I Regenerate Phase

Lifecycle

Figure 2.4 Getting on the optimal, most cost-effective path

made three findings. Costs of getting to contract fall between 0.4 percent and 2.5 percent of contract value. These costs rise as a percentage as the size of the deal increases. Thirdly, these costs rise as the percentage of IT/business processes outsourced increases.

We found ongoing outsourcing management to cost from 3 percent to 8 percent of total contract value. Our 2001 survey found the average contract management cost to be 4.2 percent of total contract value. Managing offshoring costs more, from 10 percent to 12 percent in 2000, and from 12 percent to 15 percent in 2003–04.[17]

As outsourcing becomes a core competency, wise organizations invest more in its management, even though spending more runs counter to most Boards' goal of spending less. Their real goal should be to continually spend less on contract management *per dollar outsourced*. We have found, though, that managing costs is less important than managing portfolio configuration, complexity, and risk.

Low spenders do not perform contract management; they perform what we call *contract administration*. Administering contracts may work where no significant contracts exist and the outsourced activities are relatively simple to define, discrete, and easy to monitor. But for all other situations, simply administering a contract slowly, but ultimately, leads to an expensive erosion of control over the client organization's IT and business process destinies.

To stay on the recommended, cost-effective path, in Figure 2.4, the Architect Phase puts a premium on developing an evidence-based sourcing strategy that pinpoints the services required and the outsourcing configuration that is most likely to deliver on expectations. Without this up-front work, significant issues will accumulate, and cost a lot more to resolve later in the lifecycle. Suppliers, too, recognize the eventual pain that non-architected plans can cause. As one supplier's CEO told us, "The customer from hell is the naïve buyer."

The Engage and Operate Phases do offer chances to make corrections, which contribute to ensuring valid assumptions, explicit and detailed expectations and service contracts, and sufficient management to keep all activities on target. As all too many deals have shown, without this initial architecting work and detailed, dynamic, ongoing management, high costs will show up later, typically as loss of control, inadequate service, extensive out-of-scope charges, excessive management time and effort, constant renegotiation, and a growing belief during the Regeneration Phase that the organization either needs to backsource the outsourced activities or switch to another provider.

However, it is not claimed here that following the building block process is the sole determinant of successful outcomes from outsourcing. For example, adequacy of staffing has a crucial bearing on which outcomes are actually achievable, as we found in our work on delineating core in-house capabilities for outsourcing.[18] The quality and content of plans, and managerial judgment, also play critical roles.[19] Unanticipated events, such as changes in business direction or replacement of CEO or board members, which can result from mergers or poor financial results, can also eat into the health of an outsourcing deal.

One of our profound frustrations has been to watch organizations repeat mistakes that others made over a decade ago. Another has been to watch organizations go through painstakingly long learning experiences that could easily be circumvented from the existing knowledge on outsourcing management. Our model intends to provide a missing piece to that knowledge. It answers the question: What process works best?

Appendix 2.1

The model is based on field data collected by the first author from 1994 to 2003. During that time, as an outsourcing consultant, she played the roles of both observer and participant in 100 outsourcing engagements (see Table 2.3). Her qualitative data consisted of plans, reports, contracts, evaluations, correspondence, presentations, minutes, reviews, audit findings and so on, from those 100 engagements.[20] Working iteratively through the cases, the three researchers trimmed the model to the 54 key activities that

Table 2.3 The 100 cases used to develop the model

1994	1995	1996	1997	1998	1999	2000	2001	2002	2003
1. Logistics JV – ITO	9. Defence – OO	15. Water utility – OO	25. Airline – BPO & OO	46. State govt agency – ITO	58. City council agency – ITO	71. Diversified manufacturer – ITO	85. Accounting firm – BPO	92. Supplier – ITO	96. Defence – OO
2. Petroleum company ITO	10. Federal govt dept – OO	16. Federal govt agency – ITO	26. Airline – OO	47. University – BPO	59. State govt agency – ITO	72. Accounting firm – BPO	86. Funds manager – ITO	93. Electric utility – OO	97. Electric utility – OO
3. Stock broker – ITO	11. Consumer Products – ITO	17. Medical products – ITO	27. Bank – BPO	48. State govt agency – ITO	60. Federal govt cluster – ITO	73. Federal govt agency – BPO	87. Gas utility OO	94. Electric utility OO	98. Electric Utility – OO
4. Bank – ITO	12. Electric utility – ITO	18. State govt agency – OO	28. Defence – ITO	49. State govt agency – BPO	61. City council – ITO	74. Federal govt agency – BPO	88. Supplier – BPO	95. Electic and gas utility – ITO	99. Gas utility – OO
5. Bank – ITO	13. Insurer – ITO	19. State govt dept – OO	29. Federal govt agency – ITO	50. Transport – ITO	62. City council – HRO	75. State govt agency – ITO	89. Airline – ITO		100. Federal govt agency BPO
6. State govt agency – ITO	14. State govt Cluster – ITO	20. Federal govt agency – ITO	30. Federal govt agency – BPO	51. Water utility – ITO	63. City council – BPO	76. Telecom manufactuer – ITO	90. Supplier BPO		
7. State govt authority – ITO		21. Electric utility – ITO	31. Federal govt agency – BPO	52. Industrial products – ITO	64. Bank – ITO	77. Federal govt agency – OO	91. Insurer – ITO		
8. State govt agency – OO		22. Transport – BPO	32. Federal govt agency – OO	53. University ITO	65. Insurer – BPO & OO	78. Travel company – ITO			
		23. Consumer products – ITO	33. State govt agency – OO	54. Logistics company – ITO	66. Electric utility – ITO	79. Automotive – BPO			
		24. University – ITO	34. State govt agency – ITO	55. Telecom – BPO	67. State govt agency – ITO	80. Telecom – ITO			
			35. Federal govt agency – ITO	56. Telecom – OO	68. University – OO	81. University – ITO			
			36. State govt agency – BPO	57. Federal govt agency –BPO	69. Telecom – OO	82. Telecom – OO			
			37. Insurer – BPO		70. Insurer ITO	83. State govt agency – BPO			
			38. Telecom – ITO			84. Telecom – OO			
			39. Defence – OO						
			40. Federal govt agency – BPO						
			41. Miner – ITO						
			42. Miner – ITO						
			43. Telecom – BPO						
			44. Telecom – BPO						
			45. State govt dept – BPO						

Notes: OO = operational outsourcing
ITO = IT outsourcing
BPO = business process outsourcing

had either contributed directly to the successful aspects of the deals or directly contributed to significant problems. In all, 1308 pieces of evidence were identified that justify the need for each of the 54 activities.[21]

To further test that these 54 were indeed necessary, the authors conducted seven additional case studies in five different industries. None had been a client of the first author. The authors held detailed, structured interviews with the CIO and the top contract manager in each firm. On average the contracts were worth Au$40 million a year. In total, 34 hours of interviews were conducted in 2003 and 2004. In addition, the authors reviewed documents, such as contracts, correspondence, and performance evaluations. Table 2.4 summarizes the "average importance" scores from these interviewees. As shown, every activity was rated "highly important."

Table 2.4 The importance of each activity, mean scores from the seven additional organizations

Average importance score	How important is (1=not at all, 5= very) this activity	Building block average
BB1 Investigate		4.7
1. Gather insight via experts and experienced organizations	5.0	
2. Determine and test goals/expectations	4.4	
3. Collect intelligence on market conditions and potential suppliers	4.7	
4. Investigate similar decisions and peer organizations	4.6	
BB2 Target		4.7
5. Match goals to appropriate outsourcing model/framework	4.4	
6. Identify, with objective criteria, suitable services to outsource	4.7	
7. Prepare the 7 profiles	4.9	
BB3 Strategize		4.6
8. Decide rollout approach	4.7	
9. Determine key strategic "rules"	5.0	
10. Design detailed end-to-end program	4.7	
11. Identify and source the lifecycle skills	4.6	
12. Prepare the lifecycle communications strategy	4.1	
13. Prepare business case rules and the base case	4.7	
14. Assess feasibility, risk, and impact	4.6	
BB4 Design		4.6
15. Prepare commercial and operating blueprint	4.1	
16. Develop the 4 balanced score metrics	4.3	
17. Draft SLA	4.9	
18. Draft the price framework	5.0	
19. Draft contract considering the standard 90+ issues	4.7	
20. Design the interparty relationship	4.6	

Continued

Table 2.4 Continued

Average importance score	How important is (1=not at all, 5= very) this activity	Building block average
21. Design the retained organization	4.6	
22. Design the contract-management function	5.0	
BB5 Select		4.8
23. Plan and detail the tender stages	4.9	
24. Identify right evaluation team	4.9	
25. Determine right evaluation criteria and strategy for each stage	4.9	
26. Request right, clear, and comprehensive bid data for each stage	4.7	
27. Facilitate the best responses	4.4	
28. Use interactive evaluation techniques	4.7	
29. Select supplier based on value for money	4.6	
30. Conduct the 5 due diligence on supplier	5.0	
BB6 Negotiate		5.0
31. Prepare negotiation strategy and prioritize negotiation items	5.0	
32. Conduct effective negotiations	5.0	
BB7 Transition		4.7
33. Finalize and mobilize all plans	4.9	
34. Resource transition project	4.7	
35. Manage impact on staff	4.9	
36. Manage transfers	4.4	
37. Manage Knowledge retention and transfer	4.6	
38. Implement retained organization and contract management	4.9	
39. Engineer workflows, communication channels, authorities, etc.	4.7	
40. conduct acceptance, closeout and post-implementation review	4.3	
BB8 Manage		4.7
41. Invest in the relationship	5.0	
42. Meaningful reporting and analyses	4.6	
43. Regular communication and meetings	5.0	
44. Diligent documentation and administration	4.7	
45. Manage risks and plan contingencies	4.9	
46. Manage issues, variations, and disputes	4.9	
47. Effect continuous improvement and streamlining	4.7	
48. Evaluate and audit supplier	4.3	
49. Evaluate organization both as a customer and contract manager	4.6	
BB9 Refresh		4.5
50. Ensure feasibility of options	4.9	
51. Assess contract outcomes and lessons	4.4	
52. Conduct knowledge refreshment	4.3	
53. Reassess requirements	4.6	
54. Determine the strategy and business case for each option	4.4	
Average	4.7	

This finding demonstrates that the lifecycle, as proposed, is enduring and fundamental for all outsourcing deals.[22]

Notes

1. For evidence see Cullen, S. and Willcocks, L. (2003), *Intelligent IT Outsourcing*, Butterworth Heinemann, Oxford; Kern, T. and Willcocks, L. (2001), *The Relationship Advantage: Information Technology, Outsourcing and Management*, Oxford University Press, Oxford; Kern, T., Willcocks, L., and van Heck, E. (2002), "The Winner's Curse in IT Outsourcing: How to Avoid Relational Trauma," *California Management Review*, 44, 2, 47–69; Lacity, M., and Willcocks, L. (2003), "Information Technology Sourcing Reflections," *Wirtschaftsinformatik*, Special Issue on Outsourcing, Vol. 45, 2, pp. 115–125.
2. Reported in Rohde, L. "Sainsbury, Accenture To Redo Outsourcing Pact," *Computer Weekly*, October 25, 2004, 5–6.
3. Reported in Earle, A. (2004), "End of The Affair: Bringing Outsourced Operations Back in-house," *Computerworld*, May 31. The actual report is: Diamondcluster, 2004 Global IT Outsourcing Study, Research, Spring, pp. 1–16.
4. Wighton, D. (2004), "JP Morgan Scraps IT Deal With IBM," *Financial Times*, September 16.
5. Reported by Miller, A. (2004), "Outsourcing Options and Performance Management In The Private and Public Sectors," Presentation at the Outsourcing Summit, London, November 22.
6. Collins, T. (2004), "MPs Given Little Comfort on State of Child Support Agency Systems," *Computer Weekly*, October 28.
7. Willcocks, L. and Fitzgerald, G. (1994), *A Business Guide to Information Technology Outsourcing*, Business Intelligence, London.
8. This quote is from Bob McKinnon, CIO of Commonwealth Bank, in August 2004. It is from an unpublished research project by Leslie Willcocks and David Feeny into implementing core IS capabilities.
9. Quoted in Lacity, M. and Willcocks, L. (2001), *Global Information Technology Outsourcing: In Search Of Business Advantage*, Wiley, Chichester.
10. A decade of ITO research has produced a large body of academic and practitioner literature with advice and insights. See Cullen, S., Willcocks, L. P., and Seddon, P. B. (2001), *Information Technology Outsourcing Practices in Australia*, Deloitte Touche Tohmatsu,

Melbourne. BPO is less well served but see Lacity, M. Willcocks, L., and Feeny, D. (2003), "Transforming a Back-Office Function: Lessons from BAE Systems' Experience with an Enterprise Partnership," *MISQ Executive*, Vol. 2, 2, pp. 86–103. Also Linder, J. (2004), "Transformational Outsourcing," *Sloan Management Review*, Vol. 45, 2.

11. Collins, H. (1996), "Competing Norms of Contractual Behaviour," in D. Campbell and P. Vincent-Jones (eds), *Contract and Economic Organization: Sociolegal Initiatives*. See also Kern, T. and Willcocks, L. (2001), *The Relationship Advantage: Information Technology, Sourcing and Management*, Oxford University Press, Oxford.

12. General Accounting Office, "Information Technology: Leading Commercial Practices for Outsourcing of Services," GAO-02–214, October 2001. http://www.gao.gov/new.items/d02214.pdf (viewed May 2004). Hurley, M. and Costa, C. (2001), "The Blurring Boundary of the Organisation: Outsourcing Comes Of Age," KPMG Consulting, Sydney. Kleppler, R. and Jones, W. O. (1998), *Outsourcing Information Technology Systems & Services*, Prentice Hall, New Jersey.

13. Loh, L. and Venkatraman, N. (1992), "Diffusion of Information Technology Outsourcing Influence Sources and the Kodak Effect," *Information Systems Research*, December, pp. 334–358. In our published and unpublished research, we found similar imitative behavior in subsequent rounds of outsourcing, including, more recently, in the offshore and business process outsourcing arenas. See Lacity and Willcocks, 2001, op.cit., and Cullen, Seddon, and Willcocks, 2001, op.cit.

14. To create this graph, the airline assumed that each criterion carried equal weight, thus each short-term and long-term rationale had one positive point and each barrier one negative point. Furthermore, to determine the relative strength of candidacy, the first consideration was the overall score (the number of short-term and long-term rationale, subtracted by the number of barriers). If the overall score for business functions was equal, the second consideration was the number of barriers. If the number of barriers in business functions was equal, the third consideration was the number of short-term rationale. This approach was meant to present a balanced picture of the overall case, rather than "cherry pick" the areas perceived to be easy to outsource or eliminating areas because of a single barrier.

15. In "Go Configure," *MIS*, August 2004, pp. 58–60, Cullen and Seddon define *configuration* as a high-level description of the choices the organization has made in crafting its outsourcing portfolio and deals. The three attributes of the configuration that describe the outsourcing

portfolio are (1) Scope Grouping, (2) Supplier Grouping, and (3) Financial Scale. The four attributes at the specific deal level are (1) Pricing Framework, (2) Duration, (3) Resource Ownership, and (4) Commercial Relationship.

16. The first research base is the 100-case base used as the basis of this paper. The second is a 400+ longitudinal case study database held at Warwick University. An early publication drawing on this research base this was Lacity, M. and Willcocks, L. (1998), "An Empirical Investigation of Information Technology Sourcing Practices: Lessons From Experience," *MIS Quarterly*, Vol. 22, 3, 363–408. The third research is a 2000 survey of 235 deals described in Cullen, S., Willcocks, L., and Seddon, P. (2001), *IT Outsourcing Practices in Australia*, Joint Deloitte-Touche Tohmatsu/University of Melbourne, Melbourne. This is available from scullen@cullengroup.com.au. Questions on costs were answered in detail by 78 respondents.

17. In one of our studies, the deals that outsourced over 65 percent of the IT budget averaged a 10 percent management cost, while those under 25 percent of the IT budget averaged 3 percent. Management costs fell between 1 and 10 percent of contract value. Detailed case study research allows us to make some judgments about effective spend. If one excludes from these figures the organizations having poor experiences, those doing contract administration rather than effective management, and those playing catch-up due to early lack of investment, the figures of 3 to 8 percent are reliable for domestic outsourcing, checked across our three separate studies.

18. See Lacity and Willcocks, 2001, chapter 7.

19. See Kern and Willcocks, 2001, op. cit. Also see DiRomualdo, T. and Gurbaxani, V. (1998), "Strategic Intent for IT Outsourcing," *Sloan Management Review*, Vol. 39, 4, pp. 1–26.

20. The value of the contracts ranged from Au$200,000 to Au$1.5 billion a year. Of the 100 cases, 60 percent were in the private sector, 40 percent in the public sector. Over 60 percent of the private-sector cases were in the finance (insurance, banking, funds management), ICT (information, communication and technology), or utilities (water, electricity, gas) industries. Within the public sector, the cases were chiefly state government agencies and departments. Nearly one-half of all the cases involved pure ITO initiatives. Nearly one-third were what is known as BPO, which has a large IT component but is mainly about outsourcing a corporate or head office function. And nearly one-fourth of the cases were operational outsourcing, which may have IT as an underlying enabler but is chiefly about production and core-business outsourcing.

21. As an academic note, a number of controls were applied in this research process. One researcher was a participant observer in all 100 cases. She applied the test of including in her original list of activities only those where she could directly attribute a notable benefit or problem as a result of either the activity's performance or non-performance. This test deleted a number of activities considered not important enough to include, reducing the number of key activities to 65. A further sifting by importance of activity outcomes, and frequency of activity in the 100 case samples, removed a few more. The two other researchers, both highly knowledgeable in outsourcing, then skeptically reviewed these decisions and the decision processes, taking into account a standard of research rigor expected in doctoral research. This review resulted in the 54 activities considered key to the outsourcing process.

22. The deals in the 100 cases and the subsequent seven organizations were neither "failed" deals nor unmitigated successes. They represent typical deals around the globe – each having aspects that worked and aspects that did not work. The collective experiences of these organizations formed the model presented in this paper. In addition, our findings did not differ significantly between earlier cases and later cases, with one exception. Because outsourcing management was a more established technique in the latter half of the data collection period, due to many organizations entering second-generation deals, we found more evidence supporting contract-management activities in those deals.

CHAPTER 3

The core capabilities framework for achieving high performing back offices

Leslie Willcocks and David Feeny

Introduction

In 1998, Feeny and Willcocks published the core information technology (IT) capabilities framework that identified four strategic domains (business, technology, third-party sourcing, and governance) and nine capabilities for high performing IT functions.[1] This framework was subsequently adopted by many large organizations seeking to deliver highly effective and cost-efficient IT services. This chapter extends the framework beyond IT by applying it to other back offices, including human resources, accounting, finance, and procurement. The resulting framework offers a powerful model for creating high performing back offices in terms of strategic agility, service excellence, and cost-efficiency.

The current framework is illustrated through three case studies, including a multinational organization that is several years into a large-scale outsourcing arrangement, a medium-sized organization beginning to outsource IT, and the BP-Exult[2] HR outsourcing arrangement. Senior executives in these organizations learned the importance of retaining the nine key capabilities discussed in this chapter. In comparing the three organizations, we discuss the different challenges arising in organizations of different sizes and at different stages in their ITO and BPO engagements.

The core capabilities strategy applied to back offices

Our core capabilities framework answers the questions raised by the shift in organizational strategy initiated in the early 1990s. At that time, many organizations shifted their strategies from selling vastly diversified products and services (to mitigate risks) to selling core products and services (to maximize competitive advantage). An organization, it was argued, can only be effective at a few core activities. Organizations should concentrate on developing these core capabilities to world-class. Anything else should be eliminated, minimized or outsourced.[3] But where should the line be drawn? Too many senior executives applied the model too literally, believing nearly all their back office functions qualified as non-core capabilities to be outsourced. One organization, for example, initially retained only 60 people in-house after transferring 3000 IT people to external suppliers. The organization was woefully understaffed to adequately plan for future needs, to administer outsourcing contracts, and to look after the organization's IT destiny.[4]

Our work makes a contribution by identifying where the line should be drawn for back offices. We found that high performing back offices are managed by a residual team of highly capable, demand-led, and strategy-focused people. Senior executives in these organizations view their back offices as performing "strategic," "governance" or "intelligent customer" roles. Essentially, this view emphasizes full in-house involvement for upstream activities (particularly governance and strategy) and a "procure and diligently manage" role for downstream activities (such as infrastructure, operational service, and support). A decade of case and advisory work in the ITO and BPO areas makes clear to us that retained core capabilities to strategize, keep control of the area, and manage external supply are key components of sourcing strategy.

The core capabilities framework is derived from several strands of research carried out in the 1993–2005 period.[5] In reviewing this research, organizations seemed to be converging on the core capabilities strategy from two different directions. Some organizations started with the premise that a back office should be outsourced, leaving the question: What, if any, capability should be retained in-house? These organizations largely concluded that they needed to retain contract and supplier management capabilities. By contrast, other organizations started with the premise that the back office represented an important strategic resource, leaving the question: What capabilities do we need to ensure continual exploitation? These latter organizations largely concluded that they needed capabilities to understand and articulate business-driven needs, and those that relate to developing the appropriate technical and operational platform. They were often less sophisticated in their requirements for contract and supplier management capabilities, even if they assumed that many back office services would be externally sourced in the future.

A second observation from this research was that senior executives tended to assess their back office *resources* such as headcount, budgets, physical facilities, and technology, rather than their *capabilities* to effectively manage and deploy these resources for the business's benefit. Our framework encourages senior executives to broaden their perspective from exclusive assessment of operational resources to include strategic capabilities and competencies. We define a capability as a distinctive set of human-based skills, orientations, attitudes, motivations, and behaviors that transform resources into specific business activities. Collections of capabilities, in turn, create high-level strategic competencies that positively influence business performance.

By synthesizing the learning from all the research, we can provide a rich picture of the core capabilities required in back offices over the next five to seven years.

Revisiting the Feeny–Willcocks core capabilities framework

The original Feeny–Willcocks framework was developed only for IT.[6] Here we extend the framework further by applying it to all back office functions. A constant finding from our BPO research is that IT is increasingly utilized as a process enabler in all back offices. Thus, the relevant IT capability is embedded in our expanded framework. The first step in the synthesis is represented by the four competencies of the retained back offices (see Figure 3.1). Next, we present the nine core capabilities that populate the four competencies (see Figure 3.2). We then discuss the implications and challenges this form of core retained back offices represents. We illustrate the implementation issues using three ITO and BPO case studies. From these, we derive major lessons on how high-performing back offices can be created, managed, and leveraged.

Figure 3.1 shows the four competencies of a high performing back office:

1. **The business competency is concerned with the elicitation and delivery of business requirements.** This competency is business-focused, demand-driven and concerned with defining the systems/processes to be provided, their relationship to business needs, and the inter-relationships and inter-dependencies with other systems/processes.

2. **The technical competency is concerned with ensuring that the business has access to the technical capability it needs.** This competence takes into account such issues as current price/performance, future directions, and integration potential. This competency is about defining the blueprint or architecture of the technical platform that will be used over time to support the target systems and processes. It presents the set of allowable options from which the technical implementation of each system and process must be selected.

3. **The supply competency encompasses understanding and use of the external business services market.** This competency is driven by decisions about the sourcing of back office activities. Large back offices may be sourced with a variety of sourcing options introduced in Chapter 1, including staff augmentation, fee-for-service outsourcing, and strategic partnerships. Particularly critical here are decisions on what to outsource and insource. For outsourcing, the competency entails selection, engagement, and management of third-party suppliers.

4. **The governance competence is concerned with the governance and coordination of the back office's activities relative to the organization as a whole.** A further focus here is on a strategy for delivery and actual systems/process implementation.

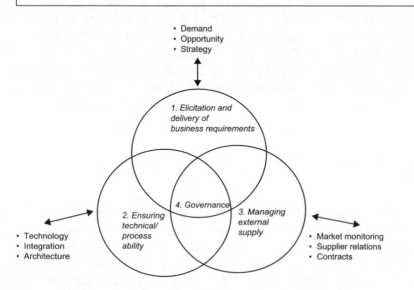

Figure 3.1 Four competencies of high performing back offices

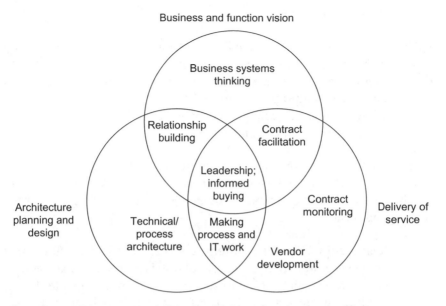

Figure 3.2 Nine core capabilities for high performing back offices

Nine core capabilities for high performing back offices

In this section, we define the nine capabilities required to render the four competencies dynamic and fully operational. The capabilities are shown in Figure 3.2. It should be noted that the nine capabilities populate seven spaces. Their placement in these spaces represents the relative contribution of a specific capability to the four competencies. Four of the capabilities primarily contribute to one competency:

- The *business systems thinking* capability primarily supports the business competency.
- The *technical process and architecture* capability primarily supports the technical competency.
- The *contract monitoring* capability and the *supplier development* capability primarily support the supply competency.

Three capabilities are placed in the intersection of two competencies because they contribute to both competencies and also serve as interfaces between two competencies:

- The *relationship building* capability contributes to and interfaces with both the business and technical competencies.
- The *contract facilitation* capability contributes to and interfaces with both the business and supply competencies.
- The *making processes and IT work* capability contributes to and interfaces with both the supply and technical competencies.

Finally, there are the governance capabilities that are placed within the intersection of all the competencies. These are the *leadership* capability and the *informed buying* capability. We now move to detailing each of the nine capabilities.

1. **The Leadership Capability integrates the back office effort with business purpose and activity.** The central task is to devise organizational structures, processes, and staffing to successfully manage the interdependencies, and to ensure that the back office function delivers value for money. Leaders also influence the overall business perception of the back office's role and contribution. They establish strong relationships at the executive level and leverage those relationships to achieve a shared vision of the back office. At the same time, leaders determine the values and culture of the back office function and instill the belief that back office staff's first duty is to contribute to the business.

2. **The Business Systems Thinking Capability ensures that back office capabilities are envisioned in every business process.** In the best practice organizations we have researched, business systems thinkers are important contributors to teams charged with business problem solving, process re-engineering, strategic development, and delivering new capabilities. Business systems thinking is about seeing how systems, processes, technologies, and skills can be integrated to support strategic intent and to achieve performance goals. Business systems thinkers help to ensure that organizations do not operate as isolated silos, but rather as integrated business units.

3. **The Relationship Building Capability gets the business constructively engaged in operational back office issues.** Relationship builders facilitate the wider dialogue by establishing understanding, trust, and cooperation between business users and back office specialists. Relationship builders develop users' understanding of the back office and its potential for their line of business. They help users and specialists work together, and ensure user ownership and satisfaction with back office services.

4. The Architecture Planning and Design Capability creates the coherent blueprint for a technical platform which responds to present and future business needs. The architect anticipates process and technology trends to ensure that the organization is consistently able to operate from an effective and efficient platform. Architects must deliver without constant investments in energy-sapping migration efforts or over-dependence on suppliers. The architect plans and shapes the increasingly IT-enabled infrastructure. They do this through developing the vision of an appropriate technical platform, and through formulating associated policies that ensure necessary integration and flexibility in IS/IT services across the firm.

5. The Making Processes and Technology Work Capability rapidly trouble-shoots problems which are being disowned by others across the technical supply chain. Operating in the overlap between the technical and supply competencies is the core capability of making processes and technology work. Process and Technology workers are needed to assess and challenge third party suppliers' claims about technical problems and proposed solutions. The capability requires the insight of an architecture planner, together with a pragmatic and short-term orientation to problem resolution. The capability requires a strong and broad understanding of technology fundamentals, rather than a deep understanding of a few technologies.

6. The Informed Buying Capability manages the back office sourcing strategy to meet the needs of the business. Informed buyers analyze the external market for relevant business and IT services. They provide leadership of the tendering, contracting, and service management processes. In an organization that has decided to outsource most of a back office function, the informed buyer is the most prominent role behind that of the back office head.

7. The Contract Facilitation Capability ensures the success of existing contracts for external business/IT services. Contract facilitators serve as liaisons between business users and thirty-party suppliers. The contract facilitator tries to ensure that problems and conflicts are resolved fairly between them. Arrangements for the delivery of back office services are complex. This action-oriented capability is needed because

- business users want one-stop shopping,
- the suppliers need the buffer to foster realistic user expectations,
- multiple suppliers need coordinating,
- it enables easier monitoring of usage and service, and
- user demand must be managed to prevent excess charges.

8. **The Contract Monitoring Capability protects the business's contractual position, present and future.** As organizations exploit the burgeoning external market for business services, contract monitoring becomes a core capability. Contract monitors hold suppliers accountable against both existing service contracts and the developing performance standards of the services market. Contract monitors produce a report card for each supplier that highlights their achievement against external benchmarks and the standards in the contract.

9. **The Supplier Development Capability identifies the potential added value from business service suppliers.** The single most threatening aspect of large-scale outsourcing is the substantial switching costs. Hence it is in the company's interest to maximize the contribution of existing suppliers. Anchored in the supply competency of our model, the supplier developer is concerned with the long-term potential for suppliers to add value. Supplier developers guard against the "mid-contract sag," which occurs when the supplier's innovation and enthusiasm wanes two or more years into the contract. Supplier developers seek to invigorate the relationship, perhaps by finding shared sources of revenue generation or new investments that benefit both parties.

Challenges and issues

The framework presents a number of serious human resource challenges. Each of the nine capabilities required to deliver the "high performance" concept implies a set of behaviors, characteristics, and skills. In contrast to the more traditional skills found in back office functions, our work suggests four key human resource developments:

1. **Organizations need to place a much greater emphasis on business skills and business orientation in nearly all the capabilities.** The back office personnel need to understand and communicate the cost/service trade-offs associated with delivering services to meet overall business needs. Some pundits further advise that back office personnel should consider the business users as *customers*. But that view can be expensive if it focuses back office personnel on meeting highly idiosyncratic needs within each business unit. A proper business orientation always balances the efficiency of shared services against the business units' preferences for customization and decentralization.

2. **Organizations need to significantly develop soft skills across all the capabilities.** In the "high performance" model there are fewer retained

staff, resulting in greater contact with business users, managers, suppliers, and each other. To effectively work in this environment, people who fulfill the nine capabilities increasingly need soft skills such as interpersonal, bridge building, leadership, communication, team building, and negotiating skills. The mix of soft skills varies across the capabilities. Bridge-building skills are most important for the capabilities that overlap two or more competencies. Leadership skills are prominent in the leadership, informed buying, and to a lesser extent, the business systems thinking capabilities. Communication, team-building, and facilitation skills are highest in the leadership, relationship building, contract facilitation, and informed buying roles. Negotiation skills are a prime requirement for informed buying, relationship building, and contract facilitation.

3. **Organizations need to attract, develop, and retain high performers.** The major shift we are observing is toward fewer personnel, but of very high quality. High performers require challenge and specific attention to their career planning needs. The people being targeted for the nine capabilities look more familiar as senior professionals within a major management consulting firm than back office staff. They are largely self-driven and job satisfaction-oriented. In practice, recruitment and retention of these high quality professionals posses major human resource management issues: How can organizations pay them enough to compete with service providers? How can organizations provide them consistently with the level of challenge they look for in the job? How can organizations provide them with a career path despite the very small numbers?

4. **Organizations need to employ enough people to adequately cover all nine capabilities.** Each capability requires a specific set of skills, attributes, and drivers. Our experience to date is that one person could deliver high performance in no more than two or three roles at any single point in time. This has considerable implications for staffing, personal and career development.

These major challenges are found in both private and public sector organizations. In several respondent organizations, and across sectors, we have witnessed a reactive rather than anticipatory approach to human resource issues associated with back office functions. Many firms have some sense of operating a core–periphery model, the notion being that core workers have superior working terms and conditions, employment security, training and development opportunities, and long-term career paths within the firm. Core workers give stability in key areas together with functional flexibility. Meanwhile non-core workers on more limited contracts offer financial and numerical flexibility. In reality, the "high performance team" concept for the back office function provides additional challenges for the wider organization, and assumes, for its operationalization, a supportive environment that was not always prevalent in organizations we studied. Outdatedness, mismatching, inflexibility, and lack of investment in the human resource policy of the wider organization often disadvantage the in-house back office function against the external labor market. Wider studies of labor markets indicate all too often a short-termism, reliance on buying in staff, lack of training, development, and career paths, and considerable neglect of human resource strategy generally.

A further human resource challenge rests with what one respondent termed "the legacy people" problem. In other words, what about existing staff that the high performance model specifically excludes? Some approaches we have observed in various combinations are: early retirement, redundancy packages, making people redundant as the in-house legacy systems become redundant, and relocation and retraining. In outsourcing situations one common response has been to transfer such staff to suppliers. One difficulty is that suppliers, understandably, prefer to take only the better-motivated and skilled staff; sometimes the result has been that the staff that remain are not sufficiently motivated, or capable, of delivering on the in-house high performance requirement.

A final challenge relates to project management capability. Note that this does not appear as a core retained capability in Figure 3.2. In dynamic business environments, the emphasis has shifted from hierarchical, functionally based organizations toward task and project-based ways of operating. The assumption here is that project management skills will be spread throughout such organizations. Project management must be an organizational core capability, and not the preserve of one function or department. However our research into ITO and BPO arrangements frequently reveal organizational project management capability as patchy at best. Yet, as we will see in the BP-Exult case below, outsourcing can involve immense organizational, human resource, and technological changes that require strong project management skills. Should these rest in the retained function or the supplier, if they are not available from the wider client organization?

Three case studies on implementing core back office capabilities

We now compare findings on two IT sourcing arrangements that explicitly adopted the Feeny–Willcocks framework, and one BPO arrangement that ran into transitional problems. The first case involves one of the largest IT outsourcing deals at the time (US$4 billion) between DuPont and its suppliers, CSC and Andersen Consulting. The deal was signed in 1997 and reconfigured in 2003/04. For comparative purposes, we also review the evolution of the IT function at State Super Financial Services (SSFS) from 2000 to 2005. SSFS is a medium-sized Australian enterprise that was gradually moving to more outsourcing over the study period. British Petroleum (BP), on the other hand, is one of the biggest oil majors in the world, which, by 1999, had over ten years' experience outsourcing IT and accounting functions. This spread allows us to explore the applicability of the core capabilities framework to both ITO and BPO in three different-sized organizations, each with distinctive sourcing strategies and implementation challenges.

In the DuPont case, we conducted 26 interviews in one round in August 2001 to discover how the model was being utilized, the challenges it presented, and the outcomes of its use, and have tracked progress since. In SSFS, a much smaller organization, we conducted four interviews over the 2000–04 period. For the BP case we draw upon conversations with four senior BP and Exult participants between 2000–04 and published studies.[7] In all three organizations, we also analyzed in-house documents relating to the function, its in-house capabilities, the progress of outsourcing, and the development and success of the IT or HR function.

Case study 1: DuPont – A global manufacturer

DuPont is a chemicals, health care, materials, and energy multinational operating in a range of segments. Its divisions include Agriculture and Nutrition, Coatings and Color Technologies, Electronic and Communication Technologies, Performance Materials, Safety and Protection, (Textiles/ Interiors/Other was divested in 2004). By the end of 2004, DuPont had US$27.3 billion revenues and 55,000 employees worldwide. Its 20 plus strategic business units operated in more than 70 countries. From 1996 DuPont strove to focus on core business competencies and has regularly divested non-core businesses. It has also focused on reduction of overhead costs and increased capital efficiency. Part of this involved IT outsourcing.

In 1997, DuPont signed a series of ten-year contracts, worth US$ 4 billion, with CSC and Accenture (then Andersen Consulting). By 2002, 80 percent of its IT spending (total: US$600 million a year) and 75 percent (3000) of its IT staff had been transferred to its alliance partners. CSC was responsible for shared infrastructure worldwide, and corporate, regional, and business specific applications, while Accenture managed the Chemical division's business enterprise applications. DuPont initially retained 100, (later reduced to 60), central staff to manage the contracts, and over 1000 distributed technical and business people to provide business IT leadership, process control computing in manufacturing, and R&D computing.

For new project work, DuPont retained the right to source from anywhere as well as from one or both sitting suppliers. As one example, by the late 1990s DuPont had identified a new US$400 million worldwide SAP/Y2K project. One supplier brought 400 SAP people on to the project. To supplement the other supplier's SAP skills, DuPont transferred 300 people from the divisions over to the supplier. The supplier then bore the costs of their SAP training. DuPont also adopted a balanced scorecard approach for benchmarking the health of its IT service silos. By 2001, DuPont had reduced its 90 percent fixed IT costs to 50 percent fixed, was getting quicker injections of skills from suppliers than it had before outsourcing, was achieving increases in some service speeds and flexibility, was probably achieving modest cost reductions on a pro rata basis (overall IT budget actually increased due to greater demand), and had given a range of its ex-employees real career development opportunities. However, by 1999, it was questioning whether it had given away too much IT technical and management expertise.

IT organization and core IS capabilities

By this date, the CIO headed two organizational units – Global Services and Alliance Operations. Global Services had 70 people providing leadership of strategic planning, architecture, security, emerging technologies, and enterprise-wide projects. Oversight of regional and specialized services was delegated to 350 people across five regions responsible for country-specific IT architecture and administration and management of regional suppliers. Global Services also had a Business Unit Support group made up of 500 employees across 20 divisions. These looked after manufacturing process and production controls, business-specific applications, and IT for central R&D. Alliance Operations consisted of 47 people who managed business unit demand for supplier services, monitored supplier service delivery, developed SLA metrics, and achieved continuous performance improvement. Of the 47, 10 dealt with Infrastructure, including oversight of the CSC deal and service responsibility for desktop, telecom, midrange, and mainframe. Another five dealt with Applications, including oversight of Accenture/CSC and liaison with four business divisions. Three employees looked after contract management, including performance scorecards, and contract dispute resolution. A further 20 people managed IT Finance, including invoices, charges to business units, audit billing accuracy, and timeliness.

While this seemed sufficient, by early 1999 DuPont began to question whether its internal capabilities were strong enough. IT leaders were often excluded from critical business discussions and decisions. Succession planning for IT leaders and core staff needed work. And employees were looking for guidance on changing skills and career paths. About this time DuPont adopted the Feeny–Willcocks framework to begin formalizing competencies, job families, personal development opportunities, and career paths. DuPont defined relationship building, leadership, contract facilitation, informed buying, and making technology work as "general competencies," and pointed to three career paths: (1) Business and IT Vision (needing business systems thinking), (2) Design of IT Architecture (requiring architecture planning) and (3) Delivery of IT Services (including supplier development and contract monitoring). In December 2000, DuPont launched an intranet-accessible career management site, enabling employees to identify required competencies – business, interpersonal, and technical – for each of its DuPont's 55 existing and prospective IT roles.

Our own analysis of DuPont's retained IT capabilities took place in July 2001. The overall finding of weaknesses in retained core capability some four years into a large-scale outsourcing arrangement was not, in fact, untypical of what we have found elsewhere.[8] On Business and IT Vision, we found the following. With limited local resources, business unit IS leaders tended to be driven to operate also in relationship building and contract facilitation modes. The focus on service delivery, automation, and firefighting diminished strategy and value creation. Business unit executives themselves commonly positioned IT as an agent of cost reduction, rather than of business value creation. Business systems thinking was generally squeezed out of the IT frame. Suppliers were not filling the gap in stimulating innovation for business value.

On IT Service Delivery, we saw the informed buying and supplier development roles needing considerable enhancement. Many business unit IT leaders needed to move from firefighting to a more strategic focus. Making technology work was often underpowered, given the IT demands. Furthermore, the variable strengths of the suppliers operating in different parts of DuPont exacerbated the making technology work capability. Neglect of the supplier development capability contributed to a number of adverse supplier behaviors and practices. The type of relationship had not moved on and this inhibited DuPont's ability to tap into the suppliers' intellectual capital. Weakness in informed buying led to limited sourcing vision, intra-DuPont learning, and limited future sourcing flexibility. As a result, the issue of how to anticipate and cope with sourcing changes over the next four to ten years was not being addressed sufficiently.

On designing IT architecture, DuPont's position fitted fairly well with our findings elsewhere. DuPont had already noted its weaknesses here and was rebuilding this capability. It needed to develop career paths and more staff for this key area. One weakness of our own model, identified in work in 2001 on building e-business infrastructure, is that architecture needs to be more closely aligned with business strategy. Our conclusion in our 2001 study was that infrastructure and architecture planning were now board-room issues because the technology platform now influenced greatly what was and was not possible as a business. The implication for DuPont was to ensure that architecture planning becomes closely co-located with business planning. Here we recommended development of career paths for this core, retained capability, with the possible quick hiring of experienced staff to fill the vital gap.

On a regional basis, we found Asia Pacific quite well adapted and lever-aging the core IS capabilities concept. Europe and South America had not yet tailored the capabilities to their environments and resource levels. Some core IS capabilities definitely needed enhancement in terms of making local resources available. In particular, contract facilitation, making tech-nology work, business vision, and contract monitoring capabilities were lacking. In terms of DuPont's overall objectives, we felt it could only move from cost reduction to business value if business executives were educated into the transformational possibilities of IT. Increased delivery speed needed more in-house project management capability and a rapid application development approach, risk-reward contracts with suppliers, a change in the bureaucratic process by which work was contracted for and assigned, architecture planning linked to business vision, and strengthened technical fixer and contract facilitation capabilities in order to leverage the operational service. Innovation could be delivered through enhanced business systems thinking, informed buying, and supplier development capabilities to unlock supplier potential and greater internal and external networking. To facilitate these moves, the core IS capabilities framework was correctly positioned for career development, but needed to be further imbedded in human resource processes, including selection, appraisal, and reward systems.

By early 2003, the competency modeling and career development self-service efforts had generated several positive results. Eighty percent of staff accessed the site in 2002 and 30 percent created career plans. Employees and managers focused on competencies rather than administrative tasks.

By 2003, the company was able to fill 90 percent of key leadership positions internally, despite the fact that it had reduced the pool of potential successors from 4000 to 1200 as a result of outsourcing. The projected shortfall of in-demand employees was reduced from 30 in 1999 to two in 2004. The strength of emerging IT leaders was recognized by business management, with 90 percent of business unit CIOs reporting to a business unit VP/General Manager as opposed to 50 percent previously. Even more importantly, DuPont felt that it had wrested back control of its IT destiny and put itself in a much better position to leverage its relationships with suppliers, and renegotiate sourcing arrangements into the future, as it began to do from 2003 onward.

Case study 2: State Super Financial Services (SSFS) – a medium-sized enterprise

SSFS Australia Limited provides professional financial planning and fund management services exclusively to current and former public sector employees and their family members. SSFS has four main products: personal retirement plans, pension funds, investment funds, and a fixed term pension plan. The company has offices in major cities in Australia, over 400 employees, and over 33,000 clients. In December 2004, it had funds in excess of AU$4.7 billion under management.

The company's strategic plan during 2002–05 identified three core competencies: attraction, conversion, and retention of clients. It established key mission success indicators needed to achieve its goal of becoming "*one of Australia's leading financial planning and funds management organisations*" (in-house strategy document).

The role of IT

In 2000, the IT function was staffed by 17 people including the CIO, a developer, and 15 support staff. Historically IT had provided a purely support role for IT infrastructure and externally sourced business applications. From 2000, IT developed an enabling capability as the company sought to gain competitive advantage from its IT investment. By 2002, a number of IT issues had been identified. SSFS had a strength in its unique in-house financial planning and marketing software. However, there was under-utilization of IT in SSFS's work processes, and the threat of loss of clients due to an inability to readily match competitors in the provision of e-commerce capabilities.

The 2002 IT action plan consisted of three broad activities:

1. exploit competitive advantage of the in-house developed software
2. achieve productivity improvements through business process automation by integrating disparate IT systems, and
3. deliver IT services to meet existing and future business needs.

An analysis of the external IT environment found four major forces to which SSFS needed to respond. First, there was an increasing focus on integration of existing IT services. This required a shift in emphasis from development to systems integration. It required sourcing appropriate skills sets and buying/building the appropriate IT infrastructure. Second, there was a greater move to outsourcing. SSFS identified a need to selectively externally source more IT services once it had identified core in-house capabilities and ways of benchmarking service provision. Third, SSFS assigned itself a watching brief on the evolution of web services for information exchange, believing this to be two to three years away from commercial adoption. Lastly, business units were looking outside the company for the information sharing vital to value creation. Therefore, SSFS needed to extend IT service delivery outside the organization, with 24 by 7 availability. This implied expanding the skills in relationship management and negotiation with business partners, and the need to increase the collaboration between employees with skills sets in legacy systems and those operating with newer technologies.

Technically, the 2002 IT strategy involved integration of the company web site, its virtual private network, its financial planning, registry, and customer relationship management (CRM) systems, together with a B2B capability through its Pillar and Master Custodian/Fund Manager software and systems. SSFS intended to develop in-house any system/software that gave it competitive advantage, but eventually to outsource the rest. While IT network and service availability compared favorably against competitors, there was a noticeable gap in e-commerce offerings. By 2003 much progress had been made on the new security, systems and network architectures, and work on the information architecture had commenced. On infrastructure, a number of weaknesses needed to be addressed. The network contained numerous single points of failure. A single failure could result in all central IT services being unavailable to a regional office. Disparate servers and business applications made information storage fragmented across a large number of servers. The data back-up strategy was complex and time-consuming, while disaster recovery was complicated. The centralized management of systems and networks was limited. All these problems would only be exacerbated by the future planned growth of the company. The new proposed infrastructure was to be scalable and modular, capable of supporting 24 by 7 applications, providing levels of redundancy, and improving back-up, recovery and disaster recovery. The infrastructure program of work carried out from 2003–05 involved enterprise database consolidation, disaster recovery upgrade, replacement of the Unix operating system on which Registry and CRM applications ran, a move to centralized storage and back-up, upgrading from Windows NT to Windows 2000, and improvement of the messaging infrastructure.

On business applications, 2002–05 saw the in-house upgrading of Financial Planning systems. The Registry system was a third-party package with limited functionality that, as a core system, needed in-house work to achieve integration with other applications. The core CRM system was a third party package not being further supported by the supplier, was costly, and needed to be replaced. In effect, 2003–05 saw twelve business application programs of work operationalized to remedy the situation.

IT organization and core IS capabilites

SSFS, under the CIO's advice, adopted a centralized IT organization structure. This was because of the small size of the company and the fact that much of the business structure itself was centralized. This allowed close scrutiny and control of IT costs, and also facilitated the task of building an IT infrastructure that adhered to a single set of architectures. By 2003, the CIO reported directly to the SSFS Managing Director. The CIO, Geoff Purcell, had under him four departments: Application Development had nine staff, IT Systems Network eight, Technology Architecture two and Project Office two. This structure, evolved in the course of 2002–03, represented a significant shift from the inherited situation of 2000 (see Figure 3.3), and was designed to facilitate the 2003–05 programs of IT.

In its forward strategy, SSFS had also explicitly adopted the Feeny–Willcocks core IS competencies framework. A piece of thinking in 2002 saw SSFS IT competencies classified into:

1. Nine core IT competencies – enabling the company to exploit IT successfully however the IT services are provided (Feeny–Willcocks framework)
2. Strategic IT services – supporting business differentiation and competitive advantage
3. Tactical IT services – supporting the provision of business services necessary for ongoing operations.

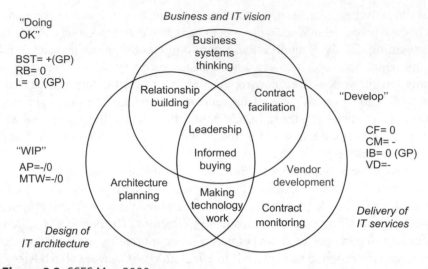

Figure 3.3 SSFS May 2000

Note: BST stands for Business Systems Thinking

Both 1 and 2, as "core," would be internally sourced. In the case of 2, the IT function would provide development and support for two applications. The PSP/Profile systems clearly differentiated the SSFS provision of financial planning advice from that of competitors. Meanwhile SPIRS (superannuation payments information reporting systems) gave SSFA competitive advantage through the information and analysis of information provided under agreements with clients. This enabled the company to managed a more targeted and effective marketing effort.

Tactical IT services, on the other hand, would be reviewed regularly, externally benchmarked, and provided through the most cost-effective means possible. This covered all non-core work in environment management, systems and network management, IT help desk, application support, project management, and applications development. In 2002, SSFS already used external suppliers for a range of IT services, including web site hosting and management, security assessment, infrastructure design, web site development, and graphical design. The updated strategy pointed to even greater outsourcing of non-core IT services.

In May 2000, the in-house core capabilities were as shown in Figure 3.3. Remembering the relatively small size of SSFS and the support role of IT at that time, the CIO's assessment was that, on the business face, SSFS were "*doing okay.*" (In the scoring system, $++$ is satisfactory while $--$ is very inadequate.) Having said that, Geoff Purcell was responsible for both leadership and business systems thinking, and there was no relationship building capability. Given the plans by 2002, all three capabilities would need significant bolstering if progress was to be made. The gaps on architecture planning and making technology work were all too obvious, with a legacy of 15 IT support staff and only one developer in-house. Implementation of the IT strategy, on SSFS's own evidence, needed significantly more capability in these areas. Likewise, in May 2000, SSFS was not at all set up to manage external IT supply, with, in fact, the CIO carrying out the informed buying role, limited contract facilitation competence, and very little contract monitoring and supplier development capability.

Not surprisingly, the 2002/03 IT strategy took explicit note of these gaps and presented a modified structure that had been developing over the previous 18 months, and which embodied the core IS capabilities more obviously. The Systems and Networks team was to be the first "port of call" for any business users with IT issues. It also planned, selected, and deployed IT infrastructure (along with the Technology and Architecture team). It also (with the Applications Development team) provided support specific to any key application utilized. This embodied aspects of the technology fixing, relationship building, and contract facilitation roles from the Feeny–Willcocks framework.

The Applications Development team was made responsible for developing applications in-house, selecting applications packages provided by suppliers, and second-level application support. This covered the technology fixer and contract facilitation roles in Figure 3.2. The Technology Architecture team was made custodian of the technical architecture. It was responsible for the review and approval of all new technology within the company, thus covering Feeny and Willcocks's architecture planning role. In 2003 SSFS also recruited a new Project Office team to work in the IT function, reflecting the large number of new IT projects. The CIO continued to carry out the leadership, informed buying and supplier development roles. Operational contract monitoring was pushed into the Systems and Network and Project Office teams.

Case study 3: British Petroleum – An oil and energy multinational

BP is a global oil, energy, and petrochemicals group. In 2004, with employees numbering 102,900, it reported US$285 billion revenues, and a profit of US$15.4 billion. With the rise in oil prices, 2005 was an even more successful year. It operates in over 100 countries. BP has a long history of back office outsourcing, beginning with selective IT outsourcing from 1987 to "total" IT outsourcing at BP Exploration from 1993. BP has outsourced its accounting function since 1992/23.[9] It has also undertaken a number of mergers in recent years, notably those with Amoco in 1998 and subsequently Arco, both of which complicated outsourcing strategy and arrangements, as we shall see. Throughout the 1990s, "core compe-tence" thinking drove BP into a number of innovative outsourcing deals, including the Human Resources (HR) deal with Exult described in this section.

Towards HR outsourcing

According to BP executives, by 1997 outsourcing further back office functions had become an imperative. Low oil prices made cost reduction a priority. BP had built up experience at managing outsourcing, especially in Europe. The merger with Amoco in 1998, and the prospect of future mergers, added scale to the argument that outsourcing HR was worth the effort. Moreover, the HR inheritance plus the merger had created a plethora of HR systems and ways of doing things that needed to be recon-ciled. Costs seemed uncompetitive and delivery uncertain. Moreover, the burden of administration was preventing the function from performing effectively in more strategic aspects of HR services, for example HR strategy, design, performance management, and regulatory issues.

Over these years, BP had considered several potential contracts, but all had fallen through. The new contract was strongly competed for by two start-up BPO suppliers, Exult and Xchanging. In late 1999, an initial seven-year US$600 million deal was signed with Exult, covering 56,000 of the 100,000 BP employees in USA and UK. Later add-ons followed when BP merged with Arco, Vastar, and Burma Castrol. By early 2004, 60,000 employees were in Exult service scope, compared with 115,000 BP staff worldwide. Exult guaranteed direct operating cost savings of 20 percent from the sixteenth month of the contract, with further gain-share once Exult had recovered defined investments and expenses.

The initial scope covered mainly transactional services, specifically payroll, benefits and compensation, training and expatriate admini-stration, supplier management, severance processing, compliance reporting, relocation, administrative aspects of employee recruitment, training and performance, and the underlying information technologies and systems. According to management, BP wished to retain "only the things that require judgement and policy," such as HR policy, strategy, professional resources, and labor relations. The effect was a possible 40 percent reduction in internal HR staff numbers. Recognizing the risks being taken, BP secured a limited ownership (less than 8%) stake in Exult, to align both parties' interests. BP wanted Exult to be economically successful by building leading edge tools and recruiting talent. This would save BP itself from having to invest in the HR area, including e-HR technologies that Exult considered one of its core capabilities. For BP, a web-enabled HR function seemed an effective way forward to take advantage of the common desktop and laptop operating environment recently established throughout BP.[10]

Putting BPO to work: Emerging challenges

In practice, both BP and Exult were taking a number of risks. Exult was a start-up with no real body of experience or best practices on which to build. HR outsourcing was a relatively new field. Exult had to staff up across the board with people who had designed or run shared service centers, BPO experts, HR professionals, and IT people with web expertise. The scope of the task was formidable, and not fully understood by BP managers themselves. Exult had to integrate multiple, diverse HR systems across BP, connect and standardize them using new technologies, while also supporting BP's line businesses which were also undergoing restructuring in the face of recent and future mergers. An overall governance steering group was formed, together with a series of joint project teams.

As the extent of the complexity emerged, it was decided to focus initial efforts on the United States and the United Kingdom only. Exult took over BP's HR administration processes in those locations in April 2000. These would be operated "as-is" and transferred to an Exult operations center later or, if passing prescribed readiness tests, transferred immediately. At the same time, Exult needed to work on delivering the e-HR web-based processes BP were expecting. There were problems immediately, with little going as originally planned. The tasks of creating HR capability, transitioning work, redesigning and delivering web-enabled process proved highly challenging. In particular, the point and click e-HR world dreamt up during the Internet "bubble" was much less practicable than imagined. The deadline for e-products was set for mid-April 2000. These products included the "International Calculator" (essentially a calculator for expatriate employees, tapping into company policies on relocation), a senior management career and data facility, and later "My Future" that helped employees look for other jobs within BP. "My Data" was a longer-term project scheduled for 2001 delivery. But the difficulties in creating a global database of peoples' skills and vital information – kept up-to-date by the employees themselves – underlined the massiveness of the under-taking. Faced with conflicting information and lack of standardized HR databases, the project had still not been completed by 2003. In practice the overall e-HR effort only really began to come to fruition in 2004.

But what of the fundamental administrative tasks to be transferred to Exult? Within 15 months of signing the contract, Exult was expected to standardize and operate up to 20 processes, usually working differently at each major site (UK, for example, had ten major sites). In 2000, it built from scratch and staffed a service center in Glasgow, to which few BP employees wanted to transfer. It had already bought a call center in Texas to service the United States. In practice, standardization of processes did not happen during transition. Faced with the struggle to staff and deliver service, a strategic decision was made (by BP and Exult) to hand things over to Exult as they were. As a result, a great deal of complexity passed into Exult's processes. On the transition date, Exult found itself managing multiple systems, with a new staff, from a central location, with little of the economies of scale and efficiency that would have come from early standardization. Moreover, Exult people at the Glasgow service center had no specialized knowledge of local site work and processes. Despite knowledge-sharing events, many BP HR people were unconvinced it was a major priority, especially with the Amoco merger needing their attention. (The same would happen during the 2002 BP–Arco merger.) Moreover, these events put additional strain on HR systems, just when they were being transitioned.

There were serious people issues in the transition phase. The actual moves were managed smoothly but in a climate of unsettling uncertainty. Senior executives supported the moves, some HR executives were skepti-cal, while users were quick to complain when HR processes did not func-tion as they should. A classic change issue emerged: the nearly 700 HR people being made redundant had site knowledge and understood the old system, its flaws, and how it could be made to work. Getting them to trans-fer the knowledge was one thing, given they were standing to lose their jobs. Another issue was Exult not having enough people to receive that knowledge.

Data conversion emerged as a big issue given BP's organizational com-plexity and continuing preference for autonomous business units where possible. Even payroll transition, especially when Amoco and Arco came on board bringing another 37,000 employees, proved very difficult indeed. This was not helped by the merging organizations all operating different HR systems (PeopleSoft, Tesseract, and Bespoke Systems). During 2001, this built to a crisis of confidence given that HR line managers seemed to be fielding a very large number of difficulties but now through a much more bureaucratized Exult set of processes. These difficulties did not cease until late 2003.

A new HR vice-president at BP helped to regain perspective on the overall project. Extra people assigned to a task force charged with developing more realistic expectations and to manage HR through the crisis. It was widely recognized that "big bang" approach was not possible – a more incremental approach was needed. It was agreed within BP that the original global strategy was unrealistic. BP would now focus only on the United States and the United Kingdom. Moreover the HR leadership in BP took accountability and ownership of the project in a way that they had not previously done. Eventually in early 2003, this led to a restructuring of the HR department. This involved the HR function being aligned as a business function, with the Exult contract on the supply side, and other HR activities on the demand side. Processes were developed for defining roles, setting expectations, and measuring results. BP followed some of the thinking inherent in Figure 3.2. Business managers now focused on the more discretionary demand activities, while HR operation managers focused on delivery of commitments, the management of the Exult relationship, and monitoring and facilitating the supplier's performance.

By late 2003 cost savings were approaching US$15 million a year, and BP had avoided US$30 million in capital investment in HR systems and processes. Exult performance was continually improving as was customer satisfaction. In addition, BP had restructured its HR function to be more strategic, more demand-led, and more e-enabled with thousands of people using the e-HR systems as they became available. If cost savings came through more slowly than planned, then the business integrations not only of Amoco and Arco but also Vastar and Burmah Castrol, were accelerated due to common HR processes and metrics. Moreover, as a result of outsourcing, BP now had much more objective HR data available, more standardized processes, and better measures.

Case Comparisons: DuPont, SSFS, and BP

DuPont. The company's experiences were not untypical of other large-scale IT outsourcing arrangements we have researched. After outsourcing 80 percent of its IT budget, DuPont discovered it had retained inadequate management and technical expertise to control its IT destiny. Mid-contract sag occurred after transition. Here the question: "how much more value and leverage could be got from the relationships?" was raised. Benchmarking was introduced for more accurate tracking of performance and as an inducement to improve. As a global outsourcing deal with two major partners, DuPont had specific issues on distribution of resources locally – in the business units – and centrally. It under-resourced the more operational capabilities (making processes and technology work, contract facilitation, and relationship building) resulting in IT managers and local CIOs having to deflect their attention into these areas and away from more strategic, business oriented activity. Moreover, despite the size of the outsourcing arrangements, DuPont had not retained enough technical or architecture planning capability either at the center or locally. This could be dangerous for big projects such as the major SAP project allied with the Y2K work from 1999. The other areas of concern were DuPont's ongoing ability to monitor and manage present and future sourcing strategy, and to develop further business value from the supplier relationships.

DuPont's IT management began addressing these issues from 1999. One result was the move towards using the core IS capabilities framework as a basis for staff development and career succession planning. Architecture planning was an interesting case in point. Given away to CSC in 1997, DuPont found it was losing control of designing its technical platform and being able to have informed discussions with suppliers. It began recreating this capability in-house from 2000. Contract monitoring, initially, had seemed detailed enough, but within two years a major benchmarking process had been introduced. DuPont thought it had resourced the business units enough, but then discovered that IT leaders there got pulled too much into operational issues, and too much doing capability was left to the supplier, run through an over-bureaucratic procurement process. Subsequently we found different business units left to deal with these issues in their own different ways. DuPont subsequently also bolstered its senior technical capability, and also its informed buying capability in order to deal with renegotiation of their outsourcing arrangements into the 2003–05 period.

SSFS. In our interviews, respondents indicated that the core IS capabilities framework was definitely valuable, and pushed skills and capabilities in the right direction to produce business value from IT exploitation. However, the relatively small size of the company, and IT management's limited access to financial resources made core IS capability evolution necessarily incremental, and ultimately partial. Given limited financial and human resources, the CIO decided to focus first on building up the technology platform, and started recruiting staff to, or training inherited staff in, the relevant core capabilities. He then focused on building the in-house team to deliver applications changes, and began developing the project office capability to manage and control projects and resources. The CIO reported human resource challenges in recruiting the right staff (though a softer local labor market in 2002–04 helped a little), and in training or making redundant inherited staff with outmoded skills sets. Moreover some full time in-house skills just seemed unavailable to a firm of this size, for example security architect skills.

IT at SSFS also operated with a money cap that restricted the full adoption of the core IS capabilities framework, and meant the spreading of the capabilities across several groups, with an inevitable diminution of the high performance component of the original model. A more complex IT environment was being built, and increasing demands were being made on the technology. All this implied more outsourcing and also the need for more of the nine core IS capabilities. However, all this was restricted by the affordability issue, and "more work with the same resources" became the keynote into late 2004.

Interestingly, in our original framework, project management was never cited as a core IS capability. We found that project management should be a core *organizational* capability. However, in this and other cases, we observed that, *with the frequent absence of such a core organizational capability*, and with a remit to move fast on building technology platforms and applications, organizations like SSFS have had to build project office and project management capability specific to IT needs quite quickly.

British Petroleum. When it comes to building retained capability, are BPO deals doomed to repeat the mistakes of earlier large-scale ITO arrangements? Undoubtedly outsourcing is a risky business.[11] Adler usefully analzses the BP–Exult deal in terms of six major risks:[12]

- The bilateral dependency risk was considerable. It was mitigated by partnering, open-book accounting, and senior line management participating in the governance structure.
- The spillover risk (the leakage of confidential information) was not anticipated, but Germany's privacy laws, for example, led to the scaling back of integration of BP's non-UK European units.
- The trust risk was mitigated early through trust building efforts plus part BP share-ownership in Exult.
- The relative proficiency risk (falsely assuming the supplier has superior proficiency to the client) occurred when BP hoped Exult's web expertise would take BP to a new HR level.
- The loss of strategic capabilities risk was mitigated by retaining HR policy, strategy, professional resources, and labor relations in-house. BP remained actively involved in high-level design of outsourced processes.

- The commitment versus flexibility risk was recognized by BP. It identified a large part of HR as non-core and needing rationalization. Outsourcing would give BP flexibility on investment, cost, and effort.

In our own analysis, BP showed particular weakness in its ability to diagnose what needed to be done on the last three risks listed, all relating to defining and building core retained HR-IT capability. Despite BP's considerable prior outsourcing experience, BP management still underestimated the degree to which retained accountability and capability were keys to making the Exult deal work. In this deal, Exult was a very willing and committed partner, but also a newly created BPO supplier. This should have flagged the need to build in-house capability very early on, along the lines indicated in Figure 3.2, was even more important than with an experienced supplier. This is perhaps most obvious in the role of retained architecture planning and design. Exult took processes and systems over as they were, and were left to sort out the resulting complexity, without having the knowledge base to do so. This was an abrogation of architecture planning and design by BP. According to one BP manager, in practice half of the problems attributed to Exult's performance were BP's fault.

In the history presented above, one can also trace the degree to which relationship building, contract facilitation, and making process/technology work capabilities were not set up in-depth within BP, thus exacerbating the difficulties Exult experienced, and causing a crisis in confidence (in late 2001) within BP about continuing with the outsourcing arrangement.

In a foreshadowing of the area we will discuss in Chapter 8 of this book, both BP and Exult greatly underestimated the knowledge issues inherent in outsourcing. Domain (local and HR) knowledge was resident in a group of people largely not being transferred to Exult and likely to be made redundant as a result of Exult taking over (compare the Xchanging–BAE deal in Chapter 6). Exult themselves was busy signing up HR, technology, and managerial knowledge even as they transitioned BP systems to service centers, and became responsible for delivering operational service. This suggests that a lot more making processes and technology work capability needed to be assigned to the project by BP than was in fact forthcoming.

While the deal had a governance and management structure of sorts, it took until early 2003 and the experience of a range of problems before BP developed a more appropriate one. This delay has parallels with DuPont's own rethinking of its retained core capability some two years into its deals with Andersen Consulting and CSC. The resulting structures have parallels with our own shown in Figure 3.2.

Learning points and conclusion

Each case provides insight into how the core capabilities can be applied, their relevance, the challenges arising, and how these were handled by each organization. Here, based on these cases, we reflect on what might be learned from attempting to implement the Feeny–Willcocks core capabilities framework.

1. Organizations need to develop long-term strategic core capability rather than being drawn into fire fighting and focusing only on the shorter-term capabilities in our model. Problems develop when any of the core IS capabilities are not suitably staffed, but there is a tendency in the first few years to neglect the capabilities with longer time-horizons – business systems thinking, governance, architecture planning for example – thus building up important issues further down the line.

2. The cases support our earlier 1998 finding that high performers with distinctive skills, capabilities, and orientations need to be appointed. The cases also indicated what we only supposed in 1998, that there would be major challenges getting organizations to develop HR policies in the areas of recruitment, pay, motivation, and retention to support the different, high performance, team-based, core capabilities mode of operating.

3. Issues of core capability development and succession emerged, which need careful management. SSFS, of course, was too small to deal with this in DuPont's more strategic manner, but instead had to stay alive to the issue and use its limited resources more opportunistically, and spread its capabilities more thinly. BP was in a position to build its own retained capability well, but got caught up in pressing priorities and an over-reliance on a start-up supplier.

4. Getting innovation and business value-added from outsourcing really does need organized, pro-active, in-house core capabilities being applied to the task. But a further challenge at all three organizations was to get the business units and power brokers there engaged with IT/HR issues. This underlined the importance of the leadership role and the business-facing capabilities in the back office function. It also points to the fact that, however empowered, the back office function cannot do it alone. Maturity of the business units' capability to manage strategically IT (or HR, procurement for example) also has to develop. We found, however, that the IT or relevant back office function has an important role to play in that process.

5. Our framework is better applied as an evolutionary process rather than as an instant fix. Particularly endorsed was the Feeny model of IT

organizations passing through Delivery, Reorientation, and Reorganization phases (see Figure 3.4).[13] Figure 3.4 shows an adapted version to include other back office functions. Core capabilities focusing on service and delivery competence are developed in the Delivery phase, more business-focused capabilities in the Re-orientation phase, with the fully fledged model being applied only in the Re-organization phase. This last phase, we find, offers the lowest risk point for large-scale outsourcing. Of the three cases, SSFS most closely followed this optimal path. BP outsourced without being in a good position internally to manage large-scale HR outsourcing. From the beginning it found itself in catch-up mode. DuPont was better placed on internal capability from the start of its deal, but still needed to revisit the Reorientation phase and also build more internal capability some three years into its outsourcing arrangement.

6. Successful implementation of the core capabilities model also related to other mitigating factors, namely governance mechanisms in place, inflexibility of outsourcing contracts and deals, the level of resourcing (numbers of staff), and supplier capabilities and responsiveness to new demands.

7. We were finding in these 2001–04 case studies that technical/process architecture capability had to be much closer to and responsive to the business units than we were finding in other case in the 1990s.

8. In the original model we positioned project management as an organizational rather than a specific IS core capability. Since then we have been getting more feedback from these cases on aspects of project management that might be distinctive to the IT or specific back office function.

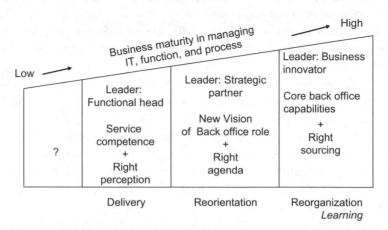

Figure 3.4 Growth states for the business, function head, and back office

In the two cases we have examined, we found the Core IS capabilities framework producing significantly better results in terms of control of IT destiny, effective working with business units, supplier management, and better control of financial aspects of IT. In allied research, and also in the BP case examined here, we are finding the model, with a few modifications, also translates well for use in business process outsourcing.[14]

This chapter has sought to provide fresh thinking on the key capabilities required in back office functions in contemporary organizations. Three research strands showed the importance of capabilities and skills, essentially human resource-based, in identifying, delivering, and operating IT for organizational advantage. In particular, organizations seemed to be making in some instances incremental, in others planned, moves toward an emergent model of the back office function as shown in Figure 3.2. Our analysis has distilled these moves into nine key capabilities and posited the need, if the promise of the outsourced back office is to be fully exploited, for a high performance retained back office function.

At the same time as developing the notion of the high performance back office function, we have been deeply aware of the challenges it poses for organizations. Historically, in back offices such as IT and HR, and in the wider organization, human resource issues have been neglected, and are still rarely the subject of anticipatory, let alone strategic action. Resource-based approaches and notions of building long-term core capabilities also appear more regularly in the academic literature and in a few high profile cases of success, than in actual organizational practices. However, there have been many encouraging signs in the organizations we have studied. Moreover, there are many indications that, if most organizations fail to move in the direction of the high performance model, then those that do would gain even more sustainable advantage than might otherwise be the case.

Notes

1. Feeny, D. and Willcocks, L. (1998), "Core IS Capabilities For Exploiting Information Technology", *Sloan Management Review*, 39, 3, pp. 9–21.
2. Exult has since been acquired by Hewitt.
3. See Hamel, G. and Heene, A. (eds.) (1994), *Competence-Based Competition*, Wiley, Chichester. Also Quinn., J. (1992), "The Intelligent Enterprise: A New Paradigm," *Academy of Management Executive*, Vol. 6, 4, pp. 44–63.

4. For IT case histories see Kern, T. and Willcocks, L. (2001), *The Relationship Advantage: Information Technologies, Sourcing and Management*, Oxford University Press, Oxford. For BPO case histories see Lawler, E., Ulrich, D., Fits-enz, J., and Madden, J. (2004), *Human Resources Business Process Outsourcing*, Wiley, San Francisco. See also Chapters 6 and 7 of the present volume. Documentation of the consequences of underpowering retained capabilities also appears in Lacity, M. and Willcocks, L., and Cullen, S. (2007), *Global IT Outsourcing: 21st Century Search for Business Advantage*, Wiley, Chichester.

5. The IT work is represented in op. cit. Feeny, D. and Willcocks, L. (1998), op. cit. The BPO research can be pursued in Feeny, D. Willcocks, L. and Lacity, M. (2005), "Taking the Measure of Outsourcing Providers," *Sloan Management Review*, Vol. 46, 3, Spring, pp. 41–48. Also Hindle, J., Willcocks, L., Feeny, D. and Lacity, M. (2003), "Value-added Outsourcing at Lloyds and BAE Systems," *Knowledge Management Review*, Vol. 6, 4, pp. 28–31. Also Lacity, M., Willcocks, L. and Feeny, D. (2003), "Transforming a Backoffice Function: Lessons from BAE Systems' Enterprise Partnership," *MISQ Executive*, Vol. 2, 2, pp. 86–103.

6. The work on the core IT function is detailed fully in Lacity, Willcocks and Cullen (2007), op.cit.

7. The most useful studies are Lawler *et al.* (2004), op. cit. J. and Adler, P. (2003), "Making The HR Outsourcing Decision," *Sloan Management Review*, Vol. 45, 1, pp. 52–60.

8. See Kern and Willcocks (2001), op. cit. and Lacity and Willcocks (2001), op.cit.

9. More detailed accounts of these developments appear in Lacity, Willcocks, and Cullen (2007), op. cit.

10. Comment from BP manager, reported in Lawler *et al.* (2004), op. cit.

11. See Lacity and Willcocks (2001), op. cit., chapter 6 for a detailed discussion.

12. See Adler (2003), op. cit.

13. Feeny, D. and Ross, J. (2000), "The Evolving Role of the CIO," in R. Zmud (ed.), *Framing the Domains of Management Research: Glimpsing the future through the Past*. Pinnaflex, Cincinnati.

14. See Feeny, D. Willcocks, L., and Lacity, M. (2005), op. cit.

CHAPTER 4

Assessing 12 supplier capabilities

David Feeny, Mary Lacity,
and Leslie Willcocks

Introduction

The IT and Business Process Outsourcing (BPO) market is large and diverse, covering everything from the outsourcing of quite simple processes or call centers to, more recently, the transformation of entire back office functions of major corporations. The supplier base is equally diverse, stretching from locally based specialists in particular applications and/or industry sectors, through offshore providers who base their appeal on their ability to provide what may be well-qualified staff at low unit labor costs, to "transformational" outsourcers who apply a combination of sophisticated management techniques and technology investment to achieve new levels of process performance. Client organizations are challenged to identify a provider whose capabilities are most appropriate for their needs.

In this chapter, we first identify three potentially critical areas of provider competency:

- **Delivery competency**, defined as the extent to which the supplier is equipped to deliver service to specification on a sustainable basis.
- **Transformation competency**, defined as the scope of supplier ability to achieve radical improvements in the quality, cost, and functionality of the outsourced service.
- **Relationship competency**, defined as the ability (and willingness) of the supplier to work in true partnership with the client, with aligned incentives operating through the life of the contract.

We then describe 12 capabilities which, based on our research experience, underpin the three target competencies. Each capability is illustrated by specific examples drawn from the outsourcing experiences of firms such as BAE Systems, Lloyd's of London, Deutsche Bank, and Bank of America.

Having first clarified which competencies are required to achieve their outsourcing goals, client organizations can evaluate potential BPO providers based on their demonstrable mastery of the capabilities relevant to achievement of those goals.

Messy back offices need transformation

In our experience, senior executives commonly express dissatisfaction with back offices such as human resources, information technology, indirect procurement, finance, and accounting. They perceive them as costing too much, providing too little, and responding too slowly. At the extreme, some of our largest companies – having grown through a series of mergers and acquisitions – face a heritage of disparate and poorly performing processes across the back office stepchildren which can only be corrected by the application of very substantial investment of dollars and scarce change management capacity. Their executives are conscious that the management attention and resource investment required will represent a diversion from what they see to be the more critical requirements of their "core" business activities. And even if they agree to commit the resources, some doubt they can create the environment for back office success: "If (back office) change was going to be achieved, it needed the injection of a catalyst by an outside party. Culturally it needed a kick up the backside" (CEO, Lloyd's of London).

Not surprisingly, rather than deal with the mess themselves, many senior executives are now outsourcing back office processes – even entire global back offices – adding to the growing army of IT and Business Process Outsourcing (BPO) providers. By now we are all familiar with the phenomenon of the back office service support call center being outsourced to "local" or "offshore" providers. We have already mentioned a number of mega-deals in Chapter 1, such as the Lloyd's of London (CEO quoted above) and BAE Systems deals with UK-based supplier Xchanging (see Chapters 6 and 7). For BAE Systems, Xchanging financed the upfront investment to transform the company's decentralized HR – scattered across 70 sites – to a shared service utility, complete with a brand new building, new business processes, and new web-enabled technology. Xchanging inducted 462 BAE Systems transferees to a front-office culture, identified and defined 400 HR services for improvement, and delivered 10 percent cost savings to BAE in the first year. For Lloyd's of

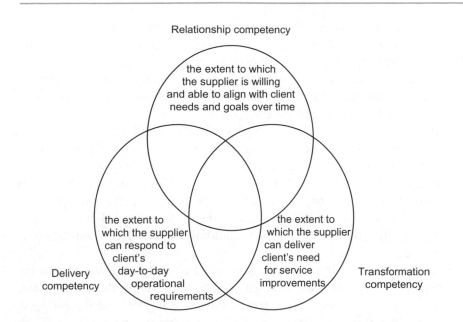

Relationship competency

the extent to which
the supplier is willing
and able to align with client
needs and goals over time

Delivery
competency

the extent to
which the supplier
can respond to
client's
day-to-day
operational
requirements

the extent to
which the supplier
can deliver
client's need
for service
improvements

Transformation
competency

Figure 4.1 Three types of competency the supplier may bring to clients

London, Xchanging financed a similar transformation for policy administration and claims processing (see Chapter 8). Beyond delivering cost
savings and service improvements to Lloyd's, Xchanging also commercial-
ized the services, sharing with Lloyd's the profits it gained from a growing
number of external customers.

In short, ITO and BPO are very large, growing, and diverse markets populated by an ever-increasing number of providers. Client organizations must
look very carefully at the goals they are seeking to achieve, and be clear
about the supplier capabilities required to achieve them. During the course
of a 17-year research program—initially focused on IT outsourcing, but now
extended to BPO—we have previously described ways to analyze appropriate
outsourcing goals and provided a widely adopted model for identifying the
capabilities which need to be retained in-house by the client.[1] In this chapter, we identify and describe the capabilities that BPO providers potentially
bring to the outsourcing relationship. Finding a supplier who provides the
capabilities appropriate to client goals is a major key to BPO success.

To greatly varying degrees, every supplier possesses competency in
three domains: delivery, transformation, and relationship (see Figure 4.1).

- The most obvious and basic domain is that of *delivery competency*,
  which determines the extent to which a supplier is able to respond to the

client's requirement for day-to-day operational services. What scope and complexity of services can this supplier sustainably provide? To what levels of cost, quality, robustness, and flexibility? No matter what level of cost saving is on offer, the client is not going to outsource unless they are confident that their minimum required standards of service will be met during the life of the contract.

- Increasingly clients have the expectation that outsourced services will in fact improve over time, providing some combination of cost/quality/functionality benefits. The *transformational competency* determines the extent to which the supplier is equipped to deliver on these formal or informal expectations. As we shall see there are several potential levers for achieving radical change and improvement, and suppliers may vary greatly in terms of which such capabilities they have convincingly mastered.

- To date, outsourcing has been dominated by fee-for-service contracts, which separate the price the client is obliged to pay for the service from the costs the supplier incurs in providing it. It has become increasingly clear that this apparently straightforward arrangement can lead, in practice, to serious ill-will and difficulty, at least during lengthy (up to ten-year) contracts. At the outset of the relationship, the client has typically used bargaining power to obtain a very attractive price. However, bargaining power shifts post-contract, and as change occurs in the business and hence its requirements – or in the factors which determine supplier costs, such as the labor market or technology – and the supplier is often perceived to be taking full advantage. Therefore, many clients will wish to give weight to the *relationship competency*. This determines the extent to which the supplier is willing and able to deliver the "win/win" relationships that more successfully align client and supplier goals and incentives over time.

Thinking about competencies in relation to outsourcing goals is the first step towards finding an appropriate supplier. Do we need a supplier whose delivery competency is geared to a "Rolls Royce" level of service? Or will a "Chevrolet" service be sufficient to meet the need? Is there clear evidence that the present service is "broken" and in need of radical change through the supplier's transformation competency? Or are we simply looking to transfer out a back office service that is already satisfactory in order to free up more management time to address core activities? Are we looking for a supplier who can easily and quickly be substituted if performance is unsatisfactory? Or do considerations such as switching costs imply that we need a long-term partner whose business success is linked over time to our own? (A common mistake is to choose a partner through a procurement process that encourages a bidding war; the resulting "winner's curse" leads to protracted hostilities as the chosen supplier seeks to restore profitability to an initially disastrous business model. The winner's curse is further explored in Chapter 5.[2])

The next challenge is to evaluate which suppliers possess the level of ability identified as appropriate to client need in each area of competency, and here we encounter a second common mistake. When evaluating competencies, client executives have a tendency to assess suppliers' *resources* such as physical facilities, technology, and workforce composition, rather than supplier *capabilities* to effectively manage and deploy these resources for the client's benefit. For example, they ask for evidence of excellent supplier employees in the technology area because they have identified technology as a key driver of the transformation required in the service. This assessment does not distinguish between suppliers because all credible suppliers have good to excellent people. But a supplier who instills in its technology people a culture of rapid and regular delivery of benefits to the business, supported by a component based platform architecture, will deliver a very different experience to the client than the supplier whose approach bundles system requirements into large infrastructure projects. Evaluation of a particular supplier capability involves understanding the infrastructure, values, and methodologies it brings to that area, as well as the processes it uses and the skills it has available. In the next section we identify the 12 capabilities we have found to underpin achievement of the three target competencies. Each is described in turn, and illustrated with examples from case studies of leading suppliers who are working with major corporate clients. The supplier capabilities model provides a tool to help clients evaluate potential providers, and may also help suppliers to assess themselves and their relative strengths versus the competition.

Twelve potential supplier capabilities

The capabilities we have identified through our research are labeled Domain Expertise, Business Management, Behavior Management, Sourcing, Technology Exploitation, Process Re-engineering, Customer Development, Planning and Contracting, Organization Design, Governance, Program Management, and Leadership. As shown in Figure 4.2, we have found that some capabilities support a single element of supplier competency, while others contribute to two or even three different domains. Each is of potential importance, depending on the competencies needed by the client.

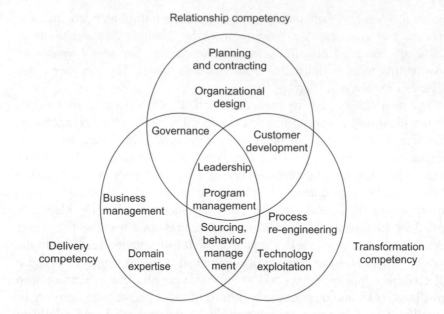

Figure 4.2 Twelve supplier capabilities

1. **Domain expertise capability.** The first and most obvious capability to assess is Domain Expertise, defined as the *supplier's capability to apply and retain sufficient professional knowledge of the target process domain to meet user requirements*. Of course, many supplier organizations acquire domain expertise through the employees transferred to them by their major clients. For example, in recent years Deutsche Bank moved its procurement people across to Accenture, Barclays transferred check-processing staff to Unisys, and Exult and Xchanging gained HR domain expertise from employees transferred by Bank of America and BAE Systems respectively. This arrangement has two potential advantages from the client point of view. First, it becomes the supplier's rather than the client's responsibility to adjust capacity, eliminate poor performers, and leverage the untapped potential of the best people. Second, both parties are assured that staff operating the service are familiar not only with the functional domain such as HR, they also understand the specifics and idiosyncrasies of the client's existing service. As the suppliers grow their own critical mass of expertise in the target domain and become more reluctant to accept more transferees, new clients will want to consider carefully the second point – does the supplier have the capability to apply domain expertise that fits their own specific context?

Other differences in client goals will impact the evaluation of domain expertise. For example, a client seeking to build external capacity to cater for periodic variations in service demand will look for a supplier's commitment to build expertise specific to their own context. The client who seeks to take advantage of low labor costs through offshore outsourcing will want to ensure it retains its own critical mass of expertise:

> It has become very clear that in order for offshore to succeed, we need to groom, reward and retain our own subject matter experts. They are the ones with the greatest knowledge of the business units and the ones who are responsible for creating the statements of work. The developers in India don't understand and can't be expected to understand the core business functions." (Senior Vice President, Fortune 500 Financial Services Company)

2. **Business management capability.** The second fundamental requirement of any BPO arrangement is that the supplier possesses the *business management capability to consistently deliver against both client service level agreements and its own required business plans*. Failure on one front will inevitably lead in time to failure on the other, but it seems that clients sometimes forget this. We have studied adversarial relationships where the clients focus on high priced items within the supplier's bundle of services and threaten to erode the supplier's margin by downsizing or eliminating these items. At the same time these clients fail to credit the supplier for other items in the bundle where unit prices are below external benchmarks of unit price. In successful relationships we find that client and supplier business managers ensure frank discussions about the supplier's business returns as well as service performance:

> We have to sit with our agency department representatives and with EDS to make expectations reasonable. We get accused by the agencies, 'Why are you siding with the supplier? You are supposed to be on our side.' But you need to be even-handed. Suppliers have to make a reasonable margin to stay in business. You don't want them to lose money because the worse their business gets, the worse your business gets. (Client Contract Manager, Australian Public Sector organization)

We saw a different example of business management in action – involving volume rather than pricing issues – in the BAE Systems procurement deal with Xchanging. During the first year of the deal it became clear to Xchanging that there was a major shortfall in the expected (£80 millions per annum) value of transactions being handled. The two parties worked hard over several months to identify additional categories of business that could be transferred to ensure that Xchanging could get back on track with its business plan, while providing the targeted savings to BAE Systems.

3. **Behavior management capability.** A common client objective when considering BPO is to seek qualitative as well as quantitative improvements in the outsourced service. Will staff transferred from their own under-appreciated "Cinderella" back office suffer further reduction in morale? Or will they exhibit new behaviors as employees of a service provider business? Clients will want to evaluate the supplier's *behavior management capability, the capability to motivate and manage people to deliver service with a "front office" culture.* Of course all major suppliers – Accenture, EDS, IBM, CSC, Unisys, HP, CGI, ACS and their like – have employees to be proud of in terms of experience, skills, and knowledge. Clients should also look for evidence that the relevant workforce will also be customer-oriented, satisfied, and empowered. How do potential suppliers orient new employees to their culture? How do they reward and incent the desired behaviors?[3]

We found one small Indian offshore supplier with an interesting behavior management capability. To overcome cultural differences, the founder and CEO hired Indians who have lived and worked in the United States to serve as project leads. To overcome substantial time zone differences, he set work hours in India from 1:00 pm to 10:00 pm to create three hours of overlap with US clients for daily communications. To reduce turnover, he involved entire, extended families in frequent parties and outings. He learned that if spouses, parents, and children are actively involved in the company, then the family conspires to retain employees. He provided several examples how this culture directly benefits his US clients, including the following anecdote. One US client needed an important deliverable by a Monday that coincided with an Indian holiday. To meet the deliverable, the team members canceled their holiday plans and worked through the weekend. Realizing the effect this had on both the team members and their families, the CEO financed an alternative weekend trip to India's version of Disneyland.

4. **Sourcing capability.** Another potentially critical contributor to meeting client goals may be the supplier's *sourcing capability, the capability to access whatever resources are required to deliver service targets.* Depending on the nature of the service, the need may be for access to economies of scale, to lower unit labor costs, to access scarce professional skills, to investment in superior infrastructure, or simply to supply management. The aforementioned deal for procurement services between BAE Systems and Xchanging was based on two of these: Xchanging's application to indirect procurement categories of the high level of professional

skills that BAE itself could only consistently attract to direct categories; and the supplier's ability to access scale by aggregating BAE's needs in these categories with those of other clients.

ATT's wish to take advantage of the high skills and low costs of the IT sector in India provides a contrasting example. Rather than build one himself, the ATT CIO persuaded IBM to create a captive IT service center in India. He was willing to trade off some costs savings in return for less risk. As of 2004, nearly 40 percent of ATT's application development work was done offshore through IBM's captive center – with reported cost savings to ATT of around 30 percent.

5. **Technology exploitation capability.** In our experience, it is often readily accepted in companies that their back office processes are suffering from years of neglect, unable to compete with core processes for the technology investment that could transform the cost, quality, and functionality of the service. Furthermore top management may be all too aware of the consistently problematic record of technology-based projects, particularly those that do not attract their own attention and active championship. Many clients are therefore strongly interested in a potential supplier's *technology exploitation capability, the capability to swiftly and effectively deploy technology in support of critical service improvement targets.* As previously rehearsed, this is a capability that requires careful evaluation by looking beyond the pure technical skills, which all major suppliers possess. What is the approach of the supplier in question? What values and behaviors do they bring to technology exploitation? What processes do they employ? What existing infrastructure do they use as a base?

As the likes of Exult (now Hewitt) and Xchanging have shown with their rapidly deployed e-enabled HR services delivered to the desk top, an excellent supplier technology exploitation capability can enable "surprise and delight." Similarly, Lloyd's of London in 2003 had the welcome experience of watching Xchanging win the "Market Initiative of the Year" award for the claims convergence program they had implemented within their contract. Xchanging was also "highly commended" in the "e-business Initiative of the Year" category.

But technology is expensive and clients will want to be sure that it is the servant, not the master of the business. CGI's approach is to jointly develop with the client an annual technology plan that identifies mutually agreed investments and projects without the need to revisit the contract. Another supplier's less fortunate client complains:

> The suppliers take your architecture where their business is going, not where you want to go. Suppliers want vanilla, our customers want

chocolate. We even have discussions on the supplier's standards. We
want to run this security environment, not their security environment
for their reasons. (Client contract manager)

6. **Process improvement capability.** Besides technology, the other prominent potential lever for service transformation is the supplier's *process
improvement capability, the capability to design and implement changes
to the service process to meet improvement targets.* For many major suppliers this is by now well-established territory and – given the prominence
gained by GE's corporate initiatives – most clients will be looking for Six
Sigma methodologies or alternatives such as Capability Maturity Model
processes. But again, it will be important to look beyond the tools to consider the people and behavior aspects. In whom are the skills vested? Who
owns the change process? Who defines what is an "improvement"? And
who benefits? We have seen too many examples – particularly in IT outsourcing – where improvements seem targeted at the convenience of the
supplier rather than the benefit of the client and the service user.

7. **Customer development capability.** *"When I became Accenture Partner
responsible for the London Stock Exchange,"* recalls David Andrews (now
CEO of Xchanging), "I found I had 200 users who complained about everything. A critical task was to change their mindsets so that they became customers." This quote goes to the heart of the supplier's *customer development
capability, which transitions "users" of an internally provided service to
"customers" who make informed choices about service level, functionality,
and the costs they incur.* BPO arrangements are usually negotiated by senior
client management, but experienced by business units and end-users who
may not share the enthusiasm. It is in the client's long-term interest to identify a supplier who can foster the user-to-customer transition. Our research
suggests three key steps the supplier will need to take:

- Establishing personal contact and understanding of service use, the pre-
cursors of trust and personal relationships
- Formal definition and communication of service required, with reporting of performance and capture of satisfaction over time
- Enactment of a business relationship in which the client feels fully
informed of service options, potential enhancements, and cost behaviors; and able to make choices to meet changing needs of the business
over time.

This might sound rather obvious, but under the still dominant form of
contracting it is not easy to achieve. In a fee-for-service deal we typically

find that the supplier sets out to provide a centrally specified service level and price package which often differs from what the user claims to have been receiving; and the supplier's management time is consumed by extensive (and central) negotiation over a long list of anomalies that pre-contract due diligence had failed to identify. The net result is that, far from the establishment of trust, the user feels neglected and hard done by and relationships are off to a rocky start. In practice we find that customer development capability works best as part of a supplier relationship competency.

8. **Planning and contracting capability.** Delivering such a relationship competency starts with the supplier's *planning and contracting capability, its capability to develop and contract for business plans which deliver "win/win" results for client and supplier over time*. The planning component involves creation of a vision of the potential prize and how it can be achieved over time. The vision and plan must be open and shared. We recall the occasion when we were asked to facilitate a workshop between putative client–supplier partners. The breakthrough came when the supplier was at last persuaded to hesitatingly reveal the extent of his ambition for new revenues from the deal; to his surprise the client executive immediately affirmed that unless the supplier succeeded in achieving at least that level of success the partnership would have failed for the client company as well. By contrast, the relatively new deal between Deutsche Bank and Accenture for procurement services clearly identifies the vision, the rewards, and the plan for their achievement. Accenture is committed to fund and create a new platform for procurement, with 200 people assigned to the development. It expects to gain a substantial new revenue stream from Deutsche Bank and the further opportunity to attract other clients to the service. Deutsche Bank sees that the plan promises to deliver 15–20 percent savings through consolidation, standardization, and re-tooling of its existing 14 procurement units – a plan for win/win. The contracting component then defines how rewards will be shared as the plan is delivered. Many variations are possible: Bank of America chose to take an equity stake in its HR services supplier Exult, as well as a share of Exult's revenues from external clients;[4] Xchanging structures its major deals as profit sharing arrangements, with open book accounting. The essential principle is that the contract enshrines win/win results from a business plan that both parties are incented to pursue.

9. **Organization design capability.** Business plans are delivered through organization structures and processes. The next question is whether the supplier demonstrates the *organization design capability*

needed to deliver the necessary resources, wherever and whenever they are needed to achieve the business plan. We find that suppliers vary greatly in terms of their organizational approach, in the choices they make and the degrees of flexibility within that. For example, some emphasize a "thin" front-end client team, which interfaces to the consolidated service units (silos) that have profit responsibility and ownership of most of the resources; all new client situations are migrated to this configuration. Clearly such arrangements – while they tap available economies of scale – may constrain ability to deliver the business plan for a specific client. At the other end of the spectrum, Xchanging allocates most of its resources to the "Enterprise Partnership" units – essentially strategic business units – it creates for each new major deal. Each enterprise partnership has its own Chief Executive, its own full executive team, and its own core resources. It is responsible and accountable for delivery of the business plan.

The second issue in supplier organizational design concerns the resource allocation process. This is an area that clients with service transformation goals will need to evaluate particularly carefully. A potential supplier may be seen to have impressive capabilities in all of the areas of transformation leverage – sourcing, technology, and process re-engineering. But the need for those capabilities will fluctuate considerably during the life of the contract. How "well geared" is the supplier to be responsive to the needs of the client (and the shared business plan) as they change over time?

10. **Governance capability.** The supplier's *governance capability refers to the capability to define and agree, to track and assess the performance of service over time.* It is likely that every supplier will point to some form of jointly staffed service review committee or Board. In the large relationship oriented deals – such as Accenture/Deutsche Bank and Xchanging/ BAE Systems – we also find a joint Board of Directors, which signals the expectation that the client is now an active partner in the enterprise (see for example Chapter 6).

The establishment of jointly staffed governance mechanisms makes a good start, but there are important follow-up questions. What reporting processes will be in place to ensure that each part of the governance structure is kept properly informed? What problem escalation procedures are defined? And what powers and sanctions are available through the governance structure? In the past we have seen joint Boards of Directors lead to managerial schizophrenia.[5] What hat does a client executive wear when they sit on the Board of the service business? Should they be pressing for more services at lower cost to benefit their host organization? Or encouraging the service business to maximize external revenues when it might divert attention from their existing service needs? We see the existence of multiple joint Boards as helping to provide checks and balances in the midst of potentially competing objectives. For example the Insurance Services deal between Lloyd's of London (25% ownership), the International Underwriting Association (25%) and Xchanging (50%) has a joint Board of Directors that is focused on achieving revenue and shared profit growth for the "Enterprise Partnership." Xchanging has a majority on this Board to ensure operational control. But service quality is protected by the separate Service Review Board on which the clients have equal membership with Xchanging. A service problem escalated to this Board requires a remedial action plan, which must be achieved in a maximum of three months. The Service Review Board has enforcement power through its ability to reduce prices. Its ultimate sanction for continual poor performance is the removal of the enterprise partnership CEO.

11. **Program management capability.** A basic assumption is that every BPO supplier needs a level of project management and change management capabilities in order to survive. Every new contract implementation requires the execution of these capabilities. But clients whose goals extend to service transformation and long-term relationship will need to look beyond these project level capabilities to evaluate the supplier's *program management capability, the capability to prioritize, coordinate, ready the organization, and deliver across a series of inter-related change projects.* Directly or indirectly our previous paragraphs have pointed to the need for a multi-phased induction and re-culturing of transferees; to a parallel transitioning of end users into customer mindsets; to technology and process based projects that deliver a series of service improvements over time; to an overarching shared business plan to which all this must contribute. This is change at a level not for the faint-hearted! Clearly it will involve methodologies and processes and high professional skills. But we suggest clients will also want to look again for values and motivations within this supplier capability. Is the supplier so proud of its sophisticated program management apparatus that it risks operating a bureaucracy that inhibits achievement of business benefit imperatives? One very experienced practitioner of the art described it this way during our research:

(Program Management) is guided by a healthy paradox. It blends the rigorous project management disciplines exemplified by world class consultants with the practicality and pragmatism that is only gained from running operations. ... It requires intellectual flexibility to vary or reverse a traditional approach according to circumstance. ... As a result there are no rules, only guidelines.

12. **Leadership capability.** While governance creates structures and processes as a context for leadership, the supplier's *leadership capability is needed to identify, communicate, and deliver the balance of activities required to achieve present and future success, for both client and provider.* In management literature generally, individual leaders are regularly credited with a surprising degree of influence on the outcomes that their businesses achieve. The general phenomenon does seem to carry across into the specifics of leading the supplier's client-facing team. After completing 76 case studies of client–supplier relationships in IT outsourcing, we found that the individuals fulfilling supplier (and indeed client) leadership roles did have considerable impact on relationship success.[6] In 80 percent of all cases the supplier was EDS, IBM, CSC, or Accenture. Although these firms were consistent in the way they contracted and governed across the case studies, 76 percent of deals were judged successful and 24 percent were not. The main differentiator between success and failure was seen to be the individuals who were leaders of the supplier (and client) account teams. If we look at how these leaders make a difference, we see three sorts of pattern:

- In unsuccessful cases, the "leader" of the supplier team was often seen to be focusing on delivery – meeting contractual service levels while delivering required margin to the host supplier company. These issues are of course important, but we have identified them earlier as business management – not leadership – capability.
- The quality of the supplier leader's personal relationship with the client leader is usually a driver of the wider relationship between client and supplier organizations.
- Least obviously but most importantly, we are finding that the quality of the relationship between the supplier leader assigned to the client and the top management at the supplier's headquarters is a critical factor in success. Because most suppliers create more of a front-end team rather than a full function business unit to serve the client, the local team is very dependent on their leader's clout with headquarters to access key resources and enact client-aligned business policies.

This recent example provides an appropriate finale to discussion of the leadership capability, and the twelve capabilities overall.

A large corporate client placed a US$200 millions contract with supplier A. Supplier A assigned "a great person" to lead the account team, but he had no clout with headquarters and could not get anything done.[7] So the client broke the contract with supplier A and signed up with supplier B. Supplier B assigned to the account a leader with great street credentials gained from managing previous large contracts. But once again the leader had no influence with Head Office, in this case because he was a recent external hire. Eventually the client called Supplier B's CEO and said, *"Send me someone who can act on your behalf."* The CEO assigned a person from Head Office, who took 18 of supplier B's best people with him to the client team. The contract has now been in effect one year and is considered a great success.

From capabilities to performance

The objective of this chapter is to provide a framework to help client companies evaluate whether suppliers possess the competencies required to address their IT and BPO requirements. We have explained and explored three supplier competencies, and the twelve supplier capabilities we find essential to their delivery. In discussing the capabilities we have tended to provide the richest version we have so far encountered. But richness is not of course necessarily goodness; richness is available at a price that can only be justified against the potential to create value. Outsourcing of a simple and stable back office process with a cost reduction objective requires a level of delivery competency, and not much more.

For example, New York City has outsourced the digitization of its (paper based) parking tickets. In 2002 this contract was moved to Ghana, Africa, when the City administration identified that the incumbent company in India had become too expensive(!).[8] But there is a sequel to the story. More recently New York has signed a contract with CGI's AMS division to manage the complete end-to-end parking violation process, now being transformed by the use of portable technology, which captures details of offending vehicles on the spot. In other words, even the simple situation may become more complex over time. As experience of BPO increases, and confidence in its benefits grows, clients will more often be seeking sophisticated – and lasting – supplier relationships.

And of course choosing a capable supplier is not enough to deliver performance. The research base that underpins this chapter suggests three imperatives for companies that wish to add value through use of the IT and BPO services market:

- To identify the competencies they should be accessing in the marketplace, client firms should think carefully about their likely future needs from any process to be outsourced. What role does this process play within the overall business model? Therefore what improvement goals for the process – cost, quality, functionality, and flexibility – make most sense over time? And given the existing versus target status of the process, what combination of delivery, transformation, and relationship competencies will be required? Our research experience has continued to confirm the selective approach we first advocated in 1996,[9] with the refinement that multiple relationships with a single supplier can be an effective approach.
- The decision to choose a particular supplier – or to extend the relationship with an existing one – should then be guided by thorough evaluation of relevant strengths in the 12 capabilities we have described. Capabilities, not skills and resources or brand name, determine the right choice.
- Last but not least, it will be essential for the client firm to stay involved in the action rather than step aside in the belief that "now it is up to the supplier." The level of involvement, and the extent and nature of client resources needed, will of course be another function of the context (see also Chapter 3, and the model we provided for the IT domain in 1998[10]). Thinking about client-side dependencies for the successful execution of each supplier capability will provide at least one level of insight into what is required.

Outsourcing has been too often, in our experience, a case of "Marry in haste, repent at leisure." As one senior executive of a major supplier observed: "*Outsourcing contracts are agreed in concept, but delivered in detail, and that's why they can break down.*" Benchmarking the 12 supplier capabilities against strategic and operational intent is at the heart of effective practice.

Notes

1. See for example Lacity, M., Willcocks, L., and Feeny, D. (1996), "The Value of Selective IT Sourcing," *Sloan Management Review*, Vol. 37, 3, pp. 13–25 and Feeny, D. and Willcocks, L. (1998), "Core IS Capabilities for Exploiting IT," *Sloan Management Review*, Vol. 39, 3, pp. 9–21 (listed as an SMR Classic).

2. For definition and analysis of the "winner's curse" phenomenon across 85 outsourcing contracts, see Kern, T. and Willcocks, L. and van Heck, E. (2002), "The Winner's Curse in IT Outsourcing: Strategies for Avoiding Relational Trauma," *California Management Review*, Vol. 44, 2, pp. 47–69.

3. For other research on motivating transitioned supplier employees, see Ho, V., Ang, S., and Straub, D. (2003), "When Subordinates Become IT Contractors: Persistent Managerial Expectations in IT Outsourcing," *MIS Quarterly*, Vol. 14, 1, pp. 66–89. Ang, S. and Slaughter, S. (2001), "Work Outcomes and Job Design for Contract Versus Permanent IS Professionals on Software Development Teams," *MIS Quarterly*, Vol. 25, 3, pp. 321–351.

4. Exult quickly won significant add-on contracts, including a US$700 millions deal with Prudential Financial, and a US$600 millions deal with International Paper. From Cagle, M.L. and Campbell, K. (2002), "Taking HR from Cost Center to Revenue Generator at Bank of America," presentation at the 2002 Outsourcing World Summit, Florida, February.

5. For discussion see Lacity, M., Feeny, D., and Willcocks, L. (2003), "Transforming a Back Office Function: Lessons from BAE Systems' Experience of Enterprise Partnership," *MIS Quarterly Executive*, Vol. 2, 2, pp. 86–103.

6. Lacity, M., and Willcocks, L. (2001), *Global Information Technology Outsourcing: Search for Business Advantage*, Wiley, Chichester.

7. Rottman, J. and Lacity, M. (2004), "Proven Practices for IT Offshore Outsourcing," *Cutter Consortium*, Vol. 5, 12, pp. 1–27.

8. Reported in *Knowledge at Wharton*, September 9, 2002.

9. Lacity, M. *et al.* (1996), op. cit.

10. Feeny, D. and Willcocks, L. (1998), op. cit.

CHAPTER 5

The winner's curse in outsourcing: How to avoid relational trauma

Thomas Kern, Leslie Willcocks, and Eric van Heck

Introduction

IT outsourcing (ITO) has evolved into a highly competitive marketplace, with consequences for how suppliers bid and secure contracts. In some instances, suppliers underbid to win the contract, resulting in the phenomenon known as the "winner's curse." *The winner's curse occurs when a supplier makes unrealistic bidding promises to ensure it wins the contract, but already knows, or subsequently discovers, that it cannot earn a profit on the engagement.* In this chapter, we report how the winner's curse can negatively affect both clients and suppliers. We present an IT outsourcing case history that illustrates the relational trauma caused by the winner's curse. We discuss how this company, and others like it, can avoid the curse.

In a field still relatively under-theorized,[1] studying the winner's curse makes a distinctive contribution to our understanding of outsourcing supplier practice. One cause of the winner's curse is the separation of the supplier's IT outsourcing bid teams from the subsequent service delivery teams. Both teams are rewarded on different, and frequently conflicting, criteria. The chapter highlights this practice (and many others) and suggests preventive strategies. It also emphasizes that in all IT outsourcing deals, client organizations need to have a carefully selected management team to actively develop, maintain, and manage the deal. Such management teams are needed to avoid or belatedly react to the damaging outcomes inherent in the winner's curse.

What clients seek from external service providers

Selecting the right IT supplier, on the right terms, poses an ongoing challenge. The difficulty frequently lies in choosing the evaluation criteria that satisfy the client's objectives for outsourcing. Commonly, the evaluation criteria are based on benefits that the internal IT organization is not able to achieve, but that the suppliers can presumably deliver. The major criteria have been based on expected financial, business, strategic, political, and/or technical benefits.[2] The most common benefits sought are financial. These include cost savings between 10 and 40 percent, improving cost control and clarity, and increasing cash flow. In addition, the general lure of ridding oneself of the "IT investment pit," and instead paying a fixed monthly sum for IT services or on a "pay-for-use" basis, remains a major financial objective. Business, strategic and/or political benefits have involved new business start-ups, process re-engineering, a refocus on the client's core competencies, assisting in managing mergers or globalization, and diminishing the often political debates about new IT projects.[3] Finally, clients have sought technical benefits from outsourcing, including access to expertise, improved services, new technologies, and technological innovation.[4] However, we do not fail to recognize that organizations typically outsource for a selected mix of the above reasons.

How clients and suppliers create the winner's curse

Clients and suppliers both contribute to the creation of the winner's curse. Clients' behaviors that contribute to the winner's curse include the following:

- Clients may excessively focus on price, compelling suppliers to bid based on small or even nil margins
- Clients may treat a bidding event as a spot purchase, ignoring the long-term nature and consequences of supplier engagements
- Clients may not adequately define requirements, forcing suppliers to bid on incomplete information

Suppliers may subsequently react by underbidding to win the contract. Suppliers do so for many reasons:

- Suppliers may need to satisfy aggressive growth targets demanded by shareholders
- Suppliers may be short of business due to recessions or increased competition

- Suppliers may be seeking entrance into new markets
- Suppliers may be seeking prestigious clients
- Suppliers may believe they can recoup the loss through contract additions
- Supplier may reward bid teams for winning the contract, but not hold them accountable for its subsequent delivery
- Suppliers may base bids on false assumptions about opportunities to improve the client's services

One could see several of these factors operating in the recessionary 2001–04 period, for example. Suppliers may be keen to enter a new market segment, want to lock out competitors, have a strategic intent to dominate certain market segments, and/or they believe that they can recoup the investment and broaden margins later. Parallel research studies frequently uncover such strategies, as we shall see later. It is precisely in such circumstances that the danger of a winner's curse arises.

Suppliers take a risk by underbidding in hopes that they can recover their costs later. For example, suppliers may seek to identify the client's service areas that urgently need attention but are excluded from the contract, so meriting excess fees. In addition, suppliers will attempt to offer additional services from their portfolio of technology capabilities, service management, and consultancy services over the life of the contract.

Suppliers may even sign a deal as a "loss leader," assuming that additional business will arise upon which they can make money. For example, in its 10-year of 1993 deal with the UK Inland Revenue, EDS made losses for several years running Inland Revenue's data centers. Profitability only emerged in the late 1990s from the economies of scale achieved by consolidating Inland Revenue's data centers with those of the Department of Social Security – a deal also run by EDS.[5]

How the nature of IT contributes to the winner's curse

Besides the client and supplier behaviors discussed in a previous section, another contributing factor is the nature of IT itself. *The overall IT environment of an organization is often too highly integrated and complex to calculate actual service costs and to define technical requirements.* Thus, suppliers often have to bid on the basis of incomplete information.

IT differs from other types of outsourcing in several respects. First, IT is not homogeneous but comprises a wide variety of activities, skills, and technologies whose differential costs and impacts cannot easily be assessed or measured. This is particularly true for IT development projects because they have so many intangibles and uncertainties. Development projects typically employ new, unstable technologies that need to work in specific business contexts where requirements keep changing. IT projects may entail turning tacit knowledge into programmed routines, which are difficult to define beforehand. Second, IT technical capability continues to evolve at a dizzying pace, making it difficult to predict IT needs with any certainty. Third, there is no simple basis for gauging the economics of IT activity – there are few industries where the underlying economics shift as fast as in IT. Fourth, IT value often lies in the cross-functional integration of business processes, and the penetration of IT into the core of organizational functioning. Such value is difficult to measure and contract for externally. Fifth, in-house IT cost tracking has been notoriously poor. This frequently makes like-for-like comparisons of in-house against supplier bids difficult to achieve. For example, in one 1999 deal we researched, supplier bids were benchmarked against an estimate of in-house costs that was subsequently found to be 70 percent understated.

All these factors came together in one telecom outsourcing deal we studied in 2001. On the supplier's calculations, it was scheduled to cover its costs in the first year and move to operational profit thereafter. The supplier actually made a US$15 million loss in the first year, a result likely to impact on the client as well as the supplier over the next four years of the contract.

The consequences of the winner's curse

The winner's curse can have dire consequences for both clients and suppliers. Since supplier account managers need to compensate for the winner's curse by concentrating on recovering costs, they may make cost/ service trade-offs that disadvantage the client. For example, case studies demonstrate that where a supplier seeks to decrease its costs, this can result in decreases in service quality and additional costs for the client.[6] As one client manager noted, "Suppliers have to make a reasonable margin to stay in business. You don't want them to lose money because the worse their business gets, the worse your business gets."[7]

A supplier's disproportionate concern for cost containment can lead to inflexibility in the interpretation of the letter and spirit of the contract, which can also lead to adversarial relationships. Thus, operational performance and the client–supplier relationship will receive less attention and suffer. As a consequence, we suggest that in winner's curse situations, suppliers will likely jeopardize the success and effectiveness of the operations and outsourcing relationship as their focus settles primarily on recovering their costs, and not on developing and maintaining the relationship and mutual objectives. A supplier might then undertake opportunistic behavior, seeking to reduce its own operational costs, often at the expense of the client, as Williamson (1975) suggests.[8]

Prior research on the winner's curse

The notion of a "winner's curse" can be traced to the study of auctions and other bidding scenarios. The winner's curse occurs if the winner of an auction or bidding event systematically bids above the actual value of the objects or service and thereby systematically incurs losses. Acceptance of a bid in general is an informative event, and the failure to incorporate such contingent information into the bidding strategy can lead to excessive bids and subsequent losses for both parties. Each bidder must recognize that she wins the object only when she has the highest signal. Failure to take into account the bad news about others' signals that comes with any victory can lead to the winner paying more, on average, than the prize is worth. This happens quite often in practice.[9]

The winner's curse occurs in *normal* auctions, in which the auctioneer is the seller (or represents the seller) and the bidders are the buyers who value the object(s) sold. The auctioneer is usually seeking a high price for the object. The winner's curse also occurs in *procurement* auctions (also called tendering), where the auctioneer is the buyer and the bidders are sellers who incur costs in supplying the object(s) bought.[10] In that case, the auctioneer is seeking a low price. Here we focus on the latter – that is, the winner's curse in a procurement auction of IT outsourcing contracts and its impact on and consequences for the relationship between the customer and the winning bidder.

Persistent overbidding in tendering situations has been observed in laboratory experiments. Kagel and Levin[11] for example report that losses due to overbidding are more common in auctions with large number of bidders, than in small numbers. But losses are likely to occur in both scenarios. Losses, however, can be minimized with awareness and experience of such tendering and auction events. Lind and Plott[12] illustrated, though, that the winner's curse is a general phenomenon exhibited by most bidders and in most bids. It all comes down to what Capen et al.[13] note: *"bidders want to win."* As we shall see, this applies in IT outsourcing as anywhere else.

Auctions have not only been a perennial feature of doing business in many sectors, but the phenomenon has been increasing with the recent development, for example, of B2B exchanges and on-line auctions. Interestingly, the theory of auctions would suggest that the winner's curse is asymmetric. The person who wins suffers the curse alone. In the *normal* auctions for physical products like cars, houses, agricultural products etc. this is usually the case. However, especially in *procurement* auctions for contracts and rights in business settings, this is not the only likely outcome. For example, a supplier winning a "cursed" deal on a B2B exchange may well cut his losses by providing lower quality products or services to the customer. A buyer winning what turns out to be a cursed deal may well drive a much harder deal in terms of service guarantee rather than price next time with the same supplier. The buyer may even remove that supplier from the favored supplier list altogether. In all sorts of markets, a winner's curse can have consequences for several parties, over months or even years. *In procurement auctions like ITO, auctions are better conceived of as relationship building exercises rather than spot purchases.*

In procurement auctions, the auctioneer could assist the bidders by providing greater clarity on the auction process and the objects' value. The auctioneer could also take steps to reduce the potential problem prior to the auction or to help the winner after the auction. One illustrative example in an IT outsourcing context occurred in the EDS–Inland Revenue deal cited by Willcocks and Kern (1998). We quote an Inland Revenue respondent who said,

> If you are minimizing bid costs, and not driving incentives down for the supplier, you are doing something really rather helpful to the potential deal down stream. Acting otherwise you can damage the relationship irrevocably.[14]

The supplier selection process

Supplier selection is a costly undertaking in terms of time, effort, and resources. One organization spent US$100 million selecting and negotiating with suppliers before finalizing a multi-billion dollar contract. But the investment in identifying the right supplier and contract bid is paramount to the success of the overall outsourcing venture.[15] Hence the criteria that generally inform the selection process is a richly researched area in outsourcing.[16] Yet we actually know very little about the consequences of a wrong selection. What are the impacts on the finances, post-contract management, and overall success of outsourcing relationships? It is here that this research and chapter make a major contribution.

Typically, the general outsourcing selection process begins in earnest with the short-listing of relevant suppliers. Clients may use an *open* short-list process, in which they advertise for suppliers to apply, or a *closed* short-list process, in which they directly approach targeted suppliers.[17] Once short-listed, clients issue a request for information (RFI)[18] to suppliers. An RFI commonly outlines the client's objectives, services, assets, transfers, and issues of relevance to its outsourcing intention. Suppliers will respond with their approach to addressing a client's outsourcing ambition, its capabilities, track record, reference sites, and associated information.[19] Those selected are then invited to tender (ITT) and issued a request for proposal (RFP). Depending on the company's approach, the tender or proposal is commonly the means by which detailed dialogues and information exchanges are initiated to further narrow down a select group of suppliers, who then define a bidding contest for the outsourcing deal.[20]

The final selection is then expected to be preceded by a phase of careful evaluation of the various supplier bids. Practice shows that clients will often choose suppliers on qualitative criteria, especially when the quantitative assessment is more or less the same for all bids. Additionally, poor in-house evaluations of costs and services by clients may also mean that over-promising by suppliers will be initially accepted as a superior bid. (In one case in 2001 we found an insurance company underestimating its in-house costs by 50 percent. Fortunately, the supplier discovered this during due diligence.) In this circumstance, a winner's curse scenario becomes more probable.

The winner's curse and other scenarios in IT outsourcing

The winner's curse, of course, is only one of several possible scenarios. Figure 5.1 illustrates the main possibilities relevant to this chapter. Logically, the supplier bids for an IT outsourcing contract against other suppliers. In Figure 5.1 the supplier experiences a winner's curse when it wins the bid but cannot generate a reasonable profit from the engagement. On one argument, the likelihood of such circumstances will increase over time, as the growing competitive pressure on suppliers will push them to compete increasingly on prices and service deliverables. As we shall see, this typically has a negative (Lose-Lose quadrant of Figure 5.1) impact on the client. However, in some cases, the winner's curse actually had

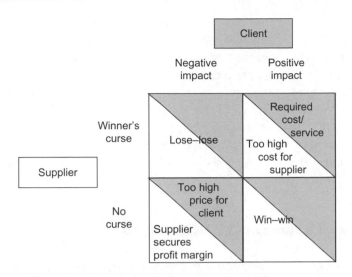

Figure 5.1 The winner's curse and other scenarios in IT outsourcing

positive impacts on the client (Lose-Win quadrant in Figure 5.1). On the other hand, the supplier may win a bid that secures its required profit margin while delivering on the client's costs and service expectations (Win-Win quadrant of Figure 5.1). But it may also be that the supplier secures its profit margins, but negatively impacts the client. As we will show in a later analysis of 85 deals, we have witnessed all four outcomes in IT outsourcing.

We posit that the operationalization of the contract and the outsourcing relationship are likely to suffer severely in a winner's curse situation. If the client controls the situation tightly, the winner's curse may only affect the supplier. However, the effect may well also be diminished services, lower number of supplier staff, and less experienced staff actually in charge of the deal. The client may well be faced with the consequences of a winner's curse, resulting in significant additional costs, and the need for increased management input to alleviate the frustrations of users and staff. Other costs may, for example, also result from not getting the much-needed new IT system and therefore remain at a competitive disadvantage. In such circumstances, the question arises whether outsourcing remains viable for the client. Some relationships we have studied cannot recover from the winner's curse and subsequently terminate contracts early.

In practice, what makes IT outsourcing distinctive is the high switching costs of "back-sourcing." In one deal we examined, a 10-year US$550 million contract was terminated after only 17 months. Additional implementation and termination costs to the client were estimated at $160 million. Not surprisingly, with such prohibitive switching costs, many clients make the judgment that continuation of a "cursed" outsourcing arrangement is the lesser of two evils. For example, one academic research study[21] found 21 of the 85 outsourcing deals were in failure mode, but only eight terminated the contract prematurely.

In the next section, we provide a first hand account of a winner's curse scenario. We show how an IT outsourcing arrangement developed into a winner's curse first for the supplier, then for the client. We discuss how other scenarios could have developed, as illustrated in Figure 5.1, and how the relationship was converted eventually into a "Win-Win" arrangement for both parties.

Relational trauma at CLIENTCO Oil[22]

CLIENTCO is an affiliate of one of the largest petroleum companies in the world. It is an integrated oil company with "upstream" activities (oil exploration and production) and "downstream" activities (refining, distribution, and sales). Plagued by ongoing cost and operational efficiency pressures, CLIENTCO has been driven to focus on their core operations and source other services from the market.

In pursuing IT outsourcing, CLIENTCO decided to engage multiple suppliers for several reasons. First, no single supplier had ever been found to deliver all of its requirements. Second, careful selection of small niche suppliers ensured that CLIENTCO's business would be of strategic significance to the supplier, assuring greater attention and control. Third, it strove to choose suppliers that closely matched their culture – a key factor in their outsourcing strategy. Amidst this multi-sourcing portfolio, we concentrate on CLIENTCO's five year, US$8 million contract signed in 1994 with Supplier A for legacy application support services.

Supplier A's selection. Supplier A was specifically asked to competitively bid against the incumbent supplier (Supplier B). Supplier B at the time was the preferred supplier, having supplied CLIENTCO with IT services for the previous seven years. But Supplier B's fees were also perceived as expensive. Consequently, Supplier A was implicitly asked to make a lower price offer, undercutting Supplier B to such an extent that it became worthwhile for CLIENTCO to switch:

> They [Supplier B] did it on a day-rate basis and they were the company that moved us the furthest forward in terms of proactively showing us how to do applications support and development better. But, at a cost. This was a Rolls-Royce service. (Senior Manager, CLIENTCO)

Supplier A's ambition to acquire a "Blue Chip" client like CLIENTCO, gave Supplier A the impetus to outbid Supplier B. However, Supplier A's low margin calculation resulted in the winner's curse. Furthermore, CLIENTCO also suffered negative consequences in the initial years of the relationship.

The specifics of the deal – the contract. In 1994, CLIENTCO signed a five-year, fixed-cost contract with Supplier A for the provision of legacy application support services. The contract was structured into two parts. One part defined the core services that had to be supplied continuously according to service level agreements. Core services were priced on a fixed monthly fee of US$73,000 for all legacy application and system services. The other part defined enhanced services that would vary according to CLIENTCO's changing requirements. Enhanced services would be priced according to agreed upon prices.

The contract was structured to assure CLIENTCO an annual cost reduction in the flat rate charges for the core services as the systems migrated from mainframe to client-server architectures: "it's reduced by $30,000 the first year, and a further $15,000 in each following year" (Customer Service Manager, Supplier A). The planned time for this was 2004.

Transition Period Difficulties. The transition period for Supplier A started in earnest mid-1994. It took over the existing service arrangements from Supplier B, and began to apply its expertise to deliver the promised cost reductions. Supplier A and CLIENTCO experienced many difficulties during the transition. Three are discussed below:

1. *Supplier A did not understand CLIENTCO's idiosyncratic requirements.* According to CLIENTCO, operationalization of the deal was a straightforward matter of delivering what the service level agreement specified. According to Supplier A, operationalization of the deal was difficult because it did not yet understand CLIENTCO's idiosyncrasies and expectations. For Supplier A, it was a new environment. There was no one whom they could initially rely on to help operationalize the contract, especially not Supplier B, the competitor, who had lost the business. Surprisingly, CLIENTCO's managers were initially not aware of these difficulties. Only in retrospect did they recognize the correlation between their idiosyncrasies and Supplier A's early problems:

> It was a difficult time because they didn't know how we worked, we weren't saying to them, : "here's five of our best people, they are going to sit and work with you," because we didn't have five people to work with them. Because the business had already been contracted. (Senior Manager, CLIENTCO)

2. *CLIENTCO held Supplier A too rigidly to the contract.* CLIENTCO had a policy of holding suppliers strictly to service level agreements. To enable this policy, CLIENTCO invested considerable time and effort on formulating a detailed contract and service level agreement:

> It's all laid down in here [the contract]. The systems are all defined as being either critical, highly critical, or low criticality. They are graded according to how critical they are to CLIENTCO and the business. And depending on whether they are critical or less critical it defines how many hours you can wait before you get a problem fixed. (Application Support Manager, Supplier A)

All supplier payments were dependent on the achievement of the stipulated services. Supplier non-performance in any way provoked the loss of any achievement bonuses. Evaluation occurred on the basis of three main performance measures: down time, the number of change requests, and the amount of time spent on specific aspects of the core services. The core service levels and their prices were annually renegotiated and updated, in an effort to ensure that costs were continually reduced, and the legacy services slowly phased out. Naturally, this put additional pressure on Supplier A's managers to identify new areas of business to compensate for losses. On average, CLIENTCO spent an additional US$67,000 a month on service additions and changes. Overall CLIENTCO was paying approximately US$ 140,000 a month in total.

3. *CLIENTCO's controlling culture increased Supplier A's costs.* The transition period also revealed CLIENTCO's strong corporate culture for the first time, to which Supplier A would need to adjust speedily. It was CLIENTCO's practice to impose its culture on any supplier wishing to do business with them. CLIENTCO's culture had a strong focus on security, safety, and control. In part, this was due to CLIENTCO's parent company, but it also emerged from the nature of their business. Working with CLIENTCO was seriously complicated by this culture. The resulting controls also increased the operating costs for the supplier substantially: *"We've had a number of suppliers tell us that our controls potentially add 25% to the cost"* (Vendor Manager, CLIENTCO).

Early relationship adjustments. These difficulties led to an initial poor service performance. This, of course, seriously hampered the development of the relationship. Managers were out to find and remedy the sources of these difficulties. They made several early adjustments.

1. *Relationship managers for both parties were replaced.* Blame was later to be apportioned to both CLIENTCO's and Supplier A's operation managers

in charge of the deal. To resolve the issue, they had to be replaced, due to ongoing confrontations. These changes were very costly for both Supplier A and CLIENTCO. However, this change in players was critical for continuation. Indeed, later, it was perceived to be a defining moment in the turnaround of the venture and relationship.

2. *Improve the client–supplier interface.* Part of the newly appointed relationship managers' remit was to ensure a better interface between Supplier A and CLIENTCO. In this respect, CLIENTCO relationship managers became much more involved in all personnel arrangements, and in the alignment of Supplier A's structure with that of CLIENTCO's. In any case, the decision to formalize the structure was to influence the growing amount of time managers spent on the relationship, rather than just focusing on the contractual requirements. It became indicative that IT outsourcing success was correlated with relationship management: *"The contract takes up 25% of our time and the rest of it takes 75%"* (Relationship Manager, CLIENTCO).

3. *Alter management processes.* However, effective relationship management depended even more so on management processes. Yet CLIENTCO had taken the management procedures and processes from its previous dealings with Supplier B and merely applied these to the operations with Supplier A. It soon became evident that these would not work with Supplier A. Consequently, during the far-reaching changes to the management structure in 1995–96, several of the management processes in terms of reporting had to be addressed. With the interaction structure already redefined, CLIENTCO then formalized its management processes, outlining particular meetings at which supplier performance would be reviewed and according to which payments were then made and bonuses granted. These meetings were key to CLIENTCO's control agenda, and gave senior managers of operations and senior functional managers an opportunity to closely monitor supplier performance. Additionally, the meetings provided the possibility for voicing any concerns or problems that had arisen and drawing senior management's attention to them. The evolving management process included ad hoc meetings, and formalized inter-organizational quarterly, monthly, and weekly meetings at different levels.

Forced to renegotiate the contract (1996). Towards the end of 1995 it had become clear to Supplier A that it was no longer able to deliver the services as originally priced and agreed. For the first one and half years, it had incurred losses. The contract was in fact costing them significant amounts of money. In consequence, services were suffering, and both sides were highly dissatisfied with the arrangements. As a result, Supplier A was forced to re-evaluate the contract and its business with CLIENTCO. In part, Supplier A had to admit that some of the problems were the result of their erroneous calculations and assumptions about CLIENTCO's business. However, this only became apparent to Supplier A during the actual operationalization of the contract:

> When Supplier A first came into the frame with us they were very much used to dealing with public utilities and councils and things like that and they found us very strange. They came in, they took our business and they made some assumptions that we were organized like a council or a utility. We had high overheads, all those sorts of things. We had excess resources working in that area. But we didn't. We'd already done all that work. They were a little bit naive to start off with. (Vendor Manager, CLIENTCO)

Consequently, in mid 1996, Supplier A was left with two real options for resolving the situation: either renegotiate or terminate the contract early. Supplier A requested contract renegotiation. CLIENTCO's response was favorable, revealing a sympathy and understanding of the supplier's situation. The stated position was that they were not interested in causing Supplier A a loss and wanted both parties to mutually benefit from the deal. Hence CLIENTCO's management agreed to revisit and evaluate the original contract. Interestingly, they found terms and price scales that essentially prohibited Supplier A from making an adequate return on their costs. Reflecting on the original state of the contract, one respondent emphasized:

> The contract that was put together was appalling. It did not take into account the availability of additional programmers as needed and the very significant price rises in the market. This thing wasn't tied to KPI's (Key Performance Indicators), it wasn't fair, they just couldn't deliver the services for us on it, so we had to go in and make some changes. (Vendor Manager, CLIENTCO)

The procedures adopted for the renegotiation cycle were as follows. Supplier A would continue to deliver on the original contract while a team on Supplier A's side would renegotiate the contract. Supplier A's team negotiated the specific changes with CLIENTCO's Contracts and Materials department and the CLIENTCO Vendor Managers. The ensuing review uncovered a number of stipulated terms that were unenforceable in business terms:

> There was a review on how much they were paying for core services because we were doing a lot more core work than we were being paid

for at the beginning [...] but also there just seemed to be a lot of unnecessary stuff in the contract which we were never going to try and do. It didn't seem to make business sense to do it. So that was taken out. (Applications Support Manager, Supplier A).

Once a section had been renegotiated and finalized, the changes were then implemented by Supplier A's account team and CLIENTCO's operational managers. This meant direct implementation and operationalization of the new terms. At times, the renegotiation phase was a trying time and relations suffered, but it was an essential process if Supplier A was to be able to continue with the outsourcing venture.

The outcomes of the renegotiation were felt to be a very positive experience for both parties. At least it ensured mutual benefit from the deal for the future: "I think to a certain extent we've both ended up walking away from that saying, 'yes we are happy with the result.' They are not getting everything they wanted, and we are not getting everything that we wanted" (Vendor Manager, CLIENTCO).

Rebuilding relations – Post-contract renegotiations (1997 onwards). The successful outcome of the renegotiation phase put the relationship back on track. First signs of the changes to come were the dramatic service performance improvements. These were so impressive that in subsequent months relations improved to such a degree that both parties agreed to develop the basis for a partnership agreement. This agreement would cover a number of operating principles, but would not embody any legal commitments whatsoever. Instead it was a rhetorical commitment:

> It's an informal thing but it's been written by both sides. We have a partnership agreement with them rather than just do this only and only this [contract]. But I don't think it's actually officially recorded anywhere. It's one of those things that Supplier A and CLIENTCO do mention a few times, we are trying very hard to work with CLIENTCO, not against them. (Application Support Manager, Supplier A)

The informal agreement was based on greater commitment by the supplier to inform CLIENTCO of any planned changes that could affect the relationship. In a sense, it was an extended promise to cooperate and collaborate more closely. The impact of this informal agreement was manifold. For one thing, it increased willingness for closer cooperation and generated a feeling of openness and trust in each other. Both parties' managers consciously worked on fostering such an environment as they not only believed in it, but also wanted to ensure each other's awareness of any difficulties or problems:

> I trust them to speak to me if ever they need anything or want to tell me anything. I think I've more or less achieved that they will phone if they've got the slightest need to talk. I also want to make sure it's a very informal relationship. That's developed quite nicely, they don't feel inhibited, they will call if they need to. (Operations Manager, CLIENTCO)

The result of these developments spurred a strong sense of loyalty on the supplier's side towards CLIENTCO. In fact, the loyalty evolved to define an ethical undertone in the operations of the venture. The benefits of these changes were felt to be of mutual advantage. In Supplier A's case, it gave rise to new opportunities for business with the IT department but also with other customers, that is a range of business units within CLIENTCO. Another benefit for Supplier A was the client IT group's willingness and openness to discuss their future developments and long-term strategy. It gave Supplier A the much sought opportunity to bid early for new and upcoming business services CLIENTCO needed. This ensured the ongoingness of their relations as well.

The benefits for CLIENTCO were increased access to technology, expertise, and skill resources, enabling them to implement projects faster and move their business forward. More importantly, CLIENTCO began actively to seek value added by offering an additional bonus award if Supplier A could show they had implemented additional innovations that added real value or generally improved CLIENTCO's operation.

Strong signs that the relationship and hence operations had improved became apparent in early 1998. Service levels were in line with CLIENTCO's demands and in most cases even exceeded stipulated services. Their service performance record was exemplary, giving raise to considerable bonuses. The operations manager from CLIENTCO explained that

> It's quite an incentive to be given that bonus for consecutive months. And just recently I think they went for seven consecutive months where the batch bonus was paid which was quite an achievement. Because that's a long time to go, a whole month without anything happening.

The relationship continued on this basis for next two years until the end of the contract. In 2001 the venture was in its second five-year contract period, having never looked back after three traumatic IT outsourcing years.

Strategies to avoid experiencing a relational trauma – Lessons learned

Before deriving the lessons learned from this case, it is useful to establish how widely applicable these lessons might be. We detailed earlier the conditions and circumstances in which a winner's curse can arise. We also argued, from the research literature, and our own research experiences, that the winner's curse is quite common, suggesting that the lessons learned from this case, are, not least through analytical generalization, highly pertinent to all contemplating or participating in IT outsourcing arrangements. Let us reinforce this point by re-analyzing from a winner's curse perspective one of the richer empirical sources available on IT outsourcing, consisting of a detailed longitudinal case research database.[23]

The research we will re-analyze examined 85 IT outsourcing arrangements and it is from Lacity and Willcocks (2001). In Figure 5.2, we chart our re-analysis of these IT outsourcing deals in terms of the impact of the original bids and contracting terms. First, it can be seen that the supplier experienced a winner's curse in nearly 20 percent of the cases, while the client experienced a negative/mixed impact in nearly 36 percent of the cases. Clearly the winner's curse and "cursed" clients are by no means rare phenomena.

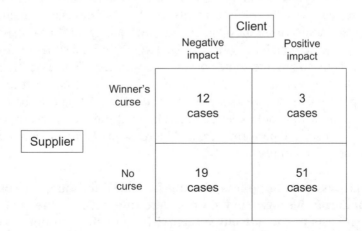

Figure 5.2 Prevalence of the winner's curse in IT outsourcing (85 cases re-analyzed from published sources)

Second, our re-analysis confirms that the left-hand quadrant IS a very risky place to be. Of the 12 deals, seven terminated early, one was terminated and restructured, one was not renewed, and three continued for differing reasons but were viewed as persistently problematic by all respondents.

Third, it is noticeable that where a supplier experiences a winner's curse, there is a high likelihood of this affecting the client negatively. There were three cases where this was not the case (top right quadrant of Figure 5.2). Two, involving a major UK retailer and an aerospace company, saw the supplier eventually move into profit as more work came on stream after the fourth year of these 10-year deals. The third was a public sector agency whose gains on an economic development package with the supplier came to be offset by the cost increases in the IT service aspects of the deal. In all three, the suppliers succeeded in removing the winner's curse, and moved into more profitable ways of operating. Fourth, and unsurprisingly, the bottom left-hand quadrant is not a stable place to be either. While ten deals did continue to their natural term, though producing very mixed results for the clients, four others were terminated early, three were renegotiated, and two saw a degree of "backsourcing" – the slow rebuilding of in-house capability during the course of the IT outsourcing contracts.

By definition, the successful IT outsourcing cases fall into the bottom right hand quadrant of Figure 5.2. What is most noticeable here is the high propensity of clients to subsequently renew contracts with the same supplier – over three quarters did so – and the disproportionately high number of selective outsourcing deals on 3–4 year terms with detailed contracts and service level agreements (SLAs). But how can stakeholders in IT outsourcing ensure they can get into this quadrant? If an outsourcing deal does not start out here, what can be done to turn the situation around? Our case helps to provide some possible answers here. The case highlights clearly the potential impact of a winner's curse on post-contract management operations. Here we will now outline what we found to be the key lessons on how to avoid experiencing relational trauma, increase in most costs, loss of service performance, and increase in dissatisfaction amongst the end-user community.

Strategic lesson 1. Suppliers bidding for an IT outsourcing contract may underbid because they do not take into account the real value and real costs of the outsourced activities and they do not take into account a correction for their own optimistic estimate because their bidding aim is to win the deal. The initial deal CLIENTCO negotiated was strongly in its favor, but the relationship as such was "cursed." The deal as agreed, gave Supplier A all too few possibilities to recover their bidding expenses and negotiation costs. In fact, Supplier A found that the venture would make a net loss to operationalize, as they had evidently mis-calculated their initial bid offer. It is interesting to examine how Supplier A could have made such an erroneous cost calculation when competitively bidding for CLIENTCO's business. The conjecture proposed by the managers at CLIENTCO seemed quite plausible – that Supplier A had made assumptions about CLIENTCO's high resource base costs and operational inefficiencies, and then was unprepared to find that CLIENTCO for the past years had been on a drive to minimize costs and rationalize, standardize, and downsize operations where possible. However, there is another plausible explanation, which in other documented cases such as the Inland Revenue,[24] British Aerospace[25] is also evident. Supplier A needed to contract with CLIENTCO to gain credibility, prestige, and references by working with a major Blue Chip organization. To Supplier A, essentially a small niche supplier, such a deal held widespread perceived benefits beyond solely making a margin on that contract. A third contributory factor was that the bid team was largely different from the group that was charged with operationalizing the contract and was rewarded on a different basis – on securing the contract, not on operational performance. The learning points are:

- Analyze carefully the reasons for, and the detail of, a low supplier bid, and whether the bid can result in a reasonable profit for the supplier.
- The supplier and client should ensure that those operationalizing the contract are influential in the supplier selection and bidding process.
- Reassess the cost/service baseline before outsourcing, and make detailed disclosure to the bidders(s).
- Fixed price contracts will create inflexibilities, possibly disadvantageous to both parties. In fact there is a considerable literature pointing out the typical problems experienced with fixed price contracts even in the IT outsourcing field.[26] Consider flexible pricing options including cost plus, market pricing, fixed fee adjusted by volume fluctuation, and benefit sharing. Track supplier costs via "open book" accounting. Allow for biannual assessment of pricing adjustments.
- Undertake a rigorous due diligence process before the contract is actually finalized.

Strategic lesson 2. A winner's curse for suppliers can result in a negative impact for the client resulting in relational trauma, renegotiation

costs, and end-user dissatisfaction or in a positive impact for the client when the supplier incurs the losses and delivers the services to the agreed levels. Its miscalculations cost Supplier A dearly in the initial one and half years, to such a degree that they were left with no other option but to ask for an early renegotiation. At this stage, CLIENTCO could have responded by emphasizing that Supplier A needed to honor the contract or pay a termination fee, but they were not interested in going down a track of complete relational failure and possible high media publicity, and instead decided to renegotiate the contract. This renegotiation proved beneficial for both parties, as services improved considerably and Supplier A in parallel was beginning to make a marginal return. The case emphasizes that a balance needs to be struck between service levels and costs. The goal must be win-win, where the supplier can make a return. In a one-sided venture, the supplier has to try to cover its costs in any way possible, which is likely to effect services, operations, and relations adversely. In addition, in situations of competitive bid circumstances the client generally has to ensure that the supplier is fully aware of the extent of the service requirements, and the client may have to spend more time on evaluating the bid proposals to avoid having to invest in costly renegotiations after such a short period of operation. The learning points are:

- An outsourcing contract will rarely be delivered satisfactorily where the supplier stands to make a loss, because this will tend to have detrimental effects on the service delivered and sour what could otherwise be a synergistic relationship.
- Renegotiation and restructuring may be better options than termination and high switching costs (see below).
- Conceive the bid as about a relationship over time, rather than a one-off win or loss.

Strategic lesson 3. Relational trauma in IT outsourcing can be overcome by initiating early contract renegotiations. Such a strategy will change service performance, the nature of the relationship, impact the management structure, and improve operational efficiency. Significant impacts on post-contract management and operations were identified in areas of contract achievement, management structure, relationship atmosphere, and operational efficiency.

Contract achievement. Unexpectedly for CLIENTCO, service levels plummeted significantly during the transition period. They remained below target and satisfaction levels for over a year. End-users commonly expect that the supplier comes in and services then improve dramatically, not least where there is pent-up demand from previous cost containment, as at CLIENTCO. Often these expectations are not achieved and rather take an unexpected downturn. CLIENTCO's case is no exception here. Adjusting to new processes, systems, and corporate cultures takes time. As the customer service manager from Supplier A noted:

> The specific stage when the trust went down is when we started, and it's extremely hard to provide a service, whatever the level of personnel is, when you don't understand the systems. Obviously systems are very different within different companies. Technology is the same and ideas of how systems work are the same but the actual specifics are very different. So when you come in cold and start to provide the service from nothing then the user will see a dip in their service from the previous supplier to you.

However, contract achievement was always going to be very difficult, as again Supplier A had made a number of assumptions about CLIENTCO's operations and requirements that, actually, did not apply; especially in terms of rationalization and standardization. It is plausible to assume that Supplier A was not fully aware of the systems and applications they were to take over and more importantly possibly lacked some of the competencies and resources to actually deliver CLIENTCO's service levels. The degree of miscalculation made by Supplier A seemed to corroborate this fact, as did the lengthy period for the actual consolidation and eventual transfer of the systems to Supplier A's headquarters. This emphasizes once again the importance of the customer evaluating the supplier's resources, skill-sets, and assumptions regarding their business.

Management structure. Selective outsourcing for cost containment on a relatively short term contract is not commonly associated with detailed *relationship* management considerations – due to the typically stable IT activities and contractual clarity of what is outsourced. In CLIENTCO's case, though, active relationship management became critical. The evidence suggests that due to the winner's curse scenario in the deal, the supplier was probably not willing to resource the venture with its most experienced managers – as a small niche supplier it most likely needed them as a sales team to attract new business. In turn, during the first year the existing account manager found it very difficult to pick-up from the previous supplier and turnaround the relationship. His problems in managing the relationship led, instead, to loggerheads with the client's manager. Therefore CLIENTCO requested a new manager, who would then face off against two newly appointed relationship managers. The reason being that SUPPLIER A obviously needed more active management. This was a decisive step to save and turnaround the venture.

The impact of a soured relationship, and consequently having to change the management team at such an early point, was very dramatic. In many ways it meant starting all over again in developing rapport and relations. For Supplier A though these changes meant improved cooperation and support in helping them to adjust to CLIENTCO's idiosyncrasies.

Relationship atmosphere. The case seemed to highlight a relational development from a strict contract controlled environment to a more trusting and cooperative environment. It is in the nature of the way CLIENTCO apparently operates that they generally endeavor to control operations:

> As far as we were initially concerned a supplier is a supplier, and we've gone out and asked them to provide X and if they don't provide X then we are going to hit them over the head until they do provide X. (Vendor Manager, CLIENTCO)

Their extensive experiences with procuring products and services from the market led them to adopt a power wielding approach. In retrospect, management by contract and the expectation to deliver according to contract reflected this culture. However, is this an appropriate approach in IT outsourcing? In this situation the control approach failed and led to the breakdown of relations. What Supplier A needed initially was some guidance in understanding CLIENTCO's operations. The parties needed to worked together to clarify the requirements and idiosyncrasies of CLIENTCO and this was clearly missing. The results were evident in the amount of conflict between account managers. Effects were disastrous for both parties. Service levels were low and Supplier A was losing money.

Improvements came with the introduction of the vendor managers who seemed to be interested in helping and cooperating to ensure both parties mutually benefited from the venture. In fact, CLIENTCO's managers quite deliberately focused their initial efforts on resolving Supplier A's problems with CLIENTCO, and so began to build trust. Cooperation between the parties was to become fundamental and it is plausible that only in this kind of context did Supplier A gather sufficient momentum to actually approach CLIENTCO to request an early contract renegotiation. The developments following the renegotiation were remarkable considering that the relations had broken down. Literally 18 months later, the parties had informally agreed to a partnership and managers from all levels were engaged in team building exercises. The environment fostered by cooperation and working through problem issues was one of openness and trust, yet the contract was still governed the deal.

Operational efficiency. The lack of a reciprocal profit for Supplier A contributed to the deficient services levels. Only through early renegotiation in 1996 was this alleviated, which of course introduced considerable extra costs for both parties in terms of time, resources to renegotiate, and subsequent development of a renewed rapport and relationship. This raises serious questions over whether CLIENTCO truly made a cost saving that year, and for the venture in general. We can assume that no matter how long contract renegotiations take it will be at significant costs to both parties.

Nevertheless, the renegotiation process assured that both parties eventually made a return on the venture and saved Supplier A from having to terminate the contract which undoubtedly would have been disastrous in terms of costs for both parties. As a matter of fact, the renegotiation helped improve relations to such an extent that other value added benefits have since emerged from the venture not only for CLIENTCO, but also for Supplier A, and in the long-term CLIENTCO's operational efficiency improved. The learning points would seem to be:

- The need for early end-user expectation management on the client side, especially during the transition period.
- Ensure that the contract management culture is conducive to supporting superior supplier performance.
- Review the in-house core management capability and skills needed for managing external supply. Consider building informed buying, contract monitoring, contract facilitation and supplier development roles from the beginning of the contract. Otherwise problems will arise making them necessary (see Chapter 3).
- There is a relationship dimension to every IT outsourcing deal that no contract can substitute for. Ensure it is managed to advantage.

Strategic lesson 4. A winner's curse can be avoided by a supplier through information gathering and bidding activities. The case findings identified a number of issues that a client organization can influence in order to avoid or at least minimize the impact of a winner's curse (see Figure 5.3). In line with general outsourcing practice these considerations would filter into a client organization's evaluation, selection, and negotiation strategy. The objective has to be control of the impact on post-contract management and the relationship.

In the case, it was evident that Supplier A suffered from having insufficient information to make an adequate assessment of CLIENTCO's requirements. The problem clearly was that Supplier A was under pressure

Causes	Adverse case outcomes
a) *Information gathering*	
• Insufficient information	
• Misinformation	Information impactedness
• Wrong assumptions	
b) *Bidding*	
• Misaligned bid offer	
• Bidding to win, no matter	Above baseline cost
• Under-estimate of resources and capabilities required	no possible profit margin
• Under-estimate of rigidity of contract	
c) *Operating*	
• Over-estimate of extra work and excess fees available.	Revenue enhancement Tactics curtailed
• Under-estimate of control and tightness of client contract management	Opportunistic behavior

Figure 5.3 Supplier perspective on the winner's curse

to make an offer for a set of services that for the past seven years had been delivered by Supplier B. The existing supplier knew exactly what the service provisions would entail, whereas Supplier A had to rely on information only partly made available by the client and the direct competitor. The resulting assumptions underpinning the Supplier A's bid was based on incomplete, incorrect, and outdated information. In terms of transaction cost theory, there is likely to have been an information asymmetry, resulting in specific knowledge concerning service specifications being fragmented and the free flow of information hampered leading to information impactedness.[27] Client organizations in turn have to ensure that no such information impactedness exists, at least, in terms of their detailed service requirements. The danger, as highlighted in this case, is missed service and technology operations that should have been part of the supplier's bid and for which the supplier has not calculated any resources.

A mis-aligned bid will entail either (1) termination, (2) supplier's opportunistic behavior (potentially damaging the client), (3) the supplier accepting the loss and supplying the agreed service for strategic reasons, or (4) renegotiation. In the case Supplier A could not achieve (2) at a profit, did not want (3) so offered (1) or (4). Clearly the client could have played a more active role in evaluating the bid suppliers made, especially in one-to-one competitive bidding circumstances, to prevent possible miscalculations of the baseline costs. Interestingly, the client culture of cost efficiency and tight control was perceived as a protection, but ultimately backfired to produce undesired results. Client organizations should ensure that suppliers have a reasonable profit margin in their deal, or else the focus on the supplier's operations will be solely on where it can recover its bidding costs and begin to make a margin. Otherwise, as what happened in the case, a supplier will seek to save on resources and employ inexperienced managers that diminish client user's satisfaction levels.

Although, the case did not provide direct evidence, there was an issue that Supplier A was confronted with a legacy system where it did not have the skills and resources to effectively handle the service and system requirements of CLIENTCO. A potentially dangerous situation, as the supplier may have to recruit resources and the capabilities from the market before it can provide the actual services. Again the client should take an active role in determining whether the supplier is sufficiently resourced in terms of capabilities and skills to handle the deal. The fundamental lesson would seem to be:

- Supplier information gathering activities are vital. The client should check to ensure that the bidders are undertaking detailed information gathering activities necessary to present a bid that will be effective in operational terms.

Strategic lesson 5. The winner's curse can be avoided by clients by detailed information provision, by building-in contingencies in the contract, and via a choice of the format of the bidding arrangements. The bidding phase is often a one-sided event, and may actually demand a more active participation of the client. We have made this clear already, especially in terms of assessing the supplier's overall resource potential, capabilities, skills, information access, bid offer, and cost calculations. Intervening early on may prevent the experience of a winner's curse for both parties and subsequent adverse impact on the relationship.

A second factor is the choice and specificities of the bidding arrangements. A key question for bidding arrangements is whether to use a single round or a multiple round sealed-bid format. The critical distinction between formats is that a multiple round scenario provides the bidders with information through the process of bidding. This information often turns out to be a double-edged sword.[28] It may stimulate competition by creating a reliable process of price discovery, by reducing the winner's curse, and by allowing efficient aggregations of items. Alternatively, the information may be used by bidders to establish and enforce collusive outcomes. Ex ante asymmetries and weak competition – as in the case – favor a single round, sealed bid design. In other cases, a multiple round bidding arrangement is likely to perform better in efficiency and revenue terms.

For the client organization some lessons would seem to be:

- Assist the supplier with the information pointed to in Strategic lesson 4;
- Maintain initial tight control but work flexibly where contract and service metrics are outrunning market prices;
- Check market prices regularly and build price recalculations into the contract;
- Consider carefully the bidding format. In different circumstances a single round or a multiple round sealed bid will be more appropriate.

Strategic lesson 6. For a customer to establish its preferred contract mode, we suggest identifying the relationship it implies and how these, and their staffing, support the service and value added it expects to receive from a supplier. The case evidence allows us to reconsider IT outsourcing in a more fundamental sense. Distilling findings from a number of previous studies, a strong relationship exists between the strategic intent a client organization chose to pursue, the kind of technical capability it needed to employ, and the type of relationship needed to match intent and supplier capability, and achieve expectations. A strong finding has also been that there are frequent misperceptions on the part of all parties as to the nature of the relationship, and what can be expected from each other as a result. Let us, firstly, classify the types of relationship we have observed, then illustrate, through examples, the importance of getting strategic intent, technical capability, and relationship definitions aligned.

The main types of IT outsourcing relationships are classified in Figure 5.4. Here strategic intent, in terms of expectations from outsourcing, is divided into whether the focus is on achieving business value and/or on achieving IT efficiencies. On the horizontal axis, technical capability refers to choosing to externally source to gain a distinctive technical leadership, or to gain access merely to technical resources that form a resource pool not otherwise available to you, in cost per quality terms. The matrix sets up four possible relationships. By far the most common is the "Technical Supply" relationship where the objective is to achieve IT efficiencies by hiring external resources. In such a relationship the fundamental focus is on cost minimization, and the rendering of IT as a variable cost. As at CLIENTCO, the major debates will center on the cost-service trade-off, and measurement systems will also be constructed around this.

Another possible relationship we call "Business Service." Here the objective is to use an external IT supplier who can improve service to the business by not only delivering more precisely on changing business

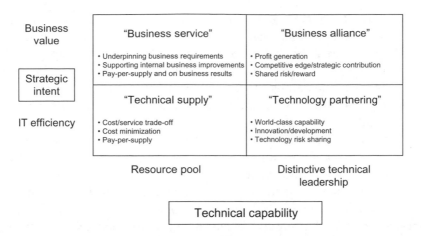

Figure 5.4 Strategic intent and capability in IT outsourcing: Identifying relationships

requirements, but also by, for example being involved in business process improvement projects. Here the contract will be about both IT efficiency for business impact, and the supplier's contribution to business improvement. Here one would expect additional processes and relationship mechanisms for involving the supplier more closely in business issues. The evaluation debate would be more on business value and suitable metrics, based on the business impact of supplier performance. In this respect it is interesting to note that on some figures business process outsourcing may grow worldwide by 10 percent a year from US$140 billion in 2005 to over US$220 billion by 2010.[29]

A third type of relationship is "Technology Partnering." BP Exploration (BPX), for example, in their 1993–98 outsourcing deals, explicitly chose three suppliers because they had best-in-class capability in particular areas. BPX expected future proofing on the technological front, with the suppliers keeping BPX abreast of leading edge technology, and also proactively innovating in technologies and their application to BPX.

Finally, too many large-scale outsourcing arrangements are presented as "Strategic Alliances." For us such an alliance assumes a working together to make offerings to the external marketplace, and sharing the risks and rewards of such endeavors. The focus here is on business expansion, the main debates will be around business goals, mutual contribution, and shared rewards. Several authors[30] found many so-called strategic alliances in IT outsourcing to be largely fee-for-service contracts; moreover the risk-reward elements were too small a part of the relationship to make a difference in terms of motivation and focus. A further example appears in the Commonwealth Bank–EDS arrangement described in Chapter 8. The bank undoubtedly secured cost savings from outsourcing its IT, but other gains were less clear. Interestingly, as a symbol for strategic alliance, the bank originally took a one-third share in EDS Australia in 1996. However this was sold back in 2005.

Clarifying these options, and when they are most suitable, is an important pre-condition for establishing the right relationship mechanisms and evaluation regimes. In practice we have seen all too many organizations contract and manage tightly for cost efficiency, but then also expect the sort of business value added that could only be got from a "Business Service" relationship, or the technical innovation and pro-activity that could only be provided through "Technology Partnering." This partly explains why BPX was disappointed with at least two of its 1993–98 suppliers. In another way, in the US$2 billion plus BAE–CSC 1993 ten-year deal, BAE managed CSC tightly though the deal ostensibly had "Business Service" and "Technology Partnering" components. It was only after several years, and after CSC had made large investments in making the IT function efficient, that BAE managers started being interested in allowing CSC to tap the other possibilities for revenue.

Cultural and financial factors often drive these misconceptions. Early on in BPX traditional cost reduction approaches prevailed in the deals though the deals had been paraded as more about technology partnering. At the same time, for example, a supplier, as at CLIENTCO, will find it difficult to sustain a "Business Service" or "Technology Partnering" orientation if the money is not going to be there. Sometimes it is lack of the right kind of partnering capability, in either or both client and supplier, as at CLIENTCO. More frequently there is a lack of clarity at the scoping and evaluation phases of IT outsourcing, to identify precisely which components require what metrics and what relationship arrangements.

Given these considerations we offer the framework in Figure 5.4 as a way for a client to think through exactly what he/she is trying to achieve with different parts of its IT outsourcing, and what the implications of this analysis might be for relationship arrangements and assessment regimes. On this, the learning points from CLIENTCO would seem to be that

- Even a "Technology Supply" outsourcing arrangement needs to be staffed and managed for its relationship dimension, not least to build in the necessary flexibility where the contract is designed poorly to deliver on stakeholder intents.

- A "Technology Supply" arrangement will inhibit severely the probability of the value added inherent in the other three forms of contracts and relationships.
- However, as in CLIENTCO, if the right core IT capabilities are in place, the relationships developed in a "Technology Supply" arrangement can lead to further opportunities for enhanced benefits in any of the other three outsourcing regimes.

Conclusions

This chapter made four distinct contributions to our understanding of IT outsourcing practice. First, we identified the phenomena of a winner's curse in the context of IT outsourcing. Second, we showed from a re-analysis of 85 IT outsourcing cases how common and problematic a winner's curse has been in IT outsourcing. Third, the detailed case history of CLIENTCO allowed for clear development of six strategic lessons. These lessons address the impacts of a winner's curse for clients and suppliers and the strategies to overcome and more importantly prevent relational trauma in an outsourcing deal. Fourth, we propose a more complex and subtle view of IT outsourcing relationships than typically analyzed in the management literature.

Concerning this last contribution, the study provides new scenarios in IT outsourcing and new directions for inquiry for managers and researcher of IT outsourcing. Thus we have described different IT outsourcing scenarios and identified different strategies for clients and suppliers to cope with the winner's curse and avoid relational trauma. We also highlight new questions for research. As one example, can we create specific tendering designs that are likely to be successful for IT outsourcing bids? We also provide a typology of types of relationship as a diagnostic tool for further research, and to help practitioners analyze their own deals and perceptions.

The experience of a winner's curse was shown to pose considerable pressures for an outsourcing venture and the relationship, to the extent that re-negotiations, or even early termination, become the only and best option. Active relationship management by competent relationship managers who can facilitate a successful and mutual turnaround of such a venture in these contexts takes on a new meaning. Regardless, though, of whether the venture and relationship is saved, significant costs will arise for both parties, raising general doubts over the financial viability of such deals in general. However awareness and understanding of how such scenarios can evolve is the starting point for avoiding a winner's curse experience.

One of our concerns is that winner's curse type deals may actually have increased, rather than diminished in the last few years, given the distinctive characteristics of the market and business pressures in the 2001–05 period in the developed economies. If this is the case, then our analysis and prescriptions have important implications for managing this legacy problem in deals going forward.

Finally, as the Internet evolves into a powerful and reliable infrastructure for electronic commerce and electronic business, new configurations are possible and feasible. E-sourcing and Application Service Provision (ASP), for example (see Chapter 10), supported by advances in technology and better crafted business models than in the e-commerce bubble era, may well see important new developments (see also Chapter 11). In such new configurations relational trauma might occur, and this chapter identifies some major lessons that client and supplier companies should consider before signing netsourcing contracts.

Notes

1. The most detailed review of theoretical perspectives used in IT outsourcing studies appears in Dibbern, J., Goles, T., Hirschheim, R., and Jayatilaka, B. (2004), "Information Systems Outsourcing: A Survey and Analysis of The Literature," *Database For Advances in Information Systems*, Vol. 35, 4, pp. 6–103.
2. DiRomualdo, A. and V. Gurbaxani (1998), "Strategic Intent for IT Outsourcing," *Sloan Management Review*, Vol. 39, 4, pp. 67–80; Lacity, M. and Willcocks, L. (1998), "An Empirical Investigation of Information Technology Sourcing Practices: Lessons from Experience," *MIS Quarterly* Vol. 22, 3, pp. 363–408. In these papers the researchers present what best practice has shown to define an IT outsourcing strategy.
3. McLellan, K., Marcolin, B., and Beamish, P. (1998), "Financial and Strategic Motivations Behind IS Outsourcing," and Sobol, M. and Apte, U. (1998), "Outsourcing Practices and Views of America's Most Effective IS Users," both in L. Willcocks and M. Lacity (eds), (1998) *Strategic Sourcing of Information Systems*, Wiley, Chichester. These two papers provide an insight into global drivers and motivators behind IT outsourcing. See also Cullen, S., Seddon, P., and Willcocks, L. (2001), *IT Outsourcing Practices in Australia*, Deloitte-Touche,

Melbourne, Joint Deloitte-Touche Tohmatsu/University of Melbourne study of over 280 plus organizations.

4. Lacity, M., Willcocks, L., and Cullen, S. (2007), *Global Information Technology Outsourcing: 21st Century Search for Business Advantage*, Wiley, Chichester, provides the most in-depth analysis of the IT outsourcing phenomenon.

5. The case is described in detail from 1993 to 2005 in Lacity, Willcocks, and Cullen (2007), op. cit.

6. Kern, T. and Willcocks, L. (2001), *The Relationship Advantage: Information Technologies, Sourcing and Management*, Oxford University Press, Oxford.

7. Lacity, M. and Willcocks, L. (2001), *Global Information Technology Outsourcing: Search for Business Advantage*, Wiley, Chichester.

8. Williamson noted that social actors will behave opportunistically if it is advantageous for them to do so. This opportunism denotes the capability and willingness of organizations to pursue their own interests at the expense of partners by withholding, for example, information. See Williamson, O. E. (1975), *Markets and Hierarchies: Analysis and Antitrust Implications, A Study in the Economics of Internal Organization*, The Free Press, New York.

9. Klemperer, P. (1999), "Auction Theory: A Guide to the Literature," *Journal of Economic Surveys*, Vol. 13, 3, pp. 227–286.

10. Klemperer, P. (1999), op. cit.

11. Kagel, J. H. and Levin, D. (1986), "The Winner's Curse and Public Information in Common Value Auctions," *American Economic Review*, Vol. 76, 5, pp. 894–920.

12. Lind, B. and Plott, C. R. (1991), "The Winner's Curse: Experiments with Buyers and Sellers," *American Economic Review*, Vol. 81, 1, pp. 335–346.

13. Capen, E.C., Clapp, R. V., Campbell, W. M. (1971), "Competitive Bidding in High-Risk Situations," *Journal of Petroleum Technology*, June , pp. 641–653.

14. Quoted in Willcocks, L. and Kern, T. (1998), "IT Outsourcing as Strategic Partnering: The Case of the UK Inland Revenue," *European Journal of Information Systems*, Vol. 7, pp. 29–45.

15. Klepper, R. and Jones, W. (1998), *Outsourcing Information Technology, Systems and Services*. Prentice Hall, New Jersey. The DuPont case appears in Lacity, Willcocks, and Cullen, (2007), op. cit.

16. A detailed summary appears in Cullen, S. and Willcocks, L. (2003), *Intelligent IT Outsourcing: Eight Building Blocks To Success*, Butterworth, Oxford.

17. Michell, V. and Fitzgerald, G. (1997), "The IT Outsourcing Market-Place: Vendors and their Selection," *Journal of Information Technology*, Vol. 12, 3, pp. 223–237. See also Cullen, S., Seddon, P., and Willcocks, L. (2006), "ITO Configuration: Research into Understanding and Defining Outsourcing Arrangements," *Journal of Strategic Information Systems* (March).

18. Cross, J. (1995), "IT Outsourcing: British Petroleum's Competitive Approach," *Harvard Business Review*, (May–June), pp. 94–102 and Huber, R. L. (1993), "How Continental Bank Outsourced its 'Crown Jewels,' " *Harvard Business Review* (January–February), pp. 121–129.

19. Cullen *et al.* (2006), op. cit.

20. Cullen and Willcocks (2003), op. cit.

21. Lacity and Willcocks (1998), op. cit.

22. To guarantee the company's and participants request for anonymity all names had to be changed.

23. See Lacity and Willcocks (2001), op. cit. The authors also make available further case study data on an open website. It is this database, updated to 2004, that we draw upon here, together with details of the cases from the written published sources. The latter are rich enough to permit an analysis of the initial deals, and of subsequent outcomes.

24. Willcocks and Kern (1998), op. cit.

25. Kern and Willcocks (2001), op. cit.

26. See for example Klepper, R. and Jones, W. (1998), *Outsourcing Information Technology, Systems and Service*, Prentice Hall, New Jersey; Strassmann, P. (1997), *The Squandered Computer*, Information Economics Press, New Canaan. In the more general theory of the firm literature see Milgrom, P. and Roberts, J. (1992), *Economics, Organization and Management*, Prentice Hall, New Jersey.

27. Williamson (1975), op. cit.

28. This is similar to the discussion in sales auctions on the difference between a multiple round, ascending auction, and sealed-bid auction; see Peter Cramton (1998), "Ascending Auctions," *European Economic Review*, Vol. 42, pp. 745–756.

29. See Willcocks and Cullen (2005), op. cit; also Chapters 1 and 11 of the present volume.

30. Lacity, M. and Hirschheim, R. (1993), *Information Systems Outsourcing: Myths, Metaphors and Realities*, Wiley, Chichester, and Ang, S. and Straub, D. (1998), "Production and Transaction Economies and Information Systems Outsourcing – A Study of The US Banking Industry," *MIS Quarterly*, Vol. 22, 4, pp. 535–552.

CHAPTER 6

Outsourcing human resources: The case of BAE systems

Mary Lacity, David Feeny, and Leslie Willcocks

Introduction: Transformational HR outsourcing

This is the first chapter where we explore deeply the outsourcing of one particular back office function, namely, human resources. For the first fifty years, HR outsourcing was limited to targeted HR activities such as payroll administration. The market for large-scale, transformational human resource outsourcing (HRO) accelerated in 1999 with the creation of two pioneering firms, Xchanging and Exult (now Hewitt). These HRO suppliers had the idea that the bulk of a large client's decentralized HR transactional services could be outsourced in order to radically reduce costs and improve services. The client's HR is transformed through the supplier's transformation levers: creation of shared services from clients' disparate HR departments, headcount reduction for redundant and low performing employees, retraining and empowerment for retained employees, process redesign and standardization, and significant technology enablement. These suppliers took over a myriad of their client's HR activities, including HR information systems, benefits administration, compensation (salary administration and job descriptions), recruitment, training, career development, and regulatory compliance. Clients kept HR strategy (budgets, policies, workforce planning, organizational design), employee performance (assessment, counseling, career paths), and liaison roles in-house. This type of transformational HRO injected the HRO market with new vitality.

Size of HRO market

The exact size of the HRO market is unknown, but there are various estimates by commercial research firms. In 2000, Gartner estimated that the HRO market was US$33.4 billion (primarily North America and Europe),[1] but that it grew to US$51 billion worldwide in 2005.[2] IDC had more modest estimates, sizing the HRO market at US$34 billion in 2005. Everest estimated a US$3.5 billion market in 2000 and a US$14.3 billion market in 2005. McKinsey had the smallest size estimates, but it primarily focused on HR IT Services – a market they estimate will be US$5 billion by 2008. Technology Partners International (TPI) and Yankee predict continued growth rates. TPI, for example found that HRO is the fastest growing and largest segment of the BPO market. Total contract value more than doubled from US$545 million in the first quarter of 2004 to US$1.7 billion in the first quarter of 2005.[3] Yankee believes the growth rate will be 10 percent annually over the next four years, reaching US$74 billion by 2009.[4] The variance in estimates is attributed to sampling differences (Everest sampled 98 transactions, Gartner sampled 120, and TPI sampled 360 BPO deals).

HRO suppliers and their customers

Coverage of the major HRO suppliers must begin with the two pioneering HRO firms, UK-based **Xchanging** and US-based **Exult** (acquired by Hewitt in 2003), both funded in 1999 by General Atlantic Partners, a US-based venture capital firm. These small, hungry suppliers were established by seasoned outsourcing gurus. David Andrews, who created Andersen Consulting's (now Accenture) successful outsourcing business in Europe, is founder and CEO of Xchanging. James Madden was recruited by General Atlantic partners to lead Exult because of his years of outsourcing leadership at Systemhouse, Booz-Allen, and Andersen Consulting in North America. Both Andrews and Madden saw the possibility of using outsourcing to radically transform large organizations plagued with duplicate, antiquated, and non-integrated HR functions into streamlined shared services organizations. Their vision, combined with seasoned experience, venture capital, and the ability to recruit top talent, attracted large contracts from large customers. Xchanging's client list includes BAE Systems, Lloyd's of London, and Deutsche Bank. Exult's client list by 2003 included Bank of America (see Chapter 8), British Petroleum (see Chapter 3),

International Paper, Circuit City, and Prudential Financial. Xchanging and Exult set a high standard for HRO by reducing client costs, increasing clients' HR services, *and* earning a profit for investors within a few years of start-up.

Given Exult's success and rapid growth rate (five-year growth of 11,929%), **Hewitt** bought them in 2003. Since buying Exult for US$690 million in stock in October of that year, Hewitt became the number one HRO supplier, closing almost US$1 billion in deals with ten companies including Marriott, Pepsico, and Sun Microsystems during the first seven months of fiscal 2005. Hewitt now holds 21 percent of all HRO deals worldwide, with competitors **Accenture** and **Fidelity** running second and third, respectively, according to an April 2005 report by Everest Research Institute.[5] Other top HRO suppliers include **ACS, AON, Cap Gemini, Convergys, EDS**, and **IBM**. What is particularly noteworthy is the move from the IT outsourcing market to BPO by both EDS and IBM (see Table 6.1).

Table 6.1 Sample of HRO suppliers and HRO customers

HRO supplier	Major customers	Number of client employees supported
Xchanging	BAE Systems, Spirit Group	Supports ~ 80,000 employees
IBM	Procter & Gamble, Dana Corporation, Oracle, Synergy	Supports ~ 300,000 employees
Fidelity	BASF, ABB, Hughes Electronics	Supports ~ 400,000 employees
Exult (now Hewitt)	PepsiCo, Bank of America, British Petroleum, Johnson & Johnson, Unisys	Supports ~ 700,000 employees
EDS	Towers Perrin	Supports ~400,000 employees
CPS Human Resource Services	Transportation & Security Administration	Supports ~40,000 employees
Convergys	Texas Health & Human Services; Home Depot	Supports ~ 400,000 employees
ACS	Delta Airlines	Supports ~ 500,000 employees
Accenture	British Telecom; British Petroleum, Citrix,	Supports ~ 500,000 employees

Sources: Table comprised from various sources, including supplier websites, Kessner (2005), Everest Research.

Promised savings from transformational HRO

Large companies have a lot of fat in their back offices, particularly since most have grown through mergers and acquisitions. After M&A (mergers and acquisitions), front offices are often integrated and streamlined, but back offices like HR are often neglected. This neglect results in over-staffed, idiosyncratic, duplicate, and incompatible back offices across business units. David Andrews estimates that the fat in back offices in the top 500 companies in the world is in the trillions.[6]

Rather than invest the necessary resources to create shared services and reduce duplication, large companies may engage BPO suppliers to eliminate the fat. According to a recent study by the Yankee Group, the average running cost for HRO providers is between US$1500 and $2000 per employee per year, saving customers up to 21 percent (see Figure 6.1 below).

But against these promised savings, it should be noted that HRO success is not guaranteed. A number of customers have prematurely terminated their HRO deals, including the 2000 British Telecom/Accenture deal, called e-peopleserve. Part of the problem was that while

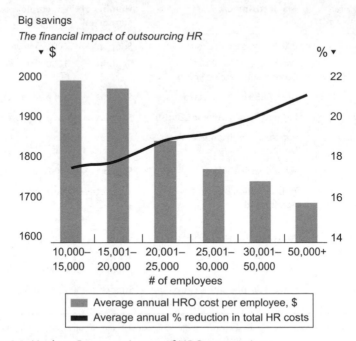

Figure 6.1 Yankee Group estimate of HRO cost savings

Source: Kersner, J. (2005), "People movers," *CFO Magazine*, June.

Accenture was focused on growing the business, BT was focused on HR cost reductions. It proved difficult to maintain a focus on service delivery to one partner at the same time as the venture was seeking to develop new business. Accenture took over the venture and transformed it into Accenture HR Services. BT remained involved in business development and has incentives to encourage this. The change in e-peopleserve's ownership also had to do with BT's desire to de-leverage its balance sheet in the wake of the telecom crash. We will see in the forthcoming case how BAE Systems and Xchanging primarily focused on BAE's HR transformation first, then sought external customers. It should be noted, however, that Xchanging had, into 2005, continued to experience difficulties in growing its HR BPO (as opposed to its HR procurement) business beyond its first client.

BAE Systems/Xchanging: A case study of transformational HRO

In this chapter, we selected an in-depth case study at BAE Systems (previously British Aerospace) as a powerful vehicle for disseminating lessons about successful back office transformation. We have been studying British Aerospace for ten years and have fully explored their ten-year, £900 million IT outsourcing relationship with Computer Sciences Corporation. (see Lacity and Willcocks 2001,[7] for the case study focusing on IT outsourcing.) In this chapter, we explore how BAE Systems incorporated lessons learned from their use of other transformation models (see Chapter 1 for discussion of back office transformation models), such as management consultants and fee-for-service relationships, when transforming their human resource function. Specifically, they sought to replicate the good aspects of management consultants (infusion of skills and expertise, ability to bypass internal resistance) while avoiding the pitfalls (lack of knowledge transfer, consultants have little accountability or ownership of results). BAE Systems sought to replicate the good aspects of fee-for-service outsourcing (variable budgeting, reduced headcount, access to global expertise) while avoiding the pitfalls (cost creep, poor alignment of customer and supplier incentives, and lack of sustainability). When outsourcing human resource management in 2001, BAE Systems and their supplier, Xchanging, employed a distinctive enterprise partnership model in which the parties created a new business, called Xchanging HR Services (XHRS). BAE Systems is both a customer and an investor to this new enterprise. By 2005, BAE Systems had already received the following benefits:

- Cost savings on baseline services
- Service improvement in many service areas
- New web-based technology capabilities rolled out to over 40,000 users in BAE Systems
- A new state-of-the art shared service center was built and occupied
- Retained BAE Systems managers now focus on more strategic activities
- Transferred BAE Systems staff have been retrained to make them more service focused
- Obtained new business, including a £500,000 deal with Spirit Group for HR services in 2005
- Partnership has earned numerous nominations and awards including UK's National Outsourcing Association (2004) and BAE's HR Excellence Award (2005).

Of course, such transformation is never painless, and BAE Systems learned many valuable lessons along the way. By sharing their experiences, we aim to help other senior executives and back office service directors successfully seek ways to cut back office costs while improving service.

BAE Systems: The customer context

British Aerospace was formed as a Government owned enterprise in 1978 from a series of independent companies in the United Kingdom (UK) aerospace industry. It brought together businesses that included military aircraft, commercial aircraft (through its share holding in Airbus), Jetstream (commuter aircraft), Dynamics (missiles), and Royal Ordinance (weapons). *Since its inception, British Aerospace fostered the independence of its operating divisions by allowing business units to be in charge of their own profitability and support services, including IT and human resources (HR).* The decentralized culture is required because each strategic business unit (SBU) operates under drastically different production, marketing, and legal environments. But the consequence is idiosyncratic, duplicate, and incompatible back offices.

In the early 1990s, British Aerospace was confronted with loss of sales due to the end of the cold war and economic recession. In 1992, it reported losses of £66 million on sales of £10 billion, and its stock prices plummeted from £7 per share to £1 per share. British Aerospace senior management sought to improve profitability by focusing on core competencies in aircraft, divesting non-core divisions, and refinancing the company. British Aerospace subsequently sold Rover, Corporate Jets, and Ballast Nedam. They outsourced some back office functions such as information technology. British Aerospace reduced headcount by 21,000 employees. As a result, profitability increased to £230 million on £11 billion in sales in 1994. But from 1997 through to 1999, British Aerospace's sales growth stagnated. Clearly, British Aerospace needed to expand their global markets.

In January of 1999, British Aerospace and GEC proposed a merger between British Aerospace and GEC's Marconi Electronic Systems to create a global aerospace and defense company called BAE Systems:

> The proposed merger with Marconi Electronic Systems is an important step in the consolidation of the industry in Europe and creates a strong and highly capable business with significant cost benefits. (Sir Richard Evans, Chairman of the Board, BAE Systems[8])

Investors were promised that the synergies from the merger would result in annual cost savings in excess of £275 million within three years of completion of the transaction. While BAE Systems would continue to invest in their core capabilities in military aircraft, weapon systems, nuclear submarines, and large commercial aircraft all support functions were mandated to deliver significant cost savings.

In the area of human resource management, BAE's Group HR Director, was charged with delivering a minimum of 15 percent cost savings with a stretch target of 40 percent on an estimated annual HR internal spend of £25 million while maintaining the same level of service. At that time in 1999, Group HR was actually a small department, focusing on senior pay and benefits, senior level development, and organizational design. Nearly all of the HR headcount, some estimated 700 people, were decentralized within the SBUs. Within the SBUs, the decentralized HR people delivered transactional activities, such as payroll, benefits administration, recruiting, and training as well as professional services such as training design, industrial relations, and HR procurement (see Figure 6.2). *According to benchmarking standards, BAE's HR function was at least 40 percent inefficient, with one HR person for every 70 employees, compared to a 1 to 200 ratio for best in class firms.[9] BAE's Group HR Director believed the only way he could deliver the mandated cost savings was to centralize much of HR into shared services.*

He assembled a team to investigate the shared services concept. The team had in mind that 80 percent of HR was probably transactional

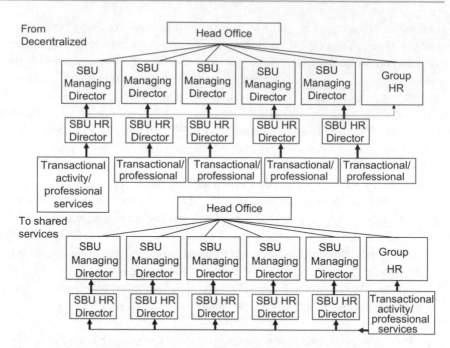

Figure 6.2 BAE Systems vision for transforming human resources

activity and only 20 percent of HR was strategic or core. Thus the team proposed a design of HR shared services that entailed a significant centralization of HR headcount and resources, leaving only HR directors and small HR teams in the SBUs.

Rejecting traditional transformation choices

Initially, the HR team considered three possibilities for implementation of shared services: do it themselves, hire a management consultancy to help with the transition, or outsource HR entirely. The pros and cons of these options were seriously debated (see Table 6.2).

Rejection of "do-it-ourselves"

The major benefit of doing it themselves was obviously that BAE Systems would directly benefit from the savings without sharing them with a third party. For this reason, many business unit managers preferred this option to

Table 6.2 BAE Systems' assessment of transformation options

Implementation option	Pros	Risks
Do-it-yourself	• Realize all the cost benefits internally • Most politically acceptable	• Senior management will not make technology investment required to implement shared service • Internal resistance from business units to centralize services • Lack of empowerment and skills of internal HR to make the quantum changes required
Management consultancy	• Infusion of external energy and skills • Ability of outsiders to bypass internal political resistance • Clear mandate from senior management that project will be done	• Large, expensive project which will likely cost escalate once consultancy is on site • Consultancy has no ultimate accountability or ownership of outcome • Lack of skills and knowledge transfer • Lack of sustainability
Fee-for-service outsourcing	• Infusion of external energy and Skills • Ability of outsiders to bypass internal political resistance • Clear mandate from senior management that project will be done • One-time savings achieved upfront • Supplier accountability for results	• Escalating costs • Lack of sustainability • Customer and supplier incentives are Misaligned • Power asymmetries develop in favor of Supplier
Enterprise partnership	• Infusion of external energy and Skills • Ability of outsiders to bypass internal political resistance • Clear mandate from senior management that project will be done • One-time savings achieved upfront and continued cost savings guaranteed for five years • Supplier accountability for results • Upfront technology investment made by supplier • Customer and supplier incentives aligned • Joint Board of Directors insures customer participation and oversight	• Start-up company, may subsequently go out of business • Business model may be overly dependent on revenues from external customers which do not materialize

hiring outsiders: "My initial feeling was, why the hell can't we do this ourselves? If we can do it ourselves, it might be a better proposition because we are not giving half of the savings away" (previously BAE Finance Director, then CFO of XHRS).

However, there were three major impediments to doing it themselves. First, the creation of shared services would require a significant investment in facilities and web-based technology, known as eHR. Given senior management's penchant for cost cuts, as well as their preference for investing only in core businesses, the HR team knew a request for HR capital funding would probably be rejected. Second, the business unit managers would resist giving up resource control: "The barons have been used to having the resource under their control" (Customer Enterprise Relationship Director, BAE Systems).

Third, senior management perceived that the internal HR staff lacked the power, enthusiasm, skills, and mentality to drive forth such a drastic change. This was not a reflection on the HR individuals themselves, just a recognition that most HR personnel historically were treated, and thus subsequently behaved, as "9:00 to 5:00" back office staff: "I was pretty clear that the organization would never make the degree of change that was necessary to get to a slick shared services organization. So long as it was part of BAE Systems, it would never have been a high priority" (Previous HR Director, then Head of Resources for XHRS).

Clearly an infusion of external energy, experience, and skills was needed.

Rejection of management consultants

The HR team considered whether to hire an outside management consultancy to manage a one-time, big-bang implementation project. The benefits of this option were the necessary infusion of energy and skills and the ability of external managers to bypass internal politics by having a direct conduit to senior BAE Systems management. Furthermore, by bringing in prestigious consultants, senior management would signal to the organization that they had committed to the project. But the HR team identified these major risks that they previously experienced with consultants: high costs, lack of accountability for and sustainability of results, and lack of skills transfer: "I don't think you can bring in consultants and expect them to do the same job because they won't" (previously BAE Finance Director, then CFO of XHRS).

Rejection of traditional outsourcing

The HR team seriously considered a traditional, fee-for-service outsourcing option, the model they had previously used with IT outsourcing. With fee-for-service outsourcing, a supplier would take over their HR assets and people and deliver services back to BAE Systems through a long-term contract. The benefits of this option included the same as the management consultancy: an external infusion of energy and skills, the ability to bypass internal politics, and the clear message that services would be centralized. Furthermore, the outsourcing supplier would be accountable for results because they would both implement and operate the shared services.

But BAE Systems was aware of three major negative consequences with fee-for-service outsourcing: escalating costs due to unbridled demand, lack of sustainability of cost savings and service levels, and power asymmetries developing in favor of the supplier. With some prior outsourcing deals, BAE Systems found that once central control of the budget is gone, demand for services – and thus costs – ran amuck. For example, BAE Systems used to provide chauffeur services in-house with a fleet of four cars. Now that chauffeurs are outsourced, there is no constraint on demand, such as "you can't have a car because they are all booked." The supplier has recently increased the fleet to 24 new Omegas to meet the unwatched demand.

BAE Systems management also feared the possible lack of sustainability with fee-for-service outsourcing. While BAE Systems enjoyed an initial one-time, upfront savings with many of their outsourcing deals, over time, it found that some suppliers lacked incentives to sustain innovation, to improve service, or to share additional cost savings with BAE Systems. Although lengthy contract negotiations upfront were designed to prevent such deterioration, the fact remained that customer and supplier incentives were never adequately aligned with fee-for-service outsourcing. Supplier margins were based on squeezing as much profit as they could from baseline service definitions while encouraging significant contract additions from decentralized users.

The final negative consequence BAE Systems experienced with fee-for-service outsourcing was power asymmetries developing in favor of the supplier. It is very difficult to award additions to a contract to an alternative supplier.

These three negative consequences of fee-for-service outsourcing all stem from the poor governance structure. With a fee-for-service outsourcing deal, every dollar from the customer's pocket is a dollar in the supplier's pocket. Because incentives are not aligned, the parties must take extreme efforts to protect their interests during lengthy contract negotiations. Global outsourcing contracts can literally occupy 10 legal boxes. Such contracts are extremely difficult to understand, monitor, and enforce.

In the midst of debating these three options in early 2000, a serendipitous fourth option emerged: "I came across this proposition which David Andrews (Founder and CEO of Xchanging) happened to land on my desk at exactly the right time. It was a different model, a partnership model" (Customer Enterprise Relationship Director, BAE Systems).

Choosing the enterprise partnership

David Andrews proposed that BAE Systems and Xchanging should form a 50/50 jointly owned enterprise. The enterprise would be operated as a strategic business unit within Xchanging, giving Xchanging the responsibility and accountability for implementation and subsequent operations. But both BAE Systems and Xchanging would sit on the Board of Directors to ensure continued customer involvement and oversight. The enterprise would initially behave as a traditional outsourcer by transferring BAE Systems HR assets and personnel to the enterprise governed by a ten-year contract. The enterprise, in turn, would implement the shared services concept and deliver HR services back to BAE Systems. But in the long run, the enterprise would further leverage the HR assets and personnel to attract external HR customers, of which profits would be shared 50/50 with BAE Systems. In addition:

- Xchanging would transfer top talent to the enterprise to ensure the necessary infusion of experience, energy, and competency.
- Xchanging would deliver guaranteed minimum cost savings for five years to BAE Systems in the form of a rebate.
- Xchanging would make an upfront invest of technology worth US$25 million, primarily to implement eHR.
- Xchanging would grant warrants in Xchanging, which could be very valuable if and when Xchanging went public.

In concept, this option offered significantly more benefits over the previous three options, while mitigating their negative consequences (see Table 6.2). But there was an obvious risk: as a start-up company, with no existing revenue stream, the potential of Xchanging experiencing financial difficulties in its first few years seemed very high. However, the HR team was impressed by Xchanging's executives and finances. Concerning executives, they concluded Xchanging's talent was world class:

> The main reason was probably to do with the individuals, what seemed to be a very high caliber of people from Xchanging. (Previous HR Director, then Head of Resources for XHRS)

> Are these people winners or losers? You just couldn't form any view other than these people are going to be winners. (Previously BAE Finance Director, then CFO of XHRS)

Concerning finances, they knew that General Atlantic Partners had provided £60 million in venture capital to Xchanging. Clearly Xchanging had cash to develop their business. The enterprise partnership was deemed the best model.

In June of 2002, a Letter of Intent was signed. Negotiations proved long and difficult because divisional managers within BAE Systems argued to de-scope the deal by retaining more than the targeted 20 percent of HR staff. A final agreement was signed on February 22, 2001, to be effective May 1, 2001.

Contract overview

The BAE Systems–Xchanging HR contract is worth at least £250 million and endures for ten years. From a BAE Systems perspective, all cost savings would be shared 50/50 in line with the ownership structure. However a proportion of these savings would be guaranteed with only Xchanging at risk. The cost savings would be delivered through a rebate mechanism. Thus, if BAE System's transferred costs were £25 million in a year, Xchanging would rebate BAE the agreed upon percentage of savings at year-end. After five years, BAE Systems and Xchanging will re-base the price using a cost-plus model for the remainder of the ten-year contract.

Much of the contract specifies how the parties will govern the enterprise, including the identification of three boards: the Board of Directors, the Service Review Board, and the Technology Review Board. The **Board of Directors** comprises Xchanging executives as well as BAE Systems HR Executives and non-HR Managing Directors. BAE Systems insisted on the latter as Board members to ensure that the enterprise is run as a business, not just an HR function. Xchanging has a majority of the Board to ensure operational control. The Board of Directors meets quarterly to do an overall business review. The **Service Review Board** is a committee, with equal BAE and Xchanging membership, charged with ensuring excellent HR service by monitoring service delivery and quickly remedying service problems. A service problem escalated to the Service Review Board requires an action plan to remedy the situation within a maximum three-month period. The Service Review Board is given teeth through provision for price reductions for inferior service or no charges for extremely poor service, but both parties would consider it a failure if these options were ever exercised. The ultimate sanction is the Board's ability to oust the Enterprise Partnership CEO for continuing poor performance. The **Technology Review Board**, also jointly populated by Xchanging and BAE Systems, was created to ensure that Xchanging's makes the promised US$25 million investment.

Implementing the enterprise partnership: May 2001–December 2002

In this time period, Xchanging successfully transferred and reoriented BAE Systems employees, defined and gained approval of 400 service levels, delivered web-based eHR, reorganized the HR function to realize the shared services vision, built and occupied a new XHRS facility, and began redesigning service processes. Each of these activities is explained in more detail.

Employee reorientation

In May 2001, 462 BAE Systems employees formally transferred into the Enterprise Partnership. The supplier celebrated their arrival with a major launch event, which included a video by the CEO of XHRS. In the video, he talks about the exciting things that the transferees will experience, how they will be more involved in the business, and how they are no longer a cost center but a profit center. The CEO also told them that all this would happen gradually over six months, but in the meantime, transferees should just conduct business as usual:

> The CEO was saying, it's business as usual today guys because we don't want to upset the service. We are not going to go around now to BAE and say, "I'm not doing that for you any more Mr. Customer because it's not in the service definition yet." We have a philosophy that says if he wants you to do something, you just do it. If there is a commercial consequence of that we will worry about it later and talk to your Line Manager but it is a yes to the customer, not a no. (Previously with BAE Systems, then Head of New Business Development for XHRS)

The transferred employees all attended a three-day induction session, where the supplier's management team addressed the staff. But the induction sessions were not only about creating a welcoming environment, but also about explaining the realities of a commercial enterprise:

> We started up by saying "these are the cost reduction commitments," I said "we'd have to double productivity in five years," I said "in so far as we can off-set that through third party revenues by effectively using spare capacity to deliver services to third parties we will, but that's what we are going to do." (CEO of XHRS)

In addition to induction training, targeted employees were intensely retrained for their new roles in process redesign, the Service 1st method, and leadership.

Defining over 400 service levels

In parallel with the employee reorientation, Xchanging implemented its service delivery plan, facilitated by a program called Service1st. Service1st is a web-enabled approach to define Xchanging's mission for BAE Systems, to identify baseline services, to identify the recipients of services, and to agree to the services in terms of standards, volume, and price. Within six months, Xchanging created 400 service levels for eight service classes:

1. Reward and recognition
2. Learning and development
3. Resource management
4. Employee documentation
5. HR information services
6. International resources
7. Pension management
8. Advisory and support service

The completed Service Definition was ratified by the Service Review Board in October 2001. The Service Review Board also ratified a procedure for changing service definitions caused by large changes in volume or changing business requirements without having to renegotiate the contract. From that point on, the Service Definition has been available live on the Internet-based version of Service1st.

Having established a trusted baseline of service definition, it serves going forward as the basis for both customers and providers to measure performance, and as the start point for any discussion of changes to requirements in the service itself or the process by which it is delivered. It was critical to Xchanging's ability to re-organize the partnership around Service Lines. And it is then the start point to help move transferees from a "back office" to a "front office" mindset:

> It is very much a relational role. Service has to make sure that we are constantly meeting our customers' expectations. And when I talk service I mean everything – it is how we are viewed, what impression we give, how the phone is answered, what does the office look like when people come into it. (Head of Service, Xchanging)

From the BAE Systems Perspective, the HR service dramatically improved:

> I do think that the service from a process, control point of view has improved extraordinarily. I think Xchanging really does have the right processes in place, they really know what they are doing on that. Some of the transformation that I have seen in some of the people that are in XHRS, especially the customer relationship managers, one or two of them, they never would have interacted with the business in the way that are doing now, they have become a lot more professional. They are a lot more understanding of what drives a business, understanding of cost base and how you actually get value out of a business, so that's been quite a nice surprise to see that happen and to see that happen so quickly. (HR Director, BAE Systems)

Managing £80 million in indirect HR spending

During the measurement exercise, BAE Systems and Xchanging recognized that HR spent much more than the direct cost to BAE Systems of £25 millions/annum; HR was also the agent for no less than £80 millions/annum of indirect procurement. This was a highly decentralized and fragmented spend for items such as cars, health care, and non-technical contract labor such as clerical staff and cleaners from an estimated 200 suppliers. BAE Systems had begun to more closely manage this spend themselves, but both parties saw huge opportunities for improvement by consolidating the buying power across BAE Systems' SBUs and across Xchanging's other customers (which now included large clients like Lloyd's of London for Policy Administration). Given the scale and scope of this HR procurement, BAE Systems and Xchanging felt it needed the attention of a separate enterprise partnership. This led to the establishment in November 2001 of Xchanging Procurement Services, a partnership deal worth £800 millions over ten years. This deal became a major story in its own right and is the subject of the next chapter.

Delivering eHR

Xchanging had committed to launch the first version of eHR, called peopleportal, within six months of signing the contract. Xchanging's CEO believed this date was realistic because Xchanging Practice Director for Technology already had a detailed technology blueprint based on reusable components. He had adopted the learning his CEO had absorbed from a previous assignment:

> I think we took it to a new level with the distinctiveness of the component-based architecture. Because typically people say you need to define functionality first, you can't build a system until you define functionality. I say you often don't define functionality for two years. We can't wait for two years, so we built a structure with components within six months, while you are deciding the functionality, we can have it up and running. And what we did was turn the model upside down. Whereas in most systems 80% of the code is functionality and 20% is the technical architecture, if you adopt a component driven approach, you can put it to 80% components and 20% functionality. Rather like cars today. They all look different but they are all the same underneath. So we did that and that enabled them to very quickly turn on functionality when they sorted out their arguments. (David Andrews, CEO of Xchanging)

At first, the Practice Director for Technology thought he could hire suppliers to actually build his design, but that quickly proved too expensive and too risky because the suppliers would retain all the knowledge of the source code. Clearly, Xchanging had to rapidly build in-house technology capability and went on a recruiting rampage. His team grew to 19 full-time technology managers, architects, and specialists supplemented by six contractor workers hired through mid-2002. The impact was profound in BAE Systems when Xchanging successfully launched the first version of peopleportal on October 4, 2001:

> I think they were absolutely astonished that we delivered on that, I don't think they expected it for one minute. (CEO, Xchanging HR Services)

> I think the peopleportal has been the first sign from within the business that something has changed, something has actually happened. … We had a lot of very good feedback, it was very good, the technology was great, it was web-based. (HR Director, BAE Systems)

Since the initial launch, Xchanging has constantly updated and integrated technology such as Oracle HR, Bond Adapt recruitment software, Talisma CRM, Consensus delegation management software, and Authoria's administration software. In 2005, BAE Systems made Andy Whelan of XHRS their Grand Finalist in their HR Excellence Award for e-enabling

HR services.[10] He was in charge of a successful project that migrated 25 HR legacy systems into one web-enabled database.

Reorganizing into shared service streams

On January 1, 2002, Xchanging HR Services was reorganized along service streams. Overall, there are seven Service Stream Heads and initially 40 service stream team leaders now in charge of cross-business services. Each service stream now operates as its own mini-business, with the same Service Heads understanding that they are responsible for further cost reductions and further streamlining. Where possible, productivity improvement should come from leveraging resources to deliver external business, but during the first year of operations, there were only a few instances in which productivity improvements were delivered from increased revenues. For example, Xchanging increased the revenue stream in the training business by £500,000 to cover the required unit cost savings.

In reality, most of the savings have come from downsizing staff. The HR staff, already reduced to 411 by April 2002, was reduced to 311 people by year-end 2002. The cost reductions have been accompanied by another round of town meetings to explain to the staff "this is what we said we were going to do at the induction, and this is what we did do."

Building and occupying a state-of-the-art, front-office facility

To house these centralized teams, David Andrews built a state-of-the-art shared service facility for Xchanging HR services. He built the facility in Preston, the center of BAE Systems' activity in North West England. This facility serves as a beacon of branding for Xchanging HR Services, complete with Xchanging's color scheme (blue and orange) and logos as the focal point of its interior design. (see Figures 6.3 and 6.4.) The new facility has also had a major impact on people's morale and perception of XHRS as a viable business:

> Space has a big impact on people's morale and the perception of their value, this is where our environmental capability comes in and the service center in Preston will be a show piece. (Head of Implementation, Xchanging)

> The main focus around that building was really to put a bit of branding out in terms of we are now Xchanging HR Services so now let's start thinking about Xchanging HR Services rather than about BAE Systems HR function. (Previously with BAE Systems, then Head of New Business Development for XHRS)

Figure 6.3 New XHRS facilities in Preston

Figure 6.4 New XHRS facilities in Preston

Redesigning business processes

Xchanging uses their own version of the Six Sigma methodology[11] to redesign business processes. The Six Sigma methodology is a strategy for satisfying the customer's needs profitably, primarily by reducing the number of defects in processes.

From a governance stand point, Xchanging implemented Six Sigma with three-tiered teams, called Master Black Belts, Black Belts, and Green Belts. Master Black Belts select the projects and mentor the Black Belts. Black Belts are employees devoted full time to the Six Sigma process, which requires an extensive training program and subsequent certification. Green Belts are part-time Black Belts who continue to work in their functional areas. Green Belts assist Black Belts with projects and integrate Six Sigma methods and tools in their daily work.

The senior leader peer review process for 640 people serves as an example of a business process redesign. Traditionally, peer review involved an extremely inefficient process of an HR person sitting down with a senior leader to fill out paperwork. Instead, Xchanging redesigned the process based more on self-service and enabled the process via the peopleportal: "What would have happened before, thirty people would have happily expanded a task to fill three months and as it is now, eight people have been busy for a month – bang! Done" (Head of Implementation, Xchanging HR Services).

Attracting new customers

Xchanging completed the HR transformation by the end of 2002, 20 months after start-up. After the transition, one of the goals of XHRS was to attract more external customers. While Xchanging was indeed expanding its business to other large clients such as Lloyd's of London, and Deutsche Bank, XHRS had not captured much additional business until 2005. In May of that year, Xchanging signed a three-year, £500,000 deal to integrate and host the payroll systems of Spirit Group, an independent managed pub company. When Spirit Group merged with pub group Scottish and Newcastle Retail last year, it boosted staff to 40,000 employees but the merger meant two separate payroll systems. Xchanging is in charge of the integration, standardization, and hosting of Spirit's Unipay system.

Case discussion and lessons on back office transformation

In this section, we describe our preliminary lessons on the effectiveness of using an enterprise partnership as a vehicle for back office transformation.

The enterprise partnership versus do-it-yourself

In their initial analysis, the BAE Systems' HR team believed that there were three impediments to trying to create a shared set of services themselves:

- Senior management will not make technology and resource investment required to implement shared service
- Internal cultural resistance from business units to centralize services
- Lack of empowerment and skills of internal HR to make the quantum changes required

The evidence suggests that the enterprise partnership model successfully solved these problems for the customer:

- Xchanging made the technology investment on behalf of the customer. Xchanging delivered the first eHR application within six months and has since released three further versions of the technology.
- Xchanging successfully centralized shared services within a year of operations, enabled by a new organizational structure and a new service center.
- Xchanging delivered a highly skilled implementation team and tool kit to kick start the change.
- Xchanging successfully empowered transferred employees by inducting them into a new culture.

This last bullet warrants further elaboration. In the over 100 outsourcing cases we previously studied,[12] customers nearly always sought a supplier with a similar culture to their own. But is this approach flawed? Certainly the BAE Systems–Xchanging partnership challenges the conventional wisdom of cultural homogeneity:

Lesson 1: The enterprise partnership model creates a clash of cultures, but cultural incompatibility may be just what you need. Nearly every person interviewed for this case – from both the customer and supplier sides – noted the cultural differences between BAE Systems and Xchanging. BAE Systems was systematically described as "risk averse," "detailed," and "cautious." This is precisely the culture BAE Systems needs to ensure safety and quality in their core products such as aircraft, submarines, and weapons. But such a culture is not helpful if the task is trying to radically transform a back office function like HR. In contrast, the Xchanging people have been consistently described as "aggressive," "winners," and "impressive." This culture is needed for a start-up company seeking to establish their reputation: "What was obvious to me, the Xchanging people were part of a small company desperate to succeed, and that desire to succeed just didn't exist in the BAE Systems HR culture" (previously BAE Finance Director, then CFO of XHRS).

Xchanging's culture demands results even if it means Xchanging bypasses a customer's bureaucracy or if it means that Xchanging has to swallow higher costs. For example, although BAE Systems was contractually required to pay an IT supplier for some IT services associated with the peopleportal, Xchanging paid the supplier to expedite the implementation process.

Xchanging's results-oriented culture was taught to the transferees through launch events, training sessions, videos, and town meetings. Lest the induction process appear oversimplified, we do note that we heard many stories about how long it took people to change. For example, one employee said it took three months to change:

> If you left work at half past six, you were having a late night at BAE. I mean, that is the BAE culture. I was in at ten to seven this morning and I'll be here at nine o'clock tonight and that is the Xchanging culture. The Xchanging guys I just could associate with very, very, very easily. From day one I felt much, much more comfortable. The hard thing was it was a damned sight harder work, much more disciplined environment, much more focused environment. It still took me a little while to make that leap – probably two or three months.

Overall, BAE Systems embraces the culture shock imputed on its transferees:

> Yes, as a business, Xchanging has placed a lot more pressure on the people in terms of responsiveness and acting in a service environment. We could never have gotten our people to do that because we couldn't have got the culture that would have taken, I don't think it would have happened. (HR Director, BAE Systems)

It's one thing to hear about the culture from senior managers, but what do the transferred employees have to say? In 2005, Professor Anthony Hesketh[13] from Lancaster University published quantitative measures on the perceptions of transferred BAE Systems employees, who are now

Xchanging employees. Specifically, he measured transferred employees:

1. perceptions of their capability,
2. their focus and importance on Xchanging's seven transformation levels (people reorientation, process redesign, service 1st, technology enablement, better sourcing (through XPS), new environment, and implementation processes), and
3. their performance.

Although Hesketh described himself as "an outsourcing skeptic," the high marks from the survey led him to conclude:

> Immediately apparent from the results is the evidence that Xchanging practices what it preaches. The strong performance goes a long way toward shattering the popular myth that back office staff are treated poorly by outsourcers. Xchanging's investment in their people is clearly paying off with high levels of employee engagement.

Management consultancy versus enterprise partnership

In their initial analysis, the BAE Systems' HR team believed that there were four impediments to trying to create a shared set of services by hiring a management consultancy:

- Consultants would identify a large, expensive project which would be likely to cost escalate once they were on site
- Consultants have no accountability or ownership of outcome
- Lack of skills and knowledge transfer
- Lack of sustainability

Concerning project size and cost, the perceived problem with management consultants, amongst our interviewees, is that they are clearly incented to identify large, complex problems:

> Two things that really got my goat in consulting, how many times do you have to get paid to select the same system? And how many times do people have to consolidate before they get it right? OK, I've got immense respect for the consulting firm I used to work for, they are an outstanding organization and the ability to take literally people straight out of university. Really good people, but I didn't like that

there was some misalignment of objectives. (Practice Director for Xchanging who previously worked for a major consulting company)

In contrast, Xchanging's partnership model subscribes to our experience of best practice:

Lesson 2: Multiple short-term implementation phases can yield faster results and pose less risk than a single, large-scale project. Our prior research has consistently found that several small projects are more productive than one large project because there can be insight and clarity each step of the way, and fewer resources spent on non-value-adding tasks such as coordination and administration.[14] The enterprise partnership model, as enacted by Xchanging, has this same view of project size:

> Innovation doesn't need to be a big idea, it can be lots of little things. … What we like doing is introducing a bit of change every three months because it has much more immediate impact rather than building a great big filthy system. (David Andrews, CEO of Xchanging)

> If you don't do it within three to six months then you don't do it. (Head of Implementation, XHRS)

For example, Xchanging implemented the first version of peopleportal within six months, and released three more value added versions within a year of operation.

One of the reasons management consultancies often identify large projects is because they view technology infrastructure as the solution to business problems. For example, consultants often view large, integrated IT systems as a client's solution for enterprise resource planning, customer relationship management, or e-business. This leads us to our next lesson.

Lesson 3: View technology not as a solution, but rather as an enabler. One of the important distinctions between Xchanging and many consultancies is their view of technology. Xchanging's executives do not view technology as a utopian panacea, but merely view technology as one of the seven important capabilities required to re-engineer a back office to front office:

> I think technology is an expensive resource, so you've got to be careful with technology, as you know you can spend a lot of money and not get a lot of value. So I think technology from our perspective is very much used when it's needed. Just because we have a service delivery platform doesn't necessarily mean that every service we deliver has to be over the Internet, if it doesn't make sense, we

shouldn't do it. So technology is a bit of a follower in this case, it definitely follows service, service is always first and it's rarely that we would be in there before process because I don't want to put technology on top of a broken process. (Technology Practice Director, Xchanging)

Specifically, Xchanging aims to process 80 percent of transactions with technology, but exceptions and peculiar transactions are best handled by capable people: "People are altogether more flexible and creative and clever to fit around a system" (Head of Implementation, XHRS).

Fee-for-service outsourcing versus the enterprise partnership model

In their initial analysis, the BAE Systems HR team rejected fee-for-service outsourcing for the following reasons:

- Escalating costs
- Customer and supplier incentives are misaligned
- Power asymmetries develop in favor of supplier
- Lack of sustainability

Senior executives naturally fret the most over the first bullet point. Costs may escalate for many reasons: the supplier has too much power and charges too much money; demand may no longer be harnessed, so the volume of services increases (thus increasing costs); and/or disaggregated spends are finally aggregated, leading to uncomfortable surprises. The enterprise partnership model discourages the first behavior through their aligned incentives, shared governance boards, and open book accounting. But the enterprise partnership model, like fee-for-service outsourcing, will experience the other two sources of cost escalation. The key is to ensure that additional demand is valid, that is, that users are demanding value adding services that the customer deems worth more than the price. And by aggregating dispersed budgets, customers finally have an opportunity to better control and manage it. These lessons are further explored in the two following lessons:

Lesson 4: When employing fee-for-service outsourcing or an enterprise partnership model, be sure to manage user demand. Prior to the partnership model, demand at BAE Systems was constrained by the number of HR staff in the SBUs. If a managing director in an SBU only wanted to hire a staff of 25 people, his unit could only demand enough HR services to occupy these 25 people. A decentralized user community of 40,000 can now demand HR resources:

> We are seeing some evidence of increased demand with Xchanging HR Services...But demand for service before XHRS was always restricted because as an HR Director, you only have the number of people that you could get your MD to agree to, so that effectively capped it. Of course, we have taken that away now and people can demand ever more and more. (Previous HR Director, then Head of Resources for XHRS)

The solution for both the fee-for-service outsourcing and enterprise partnership models is a customer liaison role that collects, prioritizes, and approves service demands (see Chapter 3 for more on this core capability). The function of this role is to ensure that additional demand adds more value than the additional costs it triggers. Although a liaison role adds to the bureaucracy and thus slows down customer service, it is vital to prevent unreasonable cost escalation. At BAE Systems, they have implemented this liaison role through their Service Review Board:

> If it's a new service or an additional higher volume of service, it will go through the service review board. The board asks what's the specification and the cost of doing it? What it doesn't do is set the strategy for what the service should be because the business sets that. Each individual business will set the strategy, if they want a new service, they will set that direction. (HR Director, BAE Systems)

Lesson 5: Both fee-for-service outsourcing and the enterprise partnership model can help customers pro-actively manage spend previously hidden in decentralized budgets. In our study of over 100 fee-for-service outsourcing cases, we found that customers typically did receive unit cost reductions on their baseline services, but that visible overall costs went up because hidden spend became illuminated after outsourcing. This illumination offers customers the opportunity to finally manage the true spend.

Certainly, BAE Systems can expect enormous benefit by consolidating the dispersed £80 million annual HR spend on miscellaneous items such as healthcare and clerical staff, now managed by a separate enterprise partnership called Xchanging Procurement Services (see Chapter 7). Within a year of operation, indirect procurement costs dropped by 12 percent, with more savings anticipated when existing procurement contacts expire and can be renegotiated.

But even removing the procurement spend from the equation, HR costs at BAE Systems appear to have risen, as more hidden HR costs are found and transferred to Xchanging HR Services, such as IT spend on HR systems and spend on temporary HR staff:

> The cost has increased quite substantially. In reality it probably isn't going up because of Xchanging. It just means that we need to probably transfer budget over that hasn't traditionally sat within the HR team, so that it's all as one and recharged against that, that total mass, rather than part left within the business. (HR Director, BAE Systems)

The difference between when and how fee-for-service outsourcers and an enterprise partnership deal with the phenomenon of hidden costs leads us to our next finding.

Lesson 6: Delaying due diligence until after the contract is in effect can speed the negotiation process and more fairly distribute the burden of newly discovered costs. With fee-for-service outsourcing, the supplier typically verifies the customer's claims on baseline costs, services, and resources prior to signing a contract. This due diligence process ensures that the supplier understands their commitments and can still generate a profit on those commitments. But due diligence slows down the negotiation process and almost never uncovers all the costs to which the supplier inadvertently commits:

> One thing in this business you cannot underestimate is, no matter how long from the outside in you try to do due diligence, you will always get it wrong. It's only when you actually go in there and start running it that you find out what's going on and the sooner you do that the better for everyone. (CEO, XHRS)

This immediately puts the customer and supplier in an adversarial position. The customer claims, "You are responsible for this, you contracted for this, it's not our fault you didn't do your homework." The supplier counters, "I am getting ripped off, I have to earn a reasonable profit, you hid these costs from us."

In contrast, the enterprise partnership model delays detailed due diligence until after the contract is signed. The customer and supplier do not need to verify all the costs beforehand because they do not contract a flat fee. Instead, the partners agree to provide a percentage of savings on the total costs transferred, including hidden costs as they become illuminated. Delaying the due diligence process under this model protects both the customer and supplier. Consider some of what Xchanging discovered after the contract was signed: An additional 15 percent of costs were uncovered, including 35 temporary HR staff, wrong salaries reported, and wrong pensions reported:

> The quality of the data about the HR function in terms of not just what salaries people were on but just who was there, how many to within 10%. Really, really surprising and if anything that experience, if I ever needed drilling home about why BAE needed to do the deal, that did it. If you can't tell how many people are in your own function within 10% to 20% what chance have you got of providing value added HR for a business? It was just shocking. (Previously BAE Finance Director, then CFO of XHRS)

At Xchanging, these costs were added to the baseline, and BAE Systems would get their agreed upon percentage of savings.

Lesson 7: The enterprise partnership model aligns incentives better than fee-for-service outsourcing. In terms of alignment, the enterprise partnership model is clearly superior to traditional outsourcing. The 50/50 shared profits and the Joint Board of Directors ensures that the parties both participate and make mutually beneficial decisions:

> It's brilliant because you have rules like the Board of Directors have to turn up for meetings. Could I get the sponsors to turn up for meetings on my previous outsourcing deals? Well, maybe, but it was hard work. When you have a Board meeting, you have to be there. You have certain duties as Board members: you have to act in the best interests of the enterprise, not your individual company. That is a big mind set change. (David Andrews, CEO of Xchanging)

The customer certainly agrees that the enterprise partnership more closely aligns the parties:

> So if it was a traditional customer/supplier relationship, you would get the instance that the customer would blame the supplier for not delivering a service. For me, the partnership means that the accountability for delivering the service into the business is mine. I have to make sure that it delivers a seamless service so that myself and my other HR directors in this business will not say "the reason this went wrong was

because Xchanging did this." If something goes wrong it's because we did it. It's very much a partner type relationship. (HR Director, BAE Systems)

The supplier concurs that the relationship is going well, partly because of the alignment:

> I think we have exceptionally good relationships with BAE Systems which have been maintained and built over this period, as opposed to any acrimony coming in. I think this is due to the approach we take. (CEO, XHRS)

However, one caveat is warranted here:

Lesson 8: Beware that the enterprise partnership model does not perfectly align incentives. In the previous chapters, we discussed how the joint governance between customers and suppliers we studied led to a managerial schizophrenia. (Because the enterprise's primary customer is also an owner, the customer has two competing goals: to maximize cost-efficient service delivery from the enterprise and to maximize the revenue of the enterprise. How can the customer do both?) While this schizophrenia has not so far been a big issue at BAE Systems, it does exist:

> I think third party business will be of great benefit financially to the partnership. It also brings in new ideas and different ways of doing things and gives the people who are doing the transactional side a different experience and perhaps different ways of doing things. But I guess one of the concerns from people in the business, if Xchanging goes out and wins more third party business, is that going to affect the service? The concern within the business will always be if that happens will the level of service drop. With all the measures that are in place I would find it would be difficult, you would spot the service dropping immediately and the contractual measures would be there to actually rein that back. (HR Director, BAE Systems)

Lesson 9: Selecting a supplier with generic business competencies rather than domain-specific knowledge may yield better results. Moving in a completely different direction, what fascinated us most about BAE Systems' selection of Xchanging is that it ignored a number of "conventional wisdoms":

- Xchanging had no track record – BAE Systems would be the first customer!
- Xchanging had no industry-specific knowledge, that is, no aerospace knowledge.
- Xchanging had little domain-specific knowledge, that is, little human resource management expertise!

Nearly every fee-for-service outsourcer positions their core capabilities in the functions they are taking over. But Xchanging claims no pre-existing competency in human resources. Instead, Xchanging believes that the talent needed to transform back offices to front offices requires six powerful cross-functional, cross-industry competencies, which they group together in the Xcellence platform:

- service excellence,
- process improvement,
- people development,
- technology enablement,
- slick physical facilities,
- efficient third-party sourcing,

And most importantly, the wisdom to know when and how to deploy these six through the seventh competency of implementation. Xchanging's enterprise partnership model absorbs the domain-specific knowledge – in this case HR knowledge – through employee transfers. Some executives from BAE Systems actually saw this lack of HR knowledge as a plus:

> I always say the best HR people are people who haven't been in the HR function all their lives. You need a different view. So the Xchanging team, although they are not HR professionals, it works probably better that they are not because if they go in understanding all the pitfalls that there may be, then they'll never make any changes, so sometimes it is better. (HR Director, BAE Systems)

Enterprise partnership model versus joint ventures

Although BAE Systems did not consider a joint venture, there are many similarities in terms of governance. We noted that joint ventures often failed because the suppliers were unable to leverage the customer investor's assets with external sales. With enterprise partnerships, the primarily focus is on transforming the customer's back office; external sales come later. But the following lesson applies:

Lesson 10: The economics of the enterprise partnership approach need to work for both parties without over-relying on third-party revenues. BAE Systems understood this lesson and will receive the guaranteed cost savings over a five-year period regardless of whether Xchanging can attract external customers to the venture. This contract item proved to be a savvy move:

> The business development in year one was almost zero because the focus was, "Let's get our act together in delivering this to BAE Systems first, before we all turn into sales people and go out and start selling ourselves." (Head of New Business Development, XHRS)

That said, if the supplier cannot earn a profit on the deal, the customer's service will invariably deteriorate. Thus, this lesson also extends to suppliers: make sure you can earn a profit on the deal even if you cannot attract external customers.

In the case of Xchanging and BAE Systems, XHRS' CEO reports that Xchanging did a make a modest profit during the first few years. Indeed, Xchanging executives note that the centralization, standardization, and downsizing reap significant savings, so generating profit is do-able with this model:

> If I only look at XHRS, we have to really work hard not to make this business work. It is pretty easy to make this business make money, the hard bit is the time scale and the growth. So you concentrate resources and put the management in place, you remove the weak people over time and you put in good technology. You really have to work to not make that add up to a significantly better position than you were in before. (CFO, XHRS)

Thus, Xchanging can earn a profit even if XRHS does not attract another customer. (But that is clearly not the goal!)

Lesson 11: Consider the enterprise model if you fit the ideal customer profile. The enterprise partnership model may work best for a customer with the following profile:

- The customer seeks substantial improvement in back office performance in costs and service.

- The customer has a substantial back office spend to make the deal large enough to attract a competent external supplier.
- The customer's back office operations are highly decentralized, allowing the opportunity for significant cost reductions from centralization and standardization.
- The customer's back office operations have not received high management attention historically, allowing the opportunity for significant cost savings and service improvement from better management.
- The customer's organization would resist centralizing and standardizing themselves due to internal political resistance, unwillingness of senior management to make the required upfront investment, or lack of skills and experience of back office staff to make the transformation.
- The customer sees the potential for sustainable, long-term development of a new business.

Conclusion: Which transformation model is best?

Because BAE Systems had a high potential for improving performance and developing HR into a sustainable business, they were looking for a long-term solution with a governance mechanism capable of aligning incentives and adapting to changes. It is very clear from the BAE Systems story and lessons that the enterprise partnership was certainly a better model than do-it-yourself, management consultancy, or fee-for-service outsourcing for this context. But BAE Systems, like many companies, use all transformation models in their organization.

To help senior executives weigh the relative advantage of these options, we have developed a matrix, which assesses the potential for performance transformation and the potential for sustainable development (see Figure 6.5). Management consultants have a proven track record of helping clients implement big-bang transformations such as reorganizing organizational structures, integrating a number of disparate existing systems, or building new systems. The focus here is on significantly improving performance, while allowing the customer to manage the ongoing result. Here one looks to the market to supply an infusion of energy and new skills not otherwise available, an ability to bypass internal political resistance, and to deliver on a clear mandate from senior management. However, our research experience has been that costs may escalate, and making the changes stick – getting them accepted, institutionalized and developed further – can be problematic.[15]

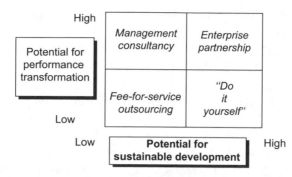

Figure 6.5 Options for "back office" performance improvement

Fee-for-service outsourcing is often targeted at incremental improvements, such as delivering the same set and level of services at a reduced cost. This model is very effective when customers can articulate requirements and wish to obtain a fair market price and competent service. Our experience has been that one-time savings are frequently achieved up-front, but there is little sustained continuous improvement, let alone transformation of performance.[16]

On the other hand, "do-it-yourself" can develop new capabilities and sustain their application, but frequently internal inertia and politics, and under-investment in the resources required often makes it a poor choice when seeking the initial performance transformation.[17] Applied to back offices, as we have seen, an all too typical scenario is lack of prioritization of management attention, financial and technical resources to make things happen.

In practice, all these models, carefully selected, focused and managed, remain viable weapons in a senior executive's arsenal. As the do-it-yourself, management consultant, and fee-for-service outsourcing models have been extensively studied, the enterprise partnership model warrants further study. By sharing BAE Systems story it is our aim to help senior executives most effectively transform their back office functions.

Notes

1. Scholl, Rebecca, "BPO at the Cross Roads," presentation At World Outsourcing Summit, Orlando, FL, 2002.
2. McIlvaine, A. (2004), "HR's Influential: BPO Pioneer James Madden," *Human Resource Executive Magazine*, April 19.

3. Bednarz, A. (2005), "HR outsourcing takes on new life," *Network World,* June 6.
4. Kersner, J. (2005), "People Movers," *CFO Magazine*, June.
5. Rafter, Michelle, (2005), "Hewitt Exults in HRO Dominance," *HR Management*, June.
6. "No Limits to Xchanging's Ambitions," *Financial News*, February 14, 2005.
7. Lacity, M. and Willcocks, L. (2001), *Global Information Technology Outsourcing: Search for Business Advantage*, Wiley, Chichester.
8. Chairman's Statement, February 24, 1999 in British Aerospace 1998 Annual Report.
9. Dickson, C. (2003), "Taking a Partnership to New Heights," *HRO Europe.com* November 7; Paton, N. (2002), "Xchanging's Sophisticated Partnership Deal," *Personnel Today*, February 5.
10. "Delivering HR Excellence 2005," BAE Systems website (www.baesystems.com).
11. Achieving "Six Sigma" in a process means that there are, on average, only 3.4 defects per million opportunities to make an error. The theory of Six Sigma suggests that profitability increases when processes are improved because defects and exceptions are expensive. Thus, Six Sigma proponents reject the notion of cost/service trade-offs, believing instead that the key to lower costs is improving service.
12. Lacity and Willcocks (2001), op. cit.
13. Hesketh, A. (2005), "Transforming Transformation: Measuring the Performance of Enterprise Partnership Outsourcing," Lancaster University Management School Working Paper.
14. Feeny, D. (1997), "Information Management: Lasting Ideas within Turbulent Times, in L. Willcocks, D. Feeny, and G. Islei (eds), *Managing IT as a Strategic Resource*, McGraw Hill, pp. xvii-xxviii; Subramanian, A. and Lacity, M. (1997), "Managing Client Server Implementations: Today's Technology, Yesterday's Lessons" *Journal of Information Technology*, Vol. 12, 3, pp. 169–186.
15. Willcocks, L., Petherbridge, P., and Olson, N. (2002), *Making IT Count: Strategy, Delivery and Infrastructure*, Butterworth, Oxford.
16. Lacity and Willcocks (2001), op. cit.
17. Willcocks, L., Feeny, D., and Islei, G. (1997), *Managing IT As A Strategic Resource*, McGraw Hill, Maidenhead.

CHAPTER 7

Outsourcing indirect procurement spend: The case of BAE Systems

Mary Lacity, Leslie Willcocks, and David Feeny

Introduction: Transformational procurement outsourcing

The previous chapter explored the use of outsourcing to transform human resources. The opportunities for cost savings are vast because HR is a labor intensive activity. Thus, the creation of technology-enabled shared services allows dramatic reductions in headcount. This chapter explores in depth the use of outsourcing to transform indirect procurement. (Procurement of direct materials and services is still considered strategic and kept in-house by most firms). This is a very different transformational model because procurement is not a labor intensive activity, but the dollars transacted are enormous. A handful of purchasing agents may transact US$100 million worth of indirect goods and services. Typically, a purchasing agent may be responsible for dozens of categories of indirect spend, and thus cannot gain deep expertise in each category. Thus, *savings from indirect procurement outsourcing come from the supplier's deep category expertise, as well as rigorous sourcing methods, tools, consolidated buying power, and the ability to attract and retain good suppliers.* Studies have shown that customers have experienced significant cost savings from outsourcing indirect procurement. Aberdeen Group, for example, found that 83 percent of 720 senior executives reported achieving significant price reductions after outsourcing procurement.[1]

Size of the procurement outsourcing market

IDC estimated that procurement outsourcing was a US$5.9 billion market in 2002, and was expected to increase to US$12 billion by 2007.[2] Most of the outsourcing market comprises indirect procurement spend on items such as office supplies, travel services, furniture, car fleets, and contract labor. This represents 60 to 80 percent of a typical company's purchasing transactions. Research firms project ambitious growth estimates for indirect procurement outsourcing. For example, TaylorHall forecasts that the procurement outsourcing market will triple by 2008.[3] Accenture claims procurement is the fastest growing BPO sector, with a survey showing that 20 percent of 220 U.S. and European companies outsourced procurement in 2003 and 50 percent plan to outsource procurement by 2006.[4]

BAE Systems and transformational indirect procurement outsourcing

Of course, transformational outsourcing of any back office poses significant challenges. All sorts of surprising issues arise when indirect spend is finally managed, such as the extent to which suppliers are inadvertently mis-paid, the shocking amount of money wasted on specific categories, duplicate orders, etc. Only by delving deeper, will senior executives be able to appraise the viability of transforming their own back office spend. For this reason, we present a case study on transformation on indirect spend in more detail. We chose the BAE and Xchanging joint enterprise called Xchanging Procurement Services (XPS) for a case study because it is one of the first enterprises to successfully tackle procurement. Enough time has elapsed since its inception in 2001 to access the outcome, unlike other large procurement outsourcing deals that were still in the early stages at time of writing, such as the seven-year deal between Accenture and Deutsche Bank signed in 2004.

As of 2005, XPS had delivered the following benefits to BAE Systems:

- An overall 12 percent reduction across all categories of spend transacted
- Improved service, including user desktop ordering from a newly developed sourcing web portal
- Profit sharing in XPS

Concerning the last point, XPS's external customers as at 2006 included Boots, United Biscuits, Novar, Carlson Wagonlit, Heywood Williams,

AMS, Compass, and Kingfisher Group. As of 2005, XPS managed £4 billion worth of spend, including:

- 10,000 fleet cars
- 10,000 engineers
- 700 tonnes of aluminium
- 5500 tonnes of Steel
- 100 million passenger miles
- 120,000 car rentals
- 100,000 hotel bookings

There is also significant evidence that XPS has attracted better suppliers and improved existing supplier relationships. As XPS renegotiated long-term contracts with suppliers, established online ordering and paid suppliers on time, suppliers increasingly report better operational efficiency. For example, the rental car giant Hertz claims that XPS has reduced their transaction costs by ten dollars per car rental by replacing telephone and fax orders with online booking. BAE Systems is sufficiently pleased with XPS to continue to transfer more categories of spend. In late 2004, BAE Systems signed a £490 million add-on for technical contract labor. This brought the total value of the deal from an initial £800 million in 2001 to £1.54 billion by late 2004.

Again, radical transformation is never painless. Throughout this case, we discuss the challenges that arose and how the partners coped with them. Specifically,

- We identify competencies needed to transform indirect spend: category expertise, sourcing methods, sourcing tools, consolidated buying power, ability to attract and retain great suppliers, and overall strategic governance.
- We discuss the benefits and limitations of five different transformation implementation options, including do-it-yourself, purchasing consultants, consortiums, e-procurement outsourcing, and enterprise partnerships.
- We assess the enterprise partnership's ability to deliver the transformation competencies as enacted at BAE Systems.
- We profile the ideal customer for the enterprise partnership model and identify four important lessons.

Six competencies needed to harness indirect procurement spend

Six competencies are needed to transform indirect spend: category expertise, sourcing methods, sourcing tools, consolidated buying power, ability to attract and retain great suppliers, and overall strategic governance.

Sourcing tools are the most visible competency needed to harness indirect spend because they are embedded in software applications customers use to analyze, source, and procure materials and services. Sourcing tools should facilitate the complete supply chain process from capturing and approving demand, translating demand into request for proposals (RFPs), soliciting suppliers, negotiating and awarding contracts, tracking receipts, and payments. Full service sourcing tools should also track customer and supplier services, including complaints, problem tracking and problem resolution. Readers will most likely be familiar with the popular sourcing tools provided by Ariba, CommerceOne, and ERP (enterprise resource planning) suppliers such as SAP and PeopleSoft. Customers may license these integrated applications, or alternatively, customers may build their own procurement applications. But simply purchasing or building tools will do nothing to reduce spend unless they are orchestrated with the other five capabilities.

Category expertise is probably the most important competency and thus is listed first in Table 7.1. Individuals who understand specific spend categories are in the best position to negotiate with suppliers. Category experts understand the value and costs of components and services and can therefore articulate demand and negotiate better prices with suppliers. In addition to understanding the specific product or service line, category experts understand the environmental context, including legal and regulatory requirements. For indirect procurement items, few companies can afford to develop in-house expertise for the breadth of materials and services required. This is why many customers seek to supplement in-house agents with outside expertise.

Sourcing methods are the procedures category experts use to define, benchmark, research, analyze, negotiate, and manage indirect spend. These methods lay out the rules of engagement for category experts and for users demanding material and services. Methods should be automated or enabled by sourcing tools.

Buying power is the ability to leverage deals from suppliers by consolidating indirect spend *within* a company and more importantly, consolidating indirect spend *across* companies.

Table 7.1 Competencies needed to transform indirect spend

1. Category expertise	"Indirect" spend is a core capability Full time experts devoted to indirect spend categories

2. Sourcing methods	Ability to baseline indirect spend and costs
	Ability to decompose indirect spend and
	  costs into commoditized units
	Ability to statistically analyze indirect spend and costs
	Ability to negotiate mutually favorable deals
	Ability to service deals, including controlling
	  price and scope creep

3. Sourcing tools	Ability to maintain correct supplier data Ability to create demand templates Ability to transform demand into RFPs Ability to facilitate user ordering, such as web portals Ability to facilitate auctions Ability to track and validate orders Ability to track and validate receipts Ability to track and pay invoices Ability to monitor service levels Ability to track and manage supplier complaints Ability to track and manage user complaints
4. Buying power	Ability to aggregate spend across units within a company Ability to aggregate spend across companies
5. Supplier appeal	Ability to offer large volumes Ability to offer long-term deals Ability to lower supplier transaction costs Ability to facilitate user orders Ability to pay supplier on time

6. Governance	Ability to align indirect spend agents'
	incentives with company interests
	Ability to reap cost cutting rewards from indirect
	  spend transformation
	Ability to keep demand variable (i.e., not
	  having to commit to huge volumes for a long
	  period of time to reap rewards)
	Ability to retain strategic decision making
	  over procurement

Supplier appeal is the ability to attract excellent suppliers, primarily by improving the supplier's sales or profitability. This is usually achieved through increased buying power by offering the supplier a bigger deal, but can also include reducing a supplier's transaction costs through efficient processes and more timely and accurate supplier payments.

Governance is the ability to govern indirect spend, to control the strategy, and to reap the financial benefits of savings. Governance becomes a major issue when outsourcing indirect procurement spend.

Table 7.1 provides a comprehensive decomposition of these capabilities. The table can be used as tool to assess a company's current sourcing competencies.

Options for transforming indirect spend

Large organizations have at least five viable options for obtaining the six transformative competencies: (1) do-it-yourself (DIY), (2) hire a purchasing consultant, (3) join a consortium exchange, (4) outsource to an e-procurement company, or (5) create an enterprise partnership. Because these approaches were discussed in previous chapters, the discussion focuses on applying these approaches specifically to indirect procurement.

Do-it-yourself. Of the six capabilities listed in Table 7.1, DIY generally would score highest on governance. In particular, if companies are able to better manage indirect spend themselves, the major benefit of DIY is that the savings are not shared with a third party. DIY would also enable the company to retain strategic decision making and to align the purchasing agents' incentives with company interests. But on the downside, the DIY option would often score lowest on developing and retaining category expertise. Frequently occurring impediments include:

- In-house purchasing agents lack interest in indirect spend categories.
- Attracting world-class experts in indirect spend is difficult because they will never have the same status or career satisfaction as direct spend agents.
- Developing in-house expertise takes too long.
- Senior management unwilling to make upfront investment required for transformation.

DIY would also be limited in terms of buying power; while spend could be aggregated within the company, it would be difficult to aggregate spend across other companies.

Purchasing consultants. This approach shares three major benefits with the other approaches that draw from outside the company. One, it brings in external energy and expertise. According to some research, customers rate large established consulting companies such as Accenture, IBM Global Services, and Cap Gemini Ernst & Young as having high caliber supply chain consultants. "The average experience levels are in the ten to fifteen year range rather than the ten to fifteen month range of years past."[5] Two, management gives a clear signal of commitment to the transformation by bringing in outsiders. Three, that commitment reduces political resistance.

But this transformation approach does have several major limitations. Consultants eventually vacate. Thus, their knowledge and expertise may not be transferred or institutionalized at the customer site, resulting in a lack of sustainability of results. Consultants' contracts are usually based on time and materials, resulting in a lessened sense of accountability and a lack of alignment between the parties. Many customers also experience cost escalation as procurement projects experience scope creep and delays.

Consortium exchanges. The main advantage of a consortium is the ability to increase the customer's buying power by consolidating spend across many organizations. But consortiums require a significant investment in enterprise development, including management and technology. Thus, the most powerful consortiums have typically been in direct spend categories. Some research has found that buyers face two risks when joining a consortium: replacing trusted suppliers with unreliable new sources and loss in customer service quality. Also, suppliers often perceive that consortiums primarily benefit customers. But the real limitation is the lack of consortiums with a comprehensive suite of indirect procurement spend categories.[6]

Outsource to e-procurement suppliers. Outsourcing e-procurement can be anything from accessing procurement software applications hosted by a supplier, outsourcing the contract monitoring and compliance of existing contracts, or outsourcing the entire procurement cycle for certain categories of spend. The outsourcing option is very complex. A major advantage of e-procurement suppliers operating in this space is that most have invested heavily in sourcing tools. The market, however, is still immature. Most start-ups are still light on category expertise, offer little opportunities to aggregate spend, and customers only engage, on average, thirty suppliers through e-sourcing. Also, if customers limit their risks by selectively sourcing different categories of spend to different suppliers, they can increase costs associated with redundant and non-standardized processes and systems.[7] Another limitation of outsourcing is that the customer and e-procurement partner rarely have aligned incentives because the customer typically pays based on number or volume of transactions. The supplier has no incentive to help reduce procurement costs but rather is incented to increase procurement volumes.

Enterprise partnership. The enterprise partnership model, as enacted by Xchanging, takes a customer's baseline indirect spend, transforms the spend using category expertise, spend aggregation, and better tools and methods to negotiate lower prices with suppliers and to improve both customer and supplier service. The savings are shared between the customer and Xchanging.

The enterprise partnership model is distinct from the other options. Compared to the do-it-yourself and purchasing consultant options, Xchanging claims that the enterprise partnership will yield better service and faster results. Figure 7.1 maps the timing and sustained value of the DIY, consulting, and enterprise partnership options. Xchanging argues that DIY would require a twelve-to-eighteen-month project to redesign three categories of spend. Management consultants would require six to twelve months to redesign up to five categories of spend. The enterprise partnership can re-engineer up to ten categories of spend within four months.

Compared to purchasing consultants, the enterprise partnership's biggest distinction is accountability and sustainability of results. Xchanging will only make money if it can lower prices for the customer, thus incentives are highly aligned with this governance mechanism. Readers will immediately question, "won't this incent Xchanging to cut corners to boost its own profits?" The customer is protected by detailed service guarantees that are reviewed monthly. Compared to the e-procurement

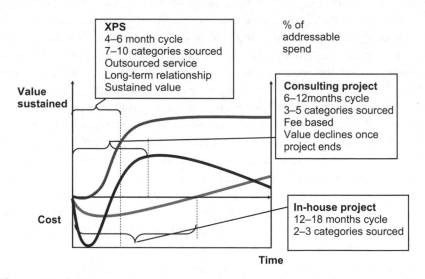

Figure 7.1 D-I-Y management consultants, and enterprise partnerships
Copyright © Xchanging

outsourcing, the enterprise model differs because of the focus on content and because technology is merely an enabler, not the solution in itself:

> We didn't want to be a dot.com. We were astute enough to see that these companies lacked content, where you only have a service and a bit of technology on the web, how do you dress that up? (CEO, XPS)

There are, however, some obvious risks, such as the supplier going out of business. But in the case of XPS, business is booming.

BAE Systems: The customer context

Of course understanding the six sourcing competencies and five transformation options at a high level does not reveal the complexities and challenges of truly transforming indirect spend. In particular, the challenges of implementing an enterprise partnership for indirect procurement warrant a detailed case study. Our research is based on 18 interviews with managers from BAE Systems and Xchanging. By interviewing multiple stakeholders, having participants verify claims, and gathering substantial documentation, the research approach objectively portrays the partnership.

The story of BAE Systems transformation began in the HR department (see Chapter 6). In the area of human resource management, HR agents, dispersed across 70 sites, were responsible for about £80 million in indirect procurement spend for travel, car fleets, contract labor, training, and stationary. Initially, BAE Systems sought to reduce indirect procurement spend by doing it themselves. They initially made good progress by consolidating some spending and re-negotiating contracts. One example is the three-year contract BAE Systems had negotiated for non-engineering contract labor. But when Xchanging took over much of BAE's HR, it became clear that there were many opportunities to further reduce indirect procurement spend.

In theory, BAE Systems, like all large organizations, had at least five viable options for further reducing indirect procurement spend: continue to do it themselves, hire a consultant, join a consortium exchange, outsource to an e-procurement company, or create an enterprise partnership. For BAE Systems, the options were clearly biased towards the enterprise partnership choice because a lot of the spend was highly integrated with the Xchanging HR Services Deal: "60% of HR services we were responsible for were delivered by external providers, so how can we not manage those as well?" (CEO, XPS).

The enterprise partnership

Given the level of success with the existing enterprise partnership with Xchanging for HR services, BAE Systems opted to use another enterprise partnership to transform indirect spend.

BAE Systems and Xchanging signed a ten-year contract for the enterprise partnership, Xchanging Procurement Services (XPS), on November 1, 2001. The initial scope of the contract covered seven categories of indirect spend:

1. Fleets (estimated to be about £25 million per year or US$46 million)
2. Non-technical contract labor (~ £25 million per year or US$46 million)
3. Learning and development (~ £25 million or US$46 million)
4. Health care (~ £5 million per year or US$9 million)
5. Permanent recruitment (~ £2 million per year or US$3.7 million)
6. Remuneration and benefits
7. Stationery

Xchanging has exclusive procurement rights in these categories. Thus, BAE Systems is obligated to purchase these items through Xchanging for the duration of the contract. BAE Systems can only go elsewhere if Xchanging fails:

> If we do not perform, there are criteria where they can go elsewhere. We have a baseline with index[8] and if we perform below that, then they have the right to go on and do market testing and if we don't put it right within a certain period of time, a couple of months, then they have the right to drop the exclusivity on that category but effectively, provided we don't screw up, we are there for ten years. (CEO, XPS)

Savings are shared 50/50 between BAE Systems and Xchanging on the baseline spend in the seven categories. In addition, as Xchanging attracts external customers to XPS besides BAE Systems, Xchanging shares 35 percent of the profits with BAE Systems. As BAE Systems transfers more spend to the enterprise, they reap 65 percent of the cost savings.

The governance of the contract entails two important joint boards: the Management Board and the Service Review Board. The Management Board's role is to oversee the relationship and to ensure success in terms of commercial benefit and delivery. The Service Review Board ensures that the service commitments are implemented and achieved.

Existing BAE Systems contracts were novated to Xchanging for ongoing management. Xchanging got a small fee to administer existing contracts. Real savings occurred after XPS renegotiated expired contracts.

The enterprise partnership deal doesn't guarantee a certain amount of savings because the customer does not have to guarantee a certain amount of spend. One of the main advantages to BAE Systems is that they did not have to guarantee Xchanging that their indirect spend would remain around the £80 million a year mark. Instead, BAE Systems benefits from the complete flexibility of variable indirect spend:

> We have a subtler model because people's requirements for these non core categories that they are purchasing can fluctuate or can even disappear, particularly in the area of resourcing – people might say, "we are on hard times next year, we are not going to have any temps next year, we are going to have a recruitment freeze or we are going to downgrade everyone's car or we are going to reel in the training budgets. We are not going to spend any money on any other deal. We are going to use it to prop up the profit and loss somewhere else" – all very regular scenarios happening in business. (Category Director, XPS)

We will see that this last contracting clause proved to be potentially devastating to XPS because they were expecting at least £80 million for the seven categories of spend to make the economics work, when only £35 million (US$65 million) was transferred initially.

XPS organization

XPS is set up to be an independent enterprise with P&L responsibility. XPS senior management includes the CEO, CFO, Head of Service, Head of Process, Head of Legal, Sales Director, Head of Implementation, and three Category Directors. This structure is the major governance mechanism, along with the contract, to ensure that the customer's and supplier's incentives are aligned, that both parties reap the rewards from indirect spend transformation, and that BAE Systems retains considerable control over strategy. The independence of XPS also helps to prevent internal political sabotage as BAE Systems' users are required to use XPS for agreed upon categories of spend.

Transition phase: November 2001 to November 2002

The XPS contract went into effect November 1, 2001. The deal was structured so that XPS, at first, only earned an administration fee. XPS did not earn real profits until spend was officially transferred. In order for spending to be transferred from BAE Systems to XPS, the baseline spend had to be measured and approved, existing legal contracts novated, or new legal contracts made to allow XPS to purchase on behalf of BAE Systems. XPS estimated that the initial benchmarking and approval activities would only take two months. Like all major outsourcing endeavors, the transition period was much longer than anticipated by the parties. It sometimes took eight months to transfer a category of spend to XPS. Two factors caused major delays:

1. XPS had to coordinate and gain approval from a large number of BAE Systems' managers.
2. The parties overestimated the amount of spend that would be transferred from the seven categories.

These two issues are explored in detail. The key learning point is that the parties did everything they could to resolve issues in the spirit of a partnership.

1. XPS had to coordinate and gain approval from a tremendous number of BAE Systems' managers. In order for XPS to transfer a category of spend, XPS had to visit up to 30 BAE Systems sites, converse with up to 50 people, and seek as many as 12 signatures from BAE Systems managers. For example, Learning and Development was a particularly challenging benchmarking area because the spend was highly decentralized and distributed to hundreds of suppliers. Just gathering the existing data was a Herculean task, and it took nearly six months to benchmark.

To complicate matters, many of the retained BAE Systems procurement managers were not fully informed of the contract, thus they did not place a high priority on meeting with XPS. Some retained procurement managers resented that procurement was being centralized, and furthermore they resented being outsourced:

> So that was a difficulty, and obviously internally some people still not believing that it was the right thing to do. It is a difficult thing to sell with some of our procurement people as well. It is almost like we are outsourcing it because you haven't done a good enough job, that could be the perception if you are not careful. (Supplier and Development Manager, BAE Systems)

Because XPS would not earn a profit until the baselines were approved, it became increasingly aggressive in seeking BAE Systems' cooperation. This XPS "task-master" approach caused friction early in the relationship. To remedy this problem, BAE Systems actually devoted more resources in terms of relationship managers to manage the XPS/BAE Systems interface. XPS learned from this experience, and now appoint dedicated relationship managers for each client.

2. The parties overestimated the amount of spend that would be transferred from the seven categories. Recall that the contract called for approximately £80 million spend to be transferred to XPS in seven categories. By the middle of the year 2002, only £30 million in spend had been transferred in these categories. For example, the partners initially thought that £25 million in learning and development was going to be transferred, but the actual number was only about 30 percent of the estimate. This underestimation threatened XPS' ability to meet their projected profitability targets.

Solving issues as partners

BAE Systems and Xchanging's executives held many strategic planning sessions to address the shortfall. The partners agreed that it was in both of their interests to transfer over the intended critical mass of spend to XPS. This would be achieved by adding eight more categories of spend, bringing the XPS controlled spend to nearly £100 million by year-end 2002. Some of the new categories included:

1. Travel (approximately £40 million; US$75 million)
2. Printing (£3 million; US$5.5 million)
3. Office furniture (£2 million; US$3.7 million)
4. Computer consumables (£1.3 million; US$2.4 million)
5. Mobile Phones

Of course, procuring fifteen smaller categories rather than seven large ones increased XPS' transaction and administration costs. The second effect was that XPS had less negotiating leverage with suppliers since the value of the deals was smaller. But the good news is that both parties have reduced the benchmarking cycle times significantly. As new categories of spend are added to scope, XPS is able to benchmark within a few months rather than eight months. And despite the added transaction and administration costs, XPS has been able to earn margins on all categories of spend, which range from a low of 5 percent to a high of 45 percent, depending on the category.

Gaining new business: 2003 to 2005

During the last few years, XPS has focused on replicating its success with BAE Systems to other customers. Some of the biggest deals include:

- a seven-year contract in 2004 with Boots for travel, marketing, resourcing, facilities management, and workplace services, worth about £400 million
- a five-year contract in 2004 with United Biscuits worth £600 million
- a £490 million add-on to the BAE Systems contract in 2004

The remainder of the story focuses on how XPS unleashes its six competencies: category expertise, methods, tools, buying power, supplier relationships, and governance to deliver benefits to BAE (and other customers) and their suppliers.

Competency 1: Obtaining category expertise. For BAE Systems, the enterprise partnership model was a better way to access category expertise than continuing to do-it-themselves. The investment to expertise and training was something BAE Systems could not see as a major priority, though inroads into indirect procurement management were still rapidly being made just before the deal setting up XPS. Thus, one of the first benefits of the XPS partnership was the development of significant category expertise.

At the start of the venture, Xchanging already had world-class sourcing experts in senior management positions. For example, consider the accomplishments of Xchanging's first Sourcing Practice Director, David Rich-Jones. David previously removed 40 percent of spend from a £100 million procurement budget and added 25 percent profits to a global building products company. Other Xchanging employees with illustrious careers in procurement include John Doherty, who delivered £54 million in savings as a senior category manager with two years at one prior site. The initial idea was that such leadership would be used to motivate, mentor, and empower the 40 targeted BAE Systems employees. But when XPS went live in November 2001, only eight of the targeted 40 people transferred from BAE Systems. BAE Systems couldn't transfer more people because there simply weren't enough experts in indirect spend, and BAE Systems wanted to retain some of those precious few experts on-site.

Xchanging was forced immediately to recruit category experts. Such specialists are extremely expensive and can have base pays as high as £130,000 with a 50 percent bonus plan. To supplement these quite expensive procurement experts, Xchanging hired nearly 30 people and trained them to become full-time category experts. Xchanging partners these new hires with existing category experts. It actually views this as a better model than hiring only existing category experts because "too many chefs might spoil the stew":

> We want to put the expert alongside a very bright, strategic thinker because the expert in our view is the solution and the problem. They will tell you very articulately why you can't do something it but if you turn that positively, they can help you actually do it. (CEO, XPS)

The strategy results in a highly effective team of category experts. In 2005, for example, XPS has four travel specialists who manage £50 million per year in spend on behalf of BAE and four other external customers. The staff has niche specialties in car, hotel, and air booking. Few companies have in-house experts who can specialize to this degree.

Competency 2: Applying sourcing excellence methods. Xchanging has many sophisticated methods for reducing a customer's costs and increasing their service levels. While a full discussion of their methods is beyond the scope of this chapter, we point to three representative examples. Portfolio management serves as an example of a strategic method, baselining and unitizing category spend serves as an example of a tactical method, and the enactment models serve as examples of the operational method.

Strategic method: Portfolio management

Because Xchanging's incentives are aligned with the customers, XPS executives are highly motivated to focus on the indirect spend categories that will reap the greatest rewards. This essentially means that XPS executives focus on the big-ticket items, tempered against the supply market characteristics. As such, XPS executives assess a customer's entire spend portfolio, and target different methods to maximize effective sourcing. Figure 7.2 provides a high-level view of the strategic portfolio analysis. Along the X-axis, XPS partners assess the level of customer business impact, including the level of spend, percentage of total spend, price volatility, impact on profitability, and relationship of product to the customer's core business. Along the Y-axis, XPS partners assess the level

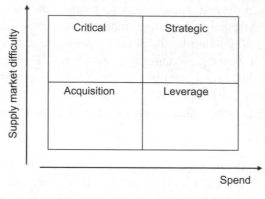

Figure 7.2 XPS portfolio analysis

of supplier risk and complexity, including the level of supplier concentration, threat of substitution, threat of new supplier entrants, buyer leverage, supplier market share, time sensitivity, and technical risk. Considering both these dimensions, four strategies for managing spend emerge:

1. **Strategic:** As the most difficult and important categories, spending is managed through strategic alliances with key suppliers, focusing on close integration between the supplier and customer.
2. **Critical:** In these categories, the customer has less leverage because the spend is smaller and the supplier environment is complex. The strategies include developing critical relationships, engaging in long-term contracts, engineering out – and, as one participant put it "at times, groveling."
3. **Acquisition:** The customer business impact is low and supplier environment is not complex. The strategies here focus on reducing transaction costs, including automation, delegation, and simplification.
4. **Leverage:** In these categories, the customer has the advantage. The sourcing strategies include adding competitors and negotiate multiple short-term contracts to procure lowest prices.

Tactical method: Baselining and unitizing category spend

We have addressed the political issues of baselining, but not the actual method itself. Obviously, the parties need a precise baseline to later calculate and distribute the savings XPS generates. But the real power of baselining is the decomposition of indirect spend to its component parts so XPS can negotiate better deals on these unbundled goods and services (see Figure 7.3). To illustrate the method and benefits of unitization, two categories of indirect spend serve as examples: car fleets and recruitment.

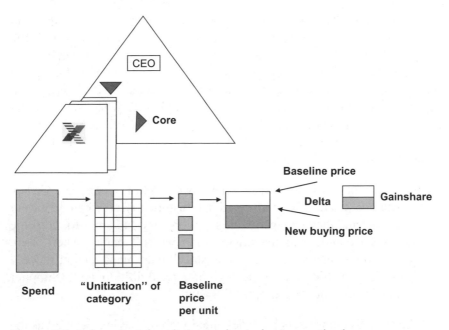

Figure 7.3 Xchanging's baselining and gainsharing method

1. **Car fleets.** Prior to Xchanging, BAE Systems managed car leases in the typical manner: it created a request for quote, invited multiple leasing companies to submit bids, and selected the best bid in terms of cost and service. The leasing companies all submitted bundled bids that were very similar. XPS decomposed the costs of car leasing into its component parts then asked suppliers to bid on these subunits, such as car purchase price, maintenance price, roadside recovery price, and financing prices:

> We went to the manufacturers separately and said no, no we don't want you to provide your standard list price, we will negotiate a price with you which we will take to you and apply your financing costs so service maintenance and repair. Disaggregating that chain is a procurement technique that you use on core materials but again, we are applying it to a non-core area where typically no one has got the time or the energy. (Category Director, XPS)

XPS has been highly successful at reducing unit costs of fleet. As of 2005, Xchanging manages one of the largest car fleets in Europe – over 10,000 vehicles.

2. **Recruitment.** The recruiting category was estimated to be worth about £2 million a year, but in reality, only £1 million was transferred to XPS. Despite the shortfall, XPS was able to generate significant savings by reducing the number of suppliers from 100 to 15. Besides reducing the transaction costs by limiting the number of suppliers, XPS was able to negotiate much better deals because the 15 suppliers now had significantly larger deals. But again, radical chance is never easy. When XPS centralized recruitment, there was significant resistance from the BAE Systems strategic business units (SBUs).

> Recruitment was an area where we hadn't done as Group. Procurement hadn't been involved in it historically, so when they went to engage and they engaged with suppliers they suddenly found some senior stakeholders in the organization weren't happy. There were some difficulties there. That whole stakeholder management piece, I guess, is something that at the beginning we didn't do well. (Supplier and Development Manager, BAE Systems)

But the BAE Systems users were delighted with the savings as well as the improved processes for recruiting:

> Recently in recruitment I had one of the businesses saying what an excellent job Xchanging did, helped them with some difficult recruitment that needed to be done. They really praised them. (Supplier and Development Manager, BAE Systems)

> From our point of the view, the recruitment process that they have employed has been successful. If I then look at some other achievements, I think the benefits that they are driving out, the signs are very good, so we have got a level of confidence that some of the benefits built into the original business model will be achieved. (Procurement Director, BAE Systems)

Operational method: Enactment models

Xchanging designed processes for contract enactment so stakeholders could easily make orders, receive goods or services, verify invoices, and make payments. Rather than a "one size fits all" model, Xchanging developed three enactment models: (1) transactional, (2) a mid-level, and (3) thick. These enactment models aim to minimize transaction costs by matching the most efficient process to the attributes of the category of spend. Each model is explained below.

1. **Transactional model.** For commodity types of indirect spend, such as stationery, Xchanging uses a transactional model in which the users place orders directly with suppliers from their desktop portal (see Figure 7.4). The supplier delivers goods and invoices directly to the users. The users pay the supplier and the supplier pays Xchanging a commission. This model was deemed the most efficient way to facilitate customer–supplier interactions and to distribute the gain shares.

Xchanging designed this model to avoid upsetting users in years to come. An alternative design would have been that the supplier invoice the user for the goods and Xchanging invoice the user for its share of savings. The financial results would be the same, but the users over time may question why they are paying Xchanging:

> You would irritate your customer, or risk irritating them by every month invoicing them for your share of the gain. So psychologically – and psychology plays a huge amount in what we do – if you were paying one hundred, far better for us to send you a new invoice for ninety than to have you pay eighty and then invoice you for ten. (CEO, XPS)

2. **Mid-level model.** For more complex types of indirect spend, such as car fleets, Xchanging uses a mid-level model (see Figure 7.5). In this model,

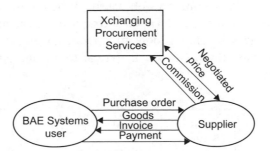

Figure 7.4 Transaction model for commodity products

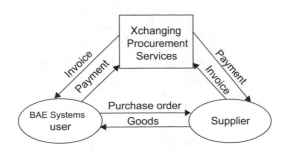

Figure 7.5 Mid-level model

the BAE Systems user again sends the order directly to the selected supplier, and the supplier delivers the goods directly to the user. Xchanging invoices the user for price of the goods plus their share of the savings. The supplier invoices Xchanging and Xchanging pays the supplier.

3. **Thick model.** For very complex services, such as contract labor, Xchanging designed the thick model. This model is used to aggregate buying power across all XPS customers (see Figure 7.6). In this model, BAE Systems user and external clients send the purchase order to Xchanging. Xchanging aggregates the orders and negotiates a favorable deal with suppliers. Xchanging invoices users and external customers for the price and both the customer's and Xchanging's share of savings. The customer receives a dividend at the end of the specified time period for its share of the savings.

Competency 3: Delivering sourcing excellence tools. Xchanging committed to invest over £7 million in new technology over the first five years. Technology is another one of Xchanging's major transformation capabilities. At XPS, the major technologies implemented the first year were the *Sourcing Workroom* to help procurement managers define, benchmark, research, analyze, negotiate, and manage categories of spend and the *Sourcing Portal* which enables users to order resources direct from their desktops.

XPS' Sourcing Workroom is a web-based online repository of methods and supply market knowledge. The Workroom links category experts to the market interfaces, baselining tools, supplier management tools, strategic sourcing plan, consortium engine, analytical tools, and supplier market

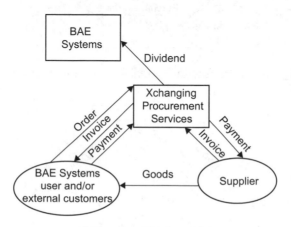

Figure 7.6 Thick model

data. The CEO describes how the Sourcing Workroom is used:

> We have a trading platform which allows us to operate the thin or the thick model depending on what we put into it and whether we just do the accounts payable or take the ordering requirements ... the software supports data capture, analysis and strategic thinking templates. There is hard data capture because otherwise it's quite a tedious task of actually going round and discovering these things, it takes time. And then it is the analysis of it and it's then the strategic thinking templates that say once you have got an analysis and unitization of it, you can then say how am I going to take this to the market. (CEO, XPS)

In addition to the Workroom, XPS launched their first version of sourcing portal on June 30, 2002. This enables users dispersed throughout BAE Systems to directly request resources from their desktop. For example, users now use the sourcing portal for recruiting. The Sourcing Portal is seen as a key enabler of scalability in that Xchanging can easily replicate the technology for its other customers:

> Instead of going into a new customer and having a number of business development meetings, we actually go in and say we will apply our technology so on every desk we will put the capability for you to order your contract labour under a portal called Xchanging Procurement Services, come back to us and you get the benefit of our behind the scenes aggregation. (CEO, XPS)

Competency 4: Increasing buying power. The two main ways to increase buying power are (1) to aggregate spend *within* a company and (2) to aggregate spend *across* companies. Xchanging has increased BAE Systems' buying power on both these dimensions. Concerning the first dimension, BAE Systems could have aggregated all the spend by themselves, but it would have taken a major effort to enforce centralized procurement, both politically and from a resource point of view. In contrast, the enterprise partnership model immediately created a centralized procurement function for indirect spend.

To ensure this increased buying power potential from consolidation, BAE Systems had to guarantee Xchanging exclusive procurement rights. But even though this is a contractual requirement, BAE Systems will never be in 100 percent compliance because no one can track users dispersed across 70 sites. However, XPS and BAE Systems senior executives realistically know that bullying the few offenders will alienate users:

> I am surprised in some of these areas how little leakage there is, given that we are so new. Now I would say that we know that we will never have 100 percent compliance and frankly probably if we try and strive for that we will just drive ourselves into the ground. ... All you do is alienate people. (Procurement Director, BAE Systems)

Concerning the ability to aggregate spend *across* companies, XPS has exceeded expectations by contracting with other external customers including, Heywood Williams, Lloyd's of London, Boots, United Biscuits, Novar, Carlson Wagonlit, Heywood Williams, AMS, Compass, and Kingfisher. In 2005, XPS controlled in excess of £3 billion in spend beyond BAE Systems. Clearly, BAE Systems could not or would not achieve such buying power on their own:

> So the real attraction for us with Xchanging was we could use the base that we, BAE, had established and the volume that we bought to actually go and get the third party revenue, because it was that third party revenue that demonstrated the great potential, by other customers that was of interest to us, because if we could make a success of this, clearly then the volume to this business would be much higher than BAE Systems could be alone, and if we could get a leverage ratio of three or four to one, then that would potentially give us a much better business opportunity that just driving around activity internally. (Procurement Director, BAE Systems)

Competency 5: Supplier relationships. The ability to attract and retain good supplier relationships is a capability required for indirect procurement transformation. After all, what good are the experts, methods, and tools if they cannot be leveraged to negotiate lower prices? The key here is to offer significant benefits to suppliers by offering larger volumes, long-term deals, lower supplier transaction costs, facilitation of user orders, and prompt supplier payment.

> Our model has to work both for clients for suppliers, otherwise why are they going to deal with us? (Category Director, XPS)

At the beginning of the venture, XPS managers were frustrated because they were not allowed to directly talk to BAE Systems suppliers. This impediment was eventually overcome as soon as the legal contracts were novated over to Xchanging. Once XPS had control of a category spend, they were able to effectively develop supplier relationships. Suppliers were very interested in working with Xchanging because of their exclusive procurement rights:

> That's very, very powerful for us as a launch pad because it means that when we talk to the car manufacturers or leasing companies or the contract labor, we are here for ten years so you get a better deal with them one way or another, they know we won't go away in a year. (CEO, XPS)

Offering suppliers long-term deals also fosters good relationships:

> And the ten year exclusive works for suppliers because they think, "well hang on a minute, if I want to deal with BAE and I have to deal with you but I know you have got a ten year deal, a ten year contract, so if I keep you on the side then I should be OK." So that's helped too. I mean, it's a threat and an opportunity for them. (Category Director, XPS)

In many instances, Xchanging really helped existing suppliers. For example, Xchanging discovered instances where suppliers were not being paid – to the tune of £12 million in one case. Xchanging analyzed the problem and discovered that the sheer size of BAE Systems was causing invoices to get lost in the decentralized organization. With the enterprise partnership, suppliers have one interface, easier user ordering through web-enabled portals, and timely and accurate payments.

Hertz claims that working through XPS has dramatically improved their efficiency. Prior to XPS, BAE employees booked car rentals using telephones and faxes. After XPS, employees book rental cars online through XPS's portal. Hertz executives report that XPS's online booking saves them up to ten dollars in processing costs per rental. Booking Service International, another supplier, claim that XPS's online booking increases their cost efficiencies by 30 percent.[9]

Competency 6: Governance. Many of the governance issues have been addressed in the context of the other competencies. Most important, we believe, is that the governance model of the enterprise partnership aligns incentives much more powerfully than a traditional outsourcing or consultancy model. In particular, XPS only generates a profit when they deliver the cost savings, thus they are highly motivated and accountable for results. To temper this highly aligned incentive for shared finances, the parties also included governance mechanisms to protect and even improve service levels. In particular, the joint Service Review Board has been an effective mechanism in this regard.

But we note that the enterprise partnership does not perfectly align incentives, as BAE Systems was motivated to reduce costs prior to transferring spend to XPS. This way, BAE Systems could reap benefits of the savings they could achieve on their own. XPS was subsequently handed a smaller piece of the pie:

> What we are finding, in fact, in a lot of the categories BAE Systems have taken a lot of the cost out. For example in stationary they have already taken twenty percent out before we have got to it, in contract labour, they had halved the margin that the contract labour suppliers were getting before we got to it. Recruitment they didn't but in a lot of the categories they had taken it out, so it is tough. (David Rich Jones, CEO, XPS)

From the customer perspective, the enterprise partnership offered the best of both worlds by extracting the easy savings themselves and passing the more difficult challenges over to the supplier. From the supplier perspective, gross deviations from their assumptions can truly hinder their ability to deliver their business plans. Clearly, the parties have to find fair ways to adapt to extreme changes in assumptions.

Conclusion

No matter what the level of current indirect procurement spend, managing spend is not optional. All senior level executives must create an enterprise spend management program to meet the needs of the organization while keeping costs low. We believe that real transformation of indirect spend requires politically difficult actions. While it is easy to prescribe consolidating spend across business units, for example, it is entirely a different matter to have enough muscle to implement it. This is why radical transformation must be initiated at top levels of an organization.

Ideal customer profile for procurement outsourcing. Our assessment is that enterprise partnership model is most suited for customers from large, global organizations with the following profile:

- Category spend is managed by multiple, decentralized budget holders, allowing the opportunity for significant savings from spend aggregation.

- The customer has a large back office spend of at least US$45 million per year in a few high volume categories, making the deal large enough to attract a competent external supplier.
- The customer's category procurement spend is such that further opportunities for significant savings and service improvement from better management are available.
- The customer's centralized procurement is not interested in indirect spend because they have more exciting challenges in core spend.
- The customer does not have the inclination or resources to corral other customers to create a stronger buying power on their own.
- The customer's organization would resist centralizing and standardizing themselves due to internal political resistance, unwillingness of senior management to make the required upfront investment, or lack of skills and experience of existing staff to make the transformation.

This profile of back office complexity, dispersion, and relative neglect can be seen as typical within companies which have grown to be large global corporations. *It arises because the customer organization simply and purposefully wants to focus on core parts of their business.* But in order for an enterprise partnership to work, the customer and supplier must be willing to truly act in the spirit and trust of a partnership. The BAE Systems/ Xchanging transition offers some powerful lessons for customers:

1. **The customer must be willing to aggressively communicate and disseminate the meaning of the partnership to all budget holders and users in the customer organization.** Large deals are negotiated by top management, but contracts are enacted in a large user community – potentially to all employees of the customer company. These decentralized users must understand the overall effects of the partnership or else they only see how a miniscule portion of the deal affects their budgets.

2. **The customer must be willing to help the partner traverse through the political and bureaucratic terrain of the customer organization.** As a corollary to the previous lesson, it is not just a matter of educating the user community, but actively managing the interface. The important thing was that once the parties recognized this lapse in communication and coordination, they devoted more people to manage the XPS/BAE Systems interfaces. These additional people helped to foster the relationship during the transition, but moved to XPS once the user community had fully adapted to the new way of sourcing.

3. **The customer must be willing to adapt flexibly to discoveries during due diligence.** Transitions are difficult. The main activities during the

transition included the immense legal work to novate existing supplier contracts and the baselining of current spend. The biggest testimony to the partnership was the way the parties adapted to the discovery that only £35 million was transferred in the seven contractual categories of spend. Both parties found a way to inject the partnership with a critical mass of spend by adding eight additional categories. A more distant customer–supplier relationship, such as a traditional fee-for-service deal, would not likely foster such adaptability.

4. **The customer and supplier align objectives with the enterprise partnership contract, but the parties must realize there is no such thing as an instant partnership.** Trust is not instantaneous, but evolves over time. We have consistently found in all of our research that the largest trust-building factor is operational delivery. Clearly, as XPS delivered the cost savings and improved service levels, the trust levels of the parties increased. Further evidence of the trust is found in both parties as BAE Systems transferred more indirect spend categories to the partnership.

> Time is a test for the marriage. If we continue to conform to each other we will have a good relationship. This will have to happen over a period of time. (CEO, XPS)[10]

Notes

1. Mazel, J. (ed.) (2004), "Outsourcing Portions of Procurement Now a Core Strategy," *Supplier Selection & Management Report*, July, Vol. 4, 7, pp. 4–6.
2. Davies, C. (2004), "The Pitfalls of Supplier Bashing," *Supply Chain Europe*, March, Vol. 13, 12, pp. 46–47.
3. Cohen, A. (2004), "Beating Outside Pressures," *Supply Management*, Vol. 9, 14, July 8, pp. 26–27.
4. Hanson, D. and Olson, E. (2005), "High Performance Via Procurement Outsourcing," *Electric Light and Power*, Jan/Feb, Vol. 83, 1, p. 18.
5. Stiffler, D. (2003), "Supply Chain Consulting: Users Want Tactical Project Expertise and Outsourcing," *AMR Research Outlook*, Friday, May 16.
6. Gochkova, A., An, A., Depenbrock, G., and Dickmann, F. (2003) "Business-to-Business Exchanges," IS 6800 Class Project, University of Missouri-St. Louis.
7. Aberdeen Group (2001) "E-Procurement: Finally Ready For Prime Time," Aberdeen Group, Research Report, Vol. 14, 2, pp. 1–12.

8. Indexing: Over time XPS will have to pay increasing prices for labor-intensive resources. BAE Systems has put some general indexes of allowable price increases each year, such as 3 percent on some types of contract labor.

9. Davies (2004), op. cit.

10. Davies (2004), op. cit.

CHAPTER 8

Managing knowledge in outsourcing: Cases in financial services

Leslie Willcocks, John Hindle, David Feeny, and Mary Lacity

Introduction

While outsourcing is currently one of the biggest business trends (and highest growth sectors),[1] it is surprising that its knowledge management implications have received so little attention. What actually happens to knowledge when clients outsource? Our research shows that most clients lack the means and experience to assign value to the knowledge they are transferring and receiving. Furthermore, most clients have no real understanding of how new knowledge can be created in outsourcing situations, let alone exploited. Nor are they inclined to assign that much importance to knowledge management because the outsourced activities are considered "non-core." But whatever the cause, managing knowledge when an organization outsources is a serious gap in practice. We address this gap by describing intellectual capital, and how it can be developed by harnessing social capital. We then apply these ideas to three outsourcing arrangements to show how intellectual, or knowledge, capital can either be a missed opportunity, or can be developed and leveraged to organizational advantage.

Understanding knowledge and intellectual capital

Most students and practitioners in knowledge management are familiar with the formulation adopted by Stewart[2] and others to describe the essential elements of intellectual capital:

- *Structural capital*, representing "the codified bodies of semi-permanent knowledge that can be transferred" and "the tools that augment the body of knowledge by bringing relevant data or expertise to people"
- *Human capital*, or "the capabilities of the individuals required to provide solutions to customers"
- *Customer capital*, or "the value of an organisation's relationships with the people with whom it does business – shared knowledge"

While there are specific investments and activities that can strengthen each of these elements, Stewart argues that creating intellectual capital is more complicated than simply hiring bright people or buying a KM (knowledge management) software program: "intellectual capital is not created from discrete wads of human, structural, and customer capital, but from the interplay among them." How, then, can organizations create the conditions, structures, and policies that encourage "interplay?" What specific actions can they take to maximize knowledge exchange and combination? We suggest there are intentional ways of creating a fourth kind of capital – social capital – which facilitates the development of trusted knowledge paths.

From a sociologist's perspective, *social capital is the value of the social network individuals belong to and their inclination to do things for each other because of that network.* Somewhat more simply, it is the value suggested by the motto from the US situation comedy Cheers, *"where everybody knows your name."* It is the value represented by trust, loyalty, and reciprocity within a community. Nahapiet and Goshal have examined the catalyst role of social capital in developing intellectual capital.[3] They identify three specific dimensions of social capital that facilitate the "interplay" that Stewart speaks of:

- the *structural dimension*, which involves the network ties and configuration and "appropriable" organization that facilitate access to people and resources, thus promoting the combining and exchange of intellectual capital
- the *cognitive dimension*, which involves the shared "cultural" context of the organization – the language, codes, and narratives that provide ways of knowing and create meaning
- the *relational dimension*, which involves trust and group identity (norms, obligations, identification), creating a sense of common motivation, purpose, and benefit.

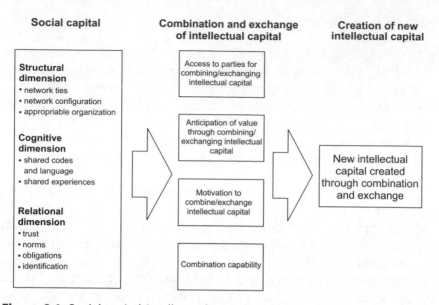

Figure 8.1 Social capital, intellectual capital, and organizational advantage
Source: Nahapiet *et al.*, 1998 (adapted).

Their research then maps the requirements for productive "interplay" – the ingredients for successful knowledge combination and exchange – against these three dimensions (see Figure 8.1). In practice, if we bring the work of Stewart and Nahapiet and Ghoshal together, this suggests a more fundamental framework for understanding types of intellectual capital and their roles in securing organizational advantage. In Figure 8.2 we show the four forms of intellectual capital. Here social capital forms the glue that brings together other forms of capital and facilitates their interplay. We also show four types of business activity ranging from relatively simple transactions, to providing more complex product solutions, offering whole business solutions, to integrated partnering activity. In practice different sectors will have a distinctive mix and balance amongst pursuing these activities. For example, back office check processing can be high on structural capital and low on human, customer, and social capital. In the London Insurance market we found social capital substituting for structural capital in highly complex negotiations over one-off insurance arrangements. The knowledge argument is that, while under certain conditions, the type of intellectual capital can substitute for each other, the further we move up the value chain to more complex activities then the more knowledge-intensive, and human-centerd work becomes, and the more an

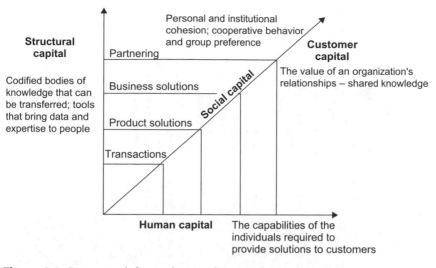

Figure 8.2 Framework for understanding intellectual capital
Source: Hindle and Willcocks from various sources.

organization needs to draw upon more and more of all four sources of intellectual capital and their interplay.

However, these conditions are difficult, if not impossible, to achieve in pure market transactions. Therefore Nahapiet and Goshal argue that organizations have a special advantage over markets in creating new intellectual capital. Moreover, they argue, the process of what Stewart calls "interplay" is recursive: social capital facilitates the development of new intellectual capital, which in turn strengthens social capital. So we face an apparent conundrum: if membership in the organization conveys such a powerful advantage in creating intellectual capital, how can outsourcing, which involves the externalization of huge swathes of people, systems, and institutional knowledge, possibly create greater advantage? Let us examine the knowledge implications of the options.

Knowledge issues in five sourcing approaches

In this section we review our research base of over 450 case studies of back office initiatives[4] covering five different options used in practice (see Figure 8.3). These were discussed also in Chapter 1 but what we are much more interested in here are the knowledge implications. All five make considerable assumptions about what will happen to knowledge – assumptions that are often belied by what happens in practice. Our main

	DIY	Management consultancy	Outsourcing IT operations	Fee-for-service BPO	Enterprise partnering
Examples	• Efficiency drives • Internal re-engineering • Technology solutions	• Analysis work • ERP • BPR • Major change initiatives	• Selective/total • Data Center/Networks • Desk-tops • Development	• Accounting • Human Resources • Call centers	– HR Transactions – Insurance settlement/claims – Procurement
Potential Benefits	– Gains accrued internally – Under in-house control/ownership – Easier to sustain gains made	– Infusion of external energy, skills – By-passing political resistance – Scale to handle work	– Hand over legacy – Reforms in-house systems development – Improves management practices – Cost savings	– Hand over non-core processes – Cost and efficiency gains – Access to skills and scale – Leverage off-shore advantages	– Cost and quality gains – Technology investment – Continuous improvement through (a) generic competencies (b) risk-reward – Securing new customers – Retaining/developing superior management and knowledge
Risks	– Inertia of Legacy • Systems • Processes • Culture – Political issues e.g. over service standardization – Lack of skills, focus, investment	– Skills not transferred – Change doesn't 'stick' – Cost escalation – Little ownership of outcomes	– Lack of innovation – Technology investment not sustained – Cost-service trade-offs – Cost of add-on services – Loss of know-how	– Motivation to invest/innovate? – One-off gains – Cost-service trade-offs – Add-on services? – Loss of know-how	

Figure 8.3 Back office performance improvement

focus below will be on outsourcing but let us look briefly at the "DIY" and "management consultancy" options.

Knowledge management: DIY and consultancy

On DIY, many case studies show that, in principle, this should be a strong option from a knowledge perspective.[5] In theory social capital should be strong, while structural, human, and customer capital may be more variable, depending on past knowledge management practices and size of organization. However, the initiative, if set up well, offers large scope for knowledge assimilation and creation, with a view to subsequent exploitation. In practice, especially with back office initiatives, we found legacy systems, processes and culture, and political issues often creating barriers, or a lower level ambition on improvement, and on knowledge creation. Moreover, back office improvement often did not attract prioritization on skills, sustained focus, and the necessary technical and financial investments.

As a result, many organizations we studied got attracted into the "management consultancy" route, looking for an infusion of human capital in the form of new skills, energy, and knowledge, and structural capital in the form of knowledge bases and best practices that could be offered as a result of the scales and specialist expertise consultancy firms. While in many cases this approach paid off, the risks often materializing were that skills and knowledge – structural and human capital – were not transferred to the client, change did not stick, and there was little internal learning or ownership of outcomes. Such initiatives lacked the glue or knowledge transfer vehicle of social capital. New knowledge was rarely created for and internalized by the client, who rarely leveraged subsequently the intellectual capital inherent in the initiative.

Knowledge and IT outsourcing

If we move to the third option, the promise from IT outsourcing is to leverage the supplier's superior management practices (structural capital) and skills (human capital), as well as plug into its scale economies arising from using a specialist IT service provider. But our own research into IT outsourcing would suggest that prospects have been disappointing for meaningful knowledge management and value creation from there.[6] Most clients report their frustration with endless cost–service debates, and significant loss of control over their IT destiny and knowledge base. Most suppliers find it difficult to deliver on their promises of innovation and value added, not least hampered by their lack of knowledge about the client's long-term business strategy.[7]

The outsourcing promise is regularly made of superior technical know-how, superior management practices, economies of scale and, increasingly, access to strategic and business advice enabling the client to refocus on strategic, core capability, and knowledge areas. More typically, our research has shown that the supplier offers technical know-how for routine solutions, with high performers in short supply. There is little influx of new technical/managerial talent, and disappointing access to the supplier's global capability and knowledge bases. Meanwhile the client does not think through thoroughly the issues of core capability and retained knowledge. As a result the client spends much time firefighting, and experiences little value-added or technical/business innovation. Over time, the client loses control over its IT or business process destiny as knowledge asymmetries develop in favor of the supplier.[8]

Like the "phantom limb sensation" that affects amputees, the loss of information and knowledge can be traumatic for both outsourcing parties unless specific and purposeful steps are undertaken to develop and sustain new information pathways and mechanisms. One route we have advocated is the retention of nine core capabilities as detailed in Chapter 3.[9] These ensure the elicitation and delivery of business requirements, the development of technical/business architecture, the managing of external supply, and the coordination and governance of these tasks. In practice, we have found all too many client organizations inadequately making these critical, initial, knowledge investments (see Chapter 3 for examples). In fact we found a more frequent pattern of focusing on contract monitoring and management, and of understaffing business facing and technology facing activities. In particular, the belief was that "technical architecture" and "making technology work" were prime outsourcing targets. Client organizations also routinely underestimate the degree of high performing "technical doing" capability they need to retain to deal with idiosyncratic business systems, non-routine problems, and the historically derived complexities of the technical infrastructure – all areas where suppliers do not play from a position of knowledge strength. Typically, in managing external suppliers, client organizations also under-invest initially in the knowledge areas of informed buying and supplier development. They also inadequately secure ways in which to build shared knowledge from relationships and interchanges back into the business – through relationship building and business systems thinking capabilities.

We find, as Chapter 3 demonstrates, that, in failing to make these knowledge investments, client organizations invariably run into a range of problems, which, together with a rising awareness of over-dependence on the supplier, leads to belated re-insourcing of these capabilities. One of the most obvious candidates we have seen here is the "technical doing" capability associated with applications development. The alternative is increasing problems as the client organization loses knowledge, control over its IT destiny, and the ability to leverage IT for business value. If these tendencies can be seen in the cases discussed in Chapter 3, then consider also Commonwealth Bank Australia.

IT outsourcing: Commonwealth Bank Australia (CBA)

In 1997 CBA signed a 10-year preferred supplier, sole source contract with EDS for improving the IT contribution to the business. The contract was worth about Au$ 700 million a year. The supplier provided knowledge capital in the form of technical expertise. Also new management processes were provided as well as business advisory and consulting skills. CBA also took a minority share (35%) interest in EDS Australia to bind client and supplier closer together and create mutual interest in pursuing a strategic relationship. From 1997–2001 CBA achieved its objectives in relation to IT cost reduction as a proportion of the bank's overall non-interest expense, while IT services were maintained largely to agreed service levels.

However, by 2000–01 CBA felt that knowledge and capability asymmetries had developed in favor of the supplier, and that the bank was losing control of its IT destiny. Nor did it always feel that it was getting the knowledge influx it required from the supplier, though it was not always in the best position to make such judgments. As a result, over the next 18 months, under its CIO Bob McKinnon, the IT function went about building up its internal capabilities, especially in the areas of technical architecture, service delivery, planning, contract monitoring, informed buying, and governance. In knowledge terms these were attempts to build the necessary structural, human, and customer capital (the customers being CBA business units) needed to leverage supplier and IT performance. Late into this process, the IT function also added business thinking and relationship building capabilities to align with business requirements and help business units identify and deliver on the potential business value of IT (see Chapter 3 for descriptions of these capabilities). Through all this the CIO emphasized the need to operate in a teaming manner both within the IT function, as well as in relationships with user staff in the business units. In this respect, this was creating social capital by which knowledge could be transferred between the parties, created, and exploited. By 2003 business units, central strategy group and the IT function were actively designing new governance mechanisms for planning for and exploiting IT. It can be seen here that a knowledge capital strategy has been put in place, but it largely treats the supplier as a bought resource, assuming little knowledge interchange, or mutual knowledge creation. By 2005, however, CBA had rebuilt its internal function from 32 to 126 people and had begun the process of redeveloping its sourcing strategy, given that the EDS contract terminated in 2006/07.

Knowledge in business process outsourcing: An IT replay?

But this approach to outsourcing restricts creation and leveraging of knowledge only to one specialist area – IT operations. Much bigger gains can arise if whole functions or processes that include IT are outsourced. This is the premise of the dramatic growth in business process outsourcing (BPO) from 2001. BPO suppliers come in many forms – as pure plays (e.g., Xchanging, Exult (acquired by Hewitt in 2003), specialist providers (e.g., in logistics Ryder, UPS; in customer care Convergys; in finance and accounting Core3), as IT outsourcers extending their range (e.g., EDS, CSC), consultants moving further into the market (e.g., Accenture), vertical specialists (e.g., McKesson in Healthcare) business service providers (e.g., Employease in HR) software providers (e.g., Genesys) or offshore providers (e.g., Wipro, Infosys). Most of these services are offered on a fee-for-service basis. The knowledge contract is to outsource non-core, (though often critical), largely back office commodities to suppliers with superior structural and human capital in the areas of business process and specific expertise. Some deals recognize the need also for closer partnering in order to get closer to the customer (to create and leverage customer capital to both parties' advantage, and also create and leverage social capital across client and service provider.

In practice, while BPO is often handled much like classic fee-for-service IT outsourcing, such deals lie much closer to the business and the knowledge implications are even greater, though, in our experience, just as neglected. One fear is that the emergent BPO market players and their clients will repeat many of the knowledge and capability mistakes made during the early 1990s IT outsourcing boom years. The potential dangers we notice here are loss of internal business process know-how, need to create requisite capability to manage the supplier, and the questions whether the supplier will be sufficiently motivated to invest knowledge and innovate in a sustained way, or if there will be only one-off gains, additional service charges, and interminable cost–service wrangles, basically over the price of knowledge and capability supplied. That said, these knowledge effects may well be disguised for a time by real cost and service improvements, simply because so many back office business processes inherited by suppliers are, in our experience, so inefficient. Let us look at the knowledge issues in one recent deal signed by Bank of America.

Business process outsourcing: Bank of America

In late 2000, Bank of America (BoA) outsourced its commodity human resource processes and services to Exult on a 10-year US$1.7 billion contract. Expected benefits included guaranteed cost savings (plus 10 percent on process, plus 40 percent for systems integration and HR self-service investment) and qualitative improvements such as speed of error rectification. Exult's job was to manage the HR back office to Six Sigma standards, and improve the shared HR service organization's performance and headcount by applying Exult's scale, expertise, and volume. Over 600 employees transferred to Exult, representing a considerable knowledge transfer. Exult took over the bank's service center in Charlotte, North Carolina in exchange for Exult stock worth US$50 million. The bank and Exult were also web portal partners, with bank employees using portal to handle HR issues, while the plan is for the bank to become the preferred provider of financial services and banking products to employees of other Exult clients. Another aspect of closer partnering is that the bank stood to gain a 3–10 percent share of revenues from third-party use of the HR service run by Exult for BoA.

Classically, as for IT, the client outsourced commodity activities to enable the IT to focus on core competencies in HR and the rest of the business. There was a large knowledge transfer of employees to Exult. Exult brought their superior knowledge and skills in the HR area, their process expertise, and their superior web-based technologies to reduce the need for the bank to make future technology and infrastructure investments. The promise was that their HR scale and specialization would reduce HR costs by over 10 percent per annum while driving innovation and improvements in HR service. By late 2003, the bank reported being very satisfied with progress on all its goals as a result of outsourcing.

The risks, however, do remain as for the earlier large-scale, mainly fee-for-service IT outsourcing deals recorded above. From a knowledge perspective, the bank could see an erosion of its ability to understand, have an informed dialogue with, and manage the supplier over HR activities and processes. Lack of in-house structural and human capital in this area could be risky, given that HR processes touch every employee. It is also not clear whether the partnering mechanisms go deep and far enough to create the social capital which will really prompt knowledge transfer, creation, and exploitation across the two organizations. Also will Exult staff, now Hewitt employees, continue to build customer capital and leverage this to make improvements in the customer's experience, or will improvements be restricted to what has been contracted for only? The client also becomes very reliant on the supplier's willingness over a long time period to provide its best managers, knowledge bases, and practices to the account. On the other hand, if, as we find in many other cases, the Bank of America HR services were not particularly efficient before they were outsourced, it may well be the case that cost reduction and improvements in HR service can be made for quite some time without much new knowledge being created or applied.

Enterprise partnering as a knowledge benchmark?

A fifth option we have researched is that of establishing a risk–reward partnership between the client and supplier (see Chapters 6 and 7). This can be applied to both IT and business process operations and improvement.

So far we have seen few of such deals in operation. The ones we have researched suggest the promise of significant cost and quality gains and technology investment as in the Exult–Bank of America deal. Additionally there is a stronger emphasis on continuous improvement through the application of generic rather than specialist competencies on the part of the supplier. Even more significant (and distinctive) is the risk–reward and joint ownership arrangement that lies at the center of such a deal, and the implications these features have for how knowledge is applied, created, and exploited. Let us look at one such deal from a more knowledge-focused perspective.

Enterprise partnering revisited: London Insurance Market outsourcing

We already looked at enterprise partnering in Chapters 6 and 7. Here, using a different case, we highlight the knowledge issues arising from the use of this governance mode. In May 2001 Lloyds of London/ Insurance Underwriters' Association (IUA) outsourced the back office policy and claims settlement systems for the London insurance markets to Xchanging. Learning from outsourcing history, the Xchanging approach introduces three key innovations. First, the Enterprise Partnership business model, which we met in Chapter 6. Xchanging Insurance Services (XIS) was set up to serve as the Lloyd's of London and IUA back office. Xchanging created a new service-providing organization that is jointly owned by client and supplier, who both share in its cost savings and profits. By assuming full responsibility for all transferred employees, moreover, Xchanging preserves transferred knowledge, service, and relationships, and establishes an organization capable of delivering service seamlessly on an "as-is" basis.

The Enterprise Partnership model entails multiple joint governance bodies: a Board of Directors, a Service Review Board, and a Technology Review Board. These governance mechanisms formally engage both client and supplier in a continuous process of joint planning and decision making, ensuring that business strategies are understood and decisions taken with full knowledge, in the best interests of the enterprise partnership rather than for the sole or lopsided benefit of one or the other party. A side benefit of this knowledge-sharing governance system is the creation of trust and mutual obligation, which reinforces the institutional relationship.

In Stewart's terms one can see clearly elements of "customer capital" being created here. But in the deeper context of Nahapiet and Goshal's social capital research, the Enterprise Partnership business model creates a robust *structural dimension*, with a formal governance network and a jointly held organization that can be "appropriated" to develop new intellectual capital and value. It also creates the necessary anticipation of value that can arise from joining Xchanging's transformational expertise with the domain-specific knowledge being transferred.

The second innovation is an Xcellence Competency model which defines seven knowledge-based capabilities used to transform the legacy back office into a profitable Enterprise Partnership: Service, People, Process, Technology, Environment, Sourcing, and Implementation (for details of the generic model see Chapter 6). Each competency is headed by a highly experienced Practice Director (an example of Stewart's "human capital"), who is responsible for establishing and maintaining the competency's explicit knowledge capital in the form of a detailed competency manual, representing, in Stewart's terms, "structural capital." Further, the Practice Director is responsible for establishing the competency in each Enterprise Partnership using mainly transferred staff. This requirement ultimately builds a community of practice at the Xchanging level across all the Enterprise Partnerships, thus promoting development and sharing of tacit knowledge and its conversion to explicit knowledge. These practice communities meet regularly, communicate online, and network with other practitioners inside and outside their organizations.

In the context of Nahapiet and Goshal's social capital model, the Xcellence competencies establish a shared *cognitive dimension*. They employ distinctive languages and "codes" that facilitate business transformation and knowledge exchange – the practice communities are rich environments for shared narratives. Further, the Xcellence platform facilitates access amongst practitioners, reinforces their expectation that they create value by sharing knowledge, and offers the ability to combine accumulated knowledge from across all the Enterprises.

The final key element of the Xchanging approach that creates significant social capital is its four-phased Implementation model: Preparation, Realignment, Streamlining, and Continuous Improvement (see Chapter 6 for more details). The purpose of the implementation model is to synchronize the significant changes that take place within the former employee population and the now-client community, and to establish and manage expectations between the partners.

This innovation contributes significantly to creating the *relational dimension* of social capital. Recognizing that staff will initially feel powerless and resentful in an outsourcing situation, and that it takes considerable time for them to re-orient themselves to new circumstances, Xchanging's implementation approach carefully stages business transformation activity to their readiness to accept and support it.

As mentioned earlier, all employees are transferred to the Enterprise Partnership on day one, and go through an intensive change program that lasts up to two years. Led by the People Competency, the process focuses on the Tuckman developmental cycle of Mourning, Forming, Storming, Norming, and Performing. The net result is the deliberate creation of a new culture – that of a dynamic, profitable business – to supplant the previous cost-centered mindset. The process is not without cost, both direct cost in creating time for employees to make the transition, and indirect cost in deferring gains until staff are fully prepared. But this effort to build group identity and trust, establish norms of behavior and performance, and instill a sense of mutual obligation yields enormous benefits in the exchange and combination of knowledge.

As at beginning of 2006 the Lloyds of London/IUA/XIS deal was well into its fifth year and was adjudged relatively successful by most participants. XIS was achieving substantial performance improvements and cost reductions for the back office of the London Insurance markets. Partly this was because it had so many major generic competencies to apply to the cause of continuous improvement. The parties were making good profits, not least because XIS was regularly securing additional clients, and in 2003 Xchanging also won an innovator of the year award for its work at Lloyds of London and for the IUA. At the same time some risks should be noted. Internal success does not guarantee competitiveness in the open market, nor additional external customers. Conflicts can arise between maximizing the enterprise partnership's profits, and minimizing the client's costs. The governance structure does rely on both sides investing the necessary effort and resources in long-term joint customer and supplier participation, decision making, and participation.

Conclusion: Competing on knowledge

Our judgment is that increasingly, under rising pressure to cut costs, compete, and deliver, both clients and suppliers need to become much more aware of the role of knowledge assimilation, creation, and application in achieving back office improvements. As such the focus will increasingly need to move to understanding in a more fine-grained way what knowledge needs to be retained, and how to guarantee a supplier will posses, create, and leverage the structural, human, and customer capital needed to deliver on ambitious outsourcing objectives and claims. The further development suggested by the Xchanging example, compared to the Commonwealth Bank and Bank of America cases, is the advantages in creating social capital as the glue that converts intellectual capital into transferred and applied knowledge for business improvement.

A knowledge-based perspective does reveal that if undertaking fee-for-service outsourcing, there are limits to what can be achieved. Our prescriptions for fee-for-service outsourcing deals have been arrived at through exhaustive research. The advice remains:

- write complete, detailed contracts;
- carry out due diligence ahead of signing the contract;
- retain core in-house capabilities;
- ensure that you and the supplier have a cultural fit;
- be sure the supplier has sector and domain knowledge and experience;
- don't outsource a "mess"; and
- write short-term (3–5 year) contracts because the circumstances and technologies will change fast.

Knowledge can be created and leveraged following this advice, but, we would contend, only to a limited extent. Both sides still bring to the party an unnecessarily constrained focus on knowledge.

But these prescriptions partly arise because knowledge assumptions and contracts between customer and supplier are often flawed, and because all too often this inhibits investment in requisite supplier and client knowledge capabilities. Changing the business, governance, and implementation models allows knowledge strategy a more central, leveraging role in outsourcing. Xchanging's innovations are interesting because they support development of intellectual and social capital essential to the sharing, creation, and exploitation of new knowledge. Instead of false signals and misdirected energy, the model actively incents and supports the creation and exploitation of new intellectual property.

At the same time, adopting something like an Xchanging enterprise partnership framework does require a new, different set of assumptions, for example,

- sign short, incomplete contracts for five years or more,
- carry out diligence after contract signing,
- let the supplier clean up your back office mess,
- create a clash of cultures if you want to see real back office improvement, and
- hire a supplier with generic rather than domain-specific competencies.

Given the history of outsourcing these modes of operating may well feel too counter-intuitive. Many may well see adopting these assumptions as too big a cultural step and too risky. At the same time, these changes in management practice on the part of both client and supplier may well be the only real way to release the knowledge potential inherent in the practice of IT and business process outsourcing. And in an ever commoditizing outsourcing market, with ever more demanding customers, it may well be that competing on knowledge becomes the new game in town.

Notes

1. See Chapters 1 and 2 for supporting statistics.
2. Stewart, T. (2001), *The Wealth Of Knowledge: Intellectual Capital and The Twenty-First Century Organization*, Nicholas Brealey, London.
3. Nahapiet, J. and Ghoshal, S. (1998), "Social Capital, Intellectual Capital and the Organizational Advantage," *Academy of Management Review*, Vol. 23, 2, pp. 242–266.
4. Represented in the following publications: Cullen, S. and Willcocks, L. (2003), *Intelligent IT Outsourcing: Eight Building Blocks To Success*, Butterworth, Oxford; Lacity, M. and Willcocks, L. (2001), *Global Information Technology Outsourcing: Search For Business Advantage*, Wiley, Chichester; Willcocks, L. and Currie, W. (1997), "Does Radical Reengineering Really Work?" in L. Willcocks, D. Feeny, and G. Islei, (eds), *Managing IT as a Strategic Resource*. McGraw Hill, Maidenhead; L. Willcocks. and Griffiths C . (1997), "Management and

Risk in Major IT Projects," in L. Willcocks, D. Feeny, and G. Islei (eds), *Managing IT as a Strategic Resource*, McGraw Hill, Maidenhead; Willcocks, L., Petherbridge, P., and Olson, N. (2002), *Making IT Count: Strategy, Delivery, Infrastructure*, Butterworth, Oxford.

5. See, for example, Willcocks and Griffiths (1997), op. cit.; Willcocks and Currie, (1997), op. cit.

6. Lacity and Willcocks (2001), op. cit.; Cullen and Willcocks (2003), op. cit.

7. Feeny, D., Willcocks, L., and Lacity, M. (2003), *Business Process Outsourcing: The Promise Of Enterprise Partnership*, Templeton Executive Briefing. Templeton College, Oxford.

8. Cullen and Willcocks (2003), op. cit.

9. Feeny, D. and Willcocks, L. (1998), "Core IS Capabilities For Exploiting Information Technology," *Sloan Management Review*, Vol. 39, 3, pp. 9–21.

CHAPTER 9

Offshoring IT work: 29 practices

Joseph Rottman and Mary Lacity

Introduction

Some management consulting firms claim clients can save 50 percent off total costs by offshoring work.[1] But in a widely cited research report,[2] IT consulting firm Gartner estimated a 50 percent failure rate for offshore outsourcing initiatives. Despite this dismal news, IT consulting firm Meta Group forecasted that the annual growth rate of offshore outsourcing will continue to grow at 20 percent reaching US$10 billion in 2005. How can executives manage risks while successfully exploiting the benefits available in remote locations such as India and China?

This chapter identifies the best, worst, and emerging practices for offshore sourcing, particularly for IT, and compares these practices with outsourcing to domestic suppliers. The practices were derived from interviews with 132 people, including customers, suppliers, and key intermediary consulting and legal firms with substantial offshore outsourcing practices (see Table 9.1). We asked participants to share their lessons on the following offshore challenges:

- How can organizations develop and implement a global sourcing portfolio?
- How can organizations mitigate risks?
- How can organizations effectively work with offshore suppliers?
- How can organizations ensure cost savings while protecting quality?

We uncovered twenty-nine proven practices for addressing offshore challenges and compared these with domestic outsourcing practices (see Table 9.2).

Six practices are equally important to domestic and offshore. Some practices for managing domestic outsourcing do indeed apply to offshore sourcing. In particular, six best practices are equally important for both domestic and offshore outsourcing: escalate the strategic importance of

Table 9.1 The research base: 132 people interviewed from 32 companies

Customer organization pseudonym	Number of participants interviewed	Supplier/Intermediary organization pseudonym	Number of participants interviewed
Aerospace	3	Large Indian supplier 1	16
Biotech	36	Large Indian supplier 2	11
Financial Services 1	4	Large global supplier 1	11
Financial Services 2	1	Large global supplier 2	7
Financial Services 3	1	Large global supplier 3	1
Financial Services 4	1	Small Indian supplier 1	3
Financial Services 5	1	Small Indian supplier 2	4
Financial Services 6	1	Intermediary consulting 1	1
Financial Services 7	1	Intermediary consulting 2	3
Financial Services 8	1	7 Legal firms	9
Insurance	1		
Manufacturer 1	3		
Manufacturer 2	3		
Retail	7		
Telecommunications	1		
Transportation	1		

Table 9.2 Proven offshore management practices

Sourcing challenge	Practices to overcome the challenge	Equally important for both domestic and offshore	More important for offshore	Unique to offshore
How can we develop and implement a global sourcing portfolio?	1. Escalate the strategic importance of new sourcing options after conquering the learning curve	X		
	2. Select an offshore sourcing destination based on business objectives			X
	3. Select an offshore sourcing model that balances costs and risks		X	
	4. Create a centralized program management office to consolidate management	X		
	5. Hire an intermediary consulting firm to serve as a broker and guide		X	
	6. Diversify the supplier portfolio to minimize risk and maximize competition	X		
How can we mitigate risks?	7. Use pilot projects to mitigate business risks	X		

Continued

Table 9.2 Continued

Sourcing challenge	Practices to overcome the challenge	Equally important for both domestic and offshore	More important for offshore	Unique to offshore
	8. Give customers a choice of sourcing location to mitigate business risks			X
	9. Hire a legal expert to mitigate legal risks		X	
	10. Unitize projects into segments to protect intellectual property		X	
	11. Openly communicate the sourcing strategy to all stakeholders to mitigate political risks		X	
	12. Use secure information links or redundant lines to mitigate infrastructure risks		X	
	13. Use fixed-priced contracts to mitigate workforce risks		X	
How can we effectively work with suppliers?	14. Design effective organizational interfaces		X	
	15. Elevate your own organization's CMM certification to close the process gap between you and your supplier			X
	16. Bring in a CMM expert with no domain expertise to flush out ambiguities in requirements			X
	17. Negotiate "Flexible CMM"			X
	18. Tactfully cross-examine, or replace, the supplier's employees to overcome cultural communication barriers		X	
	19. Require supplier to submit daily status reports			X
	20. Let the project team members meet face-to-face to foster camaraderie		X	
	21. Consider innovative techniques, such as real-time dashboards, to improve workflow verification, synchronization, and management		X	
	22. Manage bottlenecks to relieve the substantial time zone differences			X
How can we ensure cost savings while protecting quality?	23. Consider both transaction and production costs to realistically calculate overall savings		X	
	24. Size projects large enough to receive total cost savings		X	

Continued

Table 9.2 Continued

Sourcing challenge	Practices to overcome the challenge	Equally important for both domestic and offshore	More important for offshore	Unique to offshore
	25. Establish the ideal in-house/ onsite/offshore ratio only after the relationship has stabilized			X
	26. Give offshore suppliers domain specific training to protect quality and lower development costs		X	
	27. Overlap onshore presence to facilitate supplier-to-supplier knowledge transfer			X
	28. Develop meaningful career paths for subject matter experts, project managers, governance experts, and technical experts to help ensure quality	X		
	29. Create balanced scorecard metrics	X		

new sourcing options (like offshore) after conquering the learning curve, create a centralized program management office, diversify the supplier portfolio, use pilot projects to mitigate business risks, develop meaningful career paths for in-house staff, and create balanced scorecard metrics.

Fourteen practices apply to both, but are more important in offshoring. These fourteen are more important to offshore because the risks and transaction costs are greater, and the delivery teams are more remote and culturally diverse. Practices that become more important in offshoring include: select a sourcing model to balance costs and risks, openly communicate the sourcing strategy to minimize domestic worker backlash, use real-time dashboards to verify, synchronize, and manage work flows, and hire an intermediary consulting firm to serve as broker and guide to foreign countries, cultures, and suppliers.

Nine practices are unique to offshoring. One intriguing offshore practice is giving customers a choice between domestic and offshore sourcing. Program management offices can publish rates for sourcing locales and allow business unit managers to assess the trade-offs between lower costs and greater risks. Other practices unique to offshore sourcing address the rigid Capability Maturity Model (CMM) requirements used by offshore IT suppliers, bottlenecks caused by substantial time zone differences, and establishing the ideal in-house/on-site/offshore ratio.

Practices for developing and implementing a global sourcing portfolio

Most of our customer participants are veterans of domestic outsourcing. They ventured offshore primarily to seek lower costs on short-term projects, such as dealing with the impending Y2K problem in the late 1990s. Early adopters faced several challenges, and practices discussed in this section can help senior executives quickly ramp up to create a global sourcing portfolio.

Lesson 1. Escalate the strategic importance of offshore after conquering the learning curve

As discussed in Chapter 1, few organizations we studied approach offshore sourcing from a strategic perspective at the outset. Most organizations initially engage in offshore sourcing for tactical reasons, such as seeking lower labor rates for staff augmentation on specific projects. During this early adopter phase, offshore sourcing program management offices are often erected as separate entities from domestic outsourcing offices to test the concept. It is not until after pilot tests are complete, supplier relationships are established, and viability proven, that organizations seek more strategic uses of offshore resources.[3] This incremental approach may be wise because organizations may first need to gain experience with new sourcing options at an operational level before seeking more strategic objectives. Three examples will illustrate the evolutionary nature of strategic offshore exploitation.

Successful offshoring of strategic product development occurred only after several false starts. Manufacturer 1 is a Fortune 100 manufacturer of industrial equipment with over 75,000 employees spread across 20 countries. Their competitive advantage is based on innovative products with intelligent embedded software. Their business requires rapid response to changes in requirements from customers, environmental protection agencies, and other stakeholders. Manufacturer 1 has a lean headcount and could not always respond quickly to changes. Senior executives solved the problem with offshore outsourcing. They now engage three Indian suppliers to develop embedded software for their key products. The suppliers do it faster and better than the overworked in-house staff.

But success took years. The first forays offshore failed to produce any of the deliverables outlined in the statement of work. Projects were ultimately pulled back in-house and completed well behind schedule and over budget. Despite the failures, Manufacturer 1 saw promise in some aspects of the original offshore engagements. For example, as the offshore employees become more experienced with embedded software, the quality of code improved and turn-around time shortened. In addition, they learned how Manufacturer 1 interacted with business units to solicit requirements, schedules, and approvals. These improvements, coupled with the staff's increased confidence in their own abilities to manage remote employees, prompted Manufacturer 1 to try again. After implementing many of the practices discussed in this chapter, they finally succeeded in offshoring strategic product development. Today, Manufacturer 1 is an exemplar of how to create nimble networks of global IT workers.

Agility, which is enabled by offshore sourcing, is a key strategy for companies that operate in cyclical business environments. Through creative sourcing arrangements that permit speedy commitment to and divestiture of human capital, business agility allows organizations to enable flexible staffing while continuing to nurture business innovation.[4] Financial Services 1, for example, uses offshore resources primarily to enable strategic agility. For the past 15 years, it has developed captive centers in Manila and Mumbai, and various joint ventures and fee-for-service relationships with 14 Indian suppliers. During the refinancing boom, the company was able to beat competitors by quickly meeting the immense surge in demand for IT and business process services. As the refinancing boom burst, the company was able to immediately scale back resources.

Financing new product development, which is enabled by offshore, is a key strategy for small companies trying to compete with the deep pockets of larger players. A small US-based healthcare services organization wanted to develop a software product to provide information for quick response to biological terrorism. Because the organization is short on funds, it used an offshore supplier to finance the development of the new system. Under this agreement, the supplier owns the intellectual property rights but the customer organization will market the application. Both parties will share software-licensing revenues when the product goes to market.

Lesson 2. Select an offshore sourcing destination based on business objectives

Most of the literature suggests that senior executives select offshore destinations by focusing solely on relative country advantage in terms of costs and risks. Consulting firms are a major source of information for senior executives, providing comparative analyses of offshore destinations based on relative advantage of government support, labor pool characteristics, cultural compatibility, etc. We looked at several consulting firms' data, and by any set of criteria, they rank India as a top locale because of government support, tax free technology parks, existence of an excellent labor pool (by 2005 India had an IT workforce of over half a million and growing), low hourly wages (but rising), and high English proficiency. But several of our participants were concerned about India's rapid growth. Some participants believed India was becoming saturated (in particular, Bangalore), salaries would continue to rise and thus erode savings, and that the immense turnover among Indian firms, particularly for workers with 2–5 years experience, would remain high.

Because cost drivers can rapidly shift, a better way to select destinations is to use a broader set of business criteria by considering the company's strategic objectives and overall commitment to certain destinations. For example, one aerospace company selected Malaysia as their IT offshore destination because they hope to sell planes in that country. The Malaysian government required that some of the manufacturing be done in Malaysia, and the IT presence would certainly help to meet that requirement. Another hardware company selected China because they hope to sell computers there. Other participants selected offshore locations where they have existing manufacturing or R&D facilities. The existing facilities serve as a launch pad, with current employees serving as guides to the country, suppliers, and culture. One US customer chose Canada because it wanted suppliers in close physical proximity to their end customers for rapid deployment.

Lesson 3. Select an offshore sourcing model that balances costs and risks

Organizations need to access the various models for leveraging offshore resources. The four most prevalent offshore sourcing models are Captive, Joint Venture, Build-Operate-Transfer (BOT), and Fee-for-service (see Table 9.3).

With the captive model, the customer builds, owns, staffs, and operates its own offshore facility. Captive centers provide the greatest amount of control but at the price of the greatest amount of risk. For this reason, senior executives only select the captive model if they have a substantial commitment to a country in terms of a large volume of work over a long period of time. EDS, Accenture, Dell, Intel, and IBM Global Services all have captive centers. Accenture, for example, is rapidly increasing their offshore headcount. In 2005, Accenture had nearly 20,000 of its 115,000 employees

Table 9.3 Offshore sourcing models

	Captive	Joint venture	Build, operate, transfer	Fee-for-service
Description	Customer builds, owns, staffs, and operates offshore facility	Customer and supplier share ownership in offshore operations	Supplier owns, builds, staffs, and operates the facility on behalf of the customer; ownership and employees transfer to the customer after completion	Customer signs a contract for services in exchange for paying the supplier a fee
Set-up cost, financial risk, operational risk	Highest	High	Medium	Low
Ability to control	Highest	Depends on amount of ownership	Medium	Low
Example	Accenture	TRW–Satyam	PeopleSoft	Financial Services 3

offshore. By 2008, it has plans for up to 30,000 new employees in China, India, and the Philippines.

With joint ventures, the customer and supplier share ownership in the offshore facility. Customers, such as MasterCard, CSC, Perot Systems, and TRW chose this model over the captive model because they wanted to sacrifice some control in exchange for the supplier bearing most of the risk.

TRW, one of the world's largest automotive suppliers to Original Equipment Manufacturers, created a joint venture with India-based Satyam in 2000 called Satyam Manufacturing Technology. TRW owns 24 percent[5] in the venture. Satyam created offshore solution centers in Hyderabad (2001) and Chennai (2003) to initially provide ERP, CAD/CAM, supply chain management, and e-business applications to TRW before attracting additional external customers.[6] TRW benefited by avoiding the risks of a fully owned captive center while ensuring more control than a fee-for-service relationship.

With the build-operate-transfer model, the supplier owns, builds, staffs, and operates the facility on behalf of the customer. Upon completion, the supplier transfers ownership and staff to the customer. From the US perspective, this model helps by-pass legal obstacles because it is easier for a supplier to create a new facility in its own country than it is for a US organization to invest directly. Also, this model enables the US organization to benefit from the supplier's local expertise on construction, utilities, and employment.

PeopleSoft signed a three-year BOT deal with Covansys and Hexaware. The suppliers would build PeopleSoft's India Services Center and India Development Center and hire and train the employees. After three years, PeopleSoft will pay book value for the facilities and transfer the employees to PeopleSoft at no additional fee.

According to the CEO of an intermediary offshore consulting firm, however, none of his US customers actually went through with the transfer phase of the BOT model. By then, his customers were comfortable with the supplier and did not want to take over the facilities. One participant said the reason he backed out of the transfer was, "I don't know whom to call when the lights go out, and they do!"

With fee-for-service offshoring sourcing, the customer signs a contract with a service provider that has facilities and staff located offshore. The supplier owns the facilities, employs its own staff, and has its own infrastructure. Contracts are typically fixed-price or based on time and materials. By far, this is the most popular offshore outsourcing model because it poses the least amount of risk. US organizations can readily alter the volume of work sent offshore to match fluctuating demand onshore. For example, Financial Services 3 has been using Wipro since 2001 for staff augmentation (time and materials) and delivery of select projects (fixed-price). Although the Wipro relationship only represents about 5 percent of Financial Services 3's external IT spend, it has allowed Financial Services 3 to quickly ramp up or scale down without affecting the employment of in-house IT staff.

Many companies use multiple models. Some US organizations use multiple models, as illustrated by Financial Services 1. They use captive centers, joint ventures, and fee-for-service relationships with 14 Indian suppliers. Other organizations switch models after conquering the learning curve. One of our participants from Financial Services 6 began with a fee-for-service model. But as volume of work increased to 3000 full time equivalents, the customer is considering a move to a captive center. According to the Vice President of Technologies at Financial Services 6, "Once I have a very good feeling about how the Indian market is progressing, I plan to move to a captive center and recoup the margin my vendor is currently gaining."

Lesson 4. Create a centralized offshore program management office to consolidate management

Program Management Offices (PMOs) set up preferred supplier relationships, negotiate contracts, assess overall performance, define best practices, and disseminate learning. This best practice is not unique to offshore sourcing. The issue here is whether senior executives should create a separate program management office for offshore or whether to integrate offshore into an existing PMO. Participants suggest that senior executives should create a separate office if the offshore initiative represents a significant departure from domestic outsourcing practices or they intend to create a captive center or joint partnership that will require dedicated management. Senior executives should create an integrated PMO if they want business requirements to drive the supplier selection and if they want the onshore and offshore suppliers to aggressively compete. *Retail, a Fortune 100 company, used competition managed by the integrated PMO to cut the domestic supplier rates by 10 to 50 percent.* When Retail decided to integrate their offshore PMO into their existing vendor management system, the results were immediate and dramatic. Prior to exploring offshore vendors as a solution to Retail's considerable Y2K issues, they were actively engaged with 35 domestic contractors. The addition of offshore providers to the supplier portfolio caused the domestic providers to lower their costs:

> We were paying about $100 for commodity type coding (with domestic suppliers). The domestic suppliers saw the writing on the wall. We put out a bid to the approved list of domestic contractors and the current director of the PMO made it very clear that we were not going to pay those kind of prices anymore. Our domestic prices dropped from about $100 per hour to $80 and some of the rates even dropped into the $50 range for some services. (Director of Contract Management, Retail)

This integration also allowed a variety of vendors to compete head to head on capabilities and project schedule in addition to cost. This allowed Retail to compare the various value propositions from the domestic contractors with the offshore contractors and expand their understanding of the offshore market.

Lesson 5. Hire an intermediary consulting firm to serve as offshore guide to the country, suppliers, and culture

The intermediary consulting market is certainly growing fast, with players such as NeoIT, SourceQuest, Soft Access, Cincom, TPI, and Providio Technology Group. Some experts estimated that by 2005, 64 percent of offshore contracts were brokered by intermediaries.[7] One of our biotechnology companies certainly found value in hiring an intermediary: "I think it absolutely engaged us more quickly with respect to them informing the offshore vendors of our situation and setting up the arrangements. We would have just had to spend a lot more of our own time with all of that. So I think it streamlined the initial process" (Global Leadership Team member).

The intermediary consulting firms are also moving up the value chain by offering offshore project management training to US customers, training joint teams on cultural compatibility, creating transition plans, and developing project metrics.

Lesson 6. Diversify the supplier portfolio to minimize risk and maximize competition

Concerning offshore suppliers, there are many choices. Some senior executives move offshore via one of their domestic suppliers such as EDS, IBM, and Accenture. These established suppliers manage the offshore resources so the customer doesn't have to navigate through legal issues. Other customers, such as Financial Services 3, prefer to select Tier 1 offshore suppliers such as Wipro because of their maturity and stability. Other customers look for smaller niche suppliers with domain expertise. Still others select suppliers like Globalign that help customers find and engage offshore resources via large staff augmentation firms like Manpower.

The questions here are: which suppliers and how many suppliers? In Chapter 4, we covered the topic of *which suppliers* with the 12 supplier capabilities model. This model is particularly useful for customers if they have little familiarity with offshore supplier options. The model is robust enough to compare the strengths and weaknesses of large domestic suppliers, Tier 1 offshore suppliers, and offshore boutique suppliers.

Concerning the *number of suppliers*, most customers found that at least two offshore suppliers were needed to motivate continued supplier performance. In contrast, reliance on a single supplier presents significant operational and strategic risks including loss of market pressure on rates and a high concentration of intellectual property in one supplier. While maintaining engagements with multiple suppliers does entail additional transaction costs and management overhead, the use of multiple suppliers successfully mitigates many risks associated with outsourcing.[8]

Manufacturer 1 uses multi-sourcing to mitigate some of the risks associated with offshore outsourcing. It has active engagements with two large Indian firms and one small, boutique firm that specializes in embedded software development. The three suppliers compete for additional work:

> We don't want to manage a whole bunch of vendors. However we need the market pressure to make sure we are getting good prices. By letting the two large vendors and the small one bid on projects, and having the preferred list, we let them [the vendors] know that we are interested in enlarging the engagement but we are also watchful of the costs. (Director of Software Center of Excellence)

Retail successfully used one large Indian supplier for years, yet recently added three other suppliers. According to the Vice President and Director of Corporate Systems:

> Don't get me wrong. I've been extremely happy with [the large Indian supplier]. Every project they have done has been basically on time and on budget and their quality is good. I just think we need to use competition to keep the vendors honest and keep rates competitive.

Practices to mitigate offshore risks

All CIOs are aware of the risks associated with offshore sourcing including business, legal, political, infrastructure, workforce, social, and logistical risks (see Table 9.4). We asked participants to provide specific examples of successful risk mitigation practices.[9] They identified common, but important, best practices such as using pilot projects, hiring legal experts, and openly communicating the offshore initiative to assuage fear. Some identified more unique and intriguing practices, such as giving the customer a choice.

Lesson 7. Use pilot projects to mitigate business risks

Business risks such as poor quality, no cost savings, or late deliverables can stem from poor supplier selection, sending the wrong types of activities offshore, or the customer's inability to manage the supplier relationship. To help mitigate these risks, customers should consider a comprehensive pilot program to test both customer and supplier capabilities at managing offshore engagements. In addition, false starts, mistakes, and other negative occurrences can serve as valuable learning experiences to gradually build these capabilities.

Biotech brought the concept of piloting to reduce risk to a new level. Biotech chose 17 pilot projects that were mostly small in size, required

Table 9.4 Offshore outsourcing risks

Risk category	Sample risks
Business	No overall cost savings Poor quality Late deliverables
Legal	Inefficient or ineffective judicial system at offshore locale Intellectual property rights infringement Export restrictions Inflexible labor laws Difficulty obtaining visas Changes in tax laws could significantly erode savings Inflexible contracts Breech in security or privacy

Political	Backlash from internal IT staff
	Perceived as unpatriotic
	Politicians threaten to tax US
	  companies that source offshore
	Political instability within offshore country
	Political instability between United States
	  and offshore country

Workforce	Supplier employee turnover Supplier employee burnout Inexperienced supplier employees Poor communication skills of supplier employees
Social	Cultural differences Holiday and religious calendar differences
Logistical	Time zone challenges Managing remote teams Coordinating travel

frequent delivery of milestones, and gave pieces of the same project to two suppliers. For example, before Biotech decided to commit to one supplier for a Peoplesoft to SAP conversion, they gave two large Indian suppliers small pieces of the conversion. Biotech experienced much better project leadership from one of the suppliers in terms of on-site coordination, project status reporting, technical fit with Biotech, and superior daily communications. Biotech selected this supplier to complete the entire conversion. Three months later, when Biotech went live with SAP, the Indian supplier was granted an ongoing maintenance contract for seven full time equivalent employees (FTEs).

Pilot projects must be large enough to extract learning and metrics, but small enough to minimize risk. But experts do not agree on the ideal size. According to a Gartner Group Senior Researcher, an ideal pilot size is ten to fifteen people for six months. According to the CEO of an intermediary consulting firm, pilot projects should be sized at two man-years, representing a project cost between US$50,000 and US$100,000. According to Biotech, the ideal project size is four full time equivalents for four months.

Lesson 8. Give customers a choice of sourcing location to mitigate business risks

When a customer calls E-Loan, she is given a choice to process a loan within one day using an Indian-based supplier or to process the loan within two days using a US-based supplier. Such choice allows the customer to determine the priority between speed and location.

The CIO of Financial Services 4 allows strategic business units a choice for application development. The strategic business units (SBUs) can source IT from three preferred offshore suppliers managed through the offshore management program office or from domestic suppliers through the domestic office. Rates are lower with the offshore suppliers, but risks are lower with the domestic suppliers. The CIO believes the business unit managers should be the ones assessing the trade-offs.

Lesson 9. Hire a legal expert to mitigate legal risks

Hiring a legal expert for domestic outsourcing has been a standard best practice for 15 years. Many legal firms specialize in outsourcing, such as Shaw Pittman and Milbank Tweed. The need for legal expertise with offshore sourcing is even more pronounced because customers must abide by different legal systems and more regulatory requirements.

In conjunction with our research, we have spoken with nine different lawyers specializing in offshore sourcing. Lawyers help customers with tax implications, protection of intellectual property, business continuity, regulatory compliance, visa formalities, dispute resolution, and governing law. Concerning dispute resolution, all the participants focused on the goal of reducing the risks of conflicts that could lead to litigation, and for good reason. Litigation in the Indian court system is frequently a 15-year process. Also, Indian courts do not enforce legal judgments or awards made in the United States. In contrast, India will enforce arbitration, so that has become the standard clause for resolving customer/supplier disputes. Concerning tax implications, one participant said he helped a customer set up operations in Mauritius because it is a tax free zone. He also determined the amount of ownership in a joint venture required for favorable taxation and negotiated how parties would bear the costs of any tax law changes.

Concerning the protection of intellectual property (IP) rights, legal experts help by writing further assurance clauses or by establishing a chain of title from employees to the supplier to the customer.

Lesson 10. Unitize projects into segments to protect intellectual property

By 2005, several reports of sensitive data being stolen or purchased from Indian BPO suppliers had caused increased concern about the security of offshore data. In addition to legal preventions mentioned in the previous lesson, there are a number of practices customers and suppliers use to protect IP. Biotech, for example, required the offshore supplier to use Biotech's secure R&D facilities in Bangalore for sensitive data access and updates.[10] Many Indian suppliers create special security areas, which require special badges and a work-related need to gain access. Suppliers also create "clean desk" policies, which control what documents or screens can be viewed. While these practices are quite common, Manufacturer 1 had a unique strategy for protecting IP.

Managers from Manufacturer 1 are very concerned about protection of IP because they outsource the development of strategic embedded software products. To mitigate this risk, they disperse work between three suppliers (two large and one boutique) to effectively distribute the intellectual property. They view their IP as a puzzle. By distributing small pieces among three suppliers, no one supplier can assemble the puzzle on their own. According to the manager of engineering:

> We keep a very tight rein on where our IP (intellectual property) is and who has it. We never let any one development team or any one vendor see too much at one time. We feel it would be impossible for our IP to be lost through offshore sourcing.

Utilizing multiple suppliers also helps Manufacturer 1 to limit the risk of a dependence on one supplier or losing the advantages of a competitive environment (lesson 6).

Lesson 11. Openly communicate the sourcing strategy to all stakeholders to mitigate political risks[11]

At Financial Services 1, senior management viewed offshore sourcing as a potential way to decrease the immense application backlog caused by the refinancing boom. But senior management chose to keep the pilot project "low key rather than panic the IT staff while we were simply testing the waters." One day, the domestic IT staff showed up for work to find 11 people from India working in cubicles. The domestic IT staff began to panic and question the future of their careers. The Indian workers were isolated and treated with suspicion, if not contempt. The IT staff found frequent reasons for complaining about the offshore sourcing projects. Eventually, the CTO held a town meeting and told the staff that there would be no layoffs caused by offshore sourcing. However, he would replace fewer in-house IT staff lost through natural attrition.

In contrast, Biotech was very open about the offshore pilots and told the internal IT staff that offshore sourcing was about "doing more with a flat budget" and that no internal IT workers would be fired as a result of offshore sourcing. Even with open communications, there was some backlash. When dealing with the internal IT staff, a Biotech team leader noted that it is important to separate the emotional issues from the real issues:

> Different people perceive offshore outsourcing in different ways. And I guarantee, we have the full spectrum. We were aware of that and wanted to be sure that it did not impact our workforce in a negative way. So we spent a great deal of time to keep the communications as transparent as possible without trying to needlessly scare people. So it's a tricky balance. I understand that there are some companies that have approached this and they've said we're just going to replace everybody this way. And they tell all of their people that and then they say, now help us make it happen. It's a really bad way to do things. (Global Leadership Team member)

Lesson 12. Use secure information links or redundant lines to mitigate infrastructure risks

Early articles on offshore sourcing focused on poor infrastructure quality in low cost countries as a major risk factor. Our participants reported only minor problems – mostly with teleconferencing capabilities – because in India, at least, the infrastructure has improved. First, many clients – such as Financial Services 3 – use secure communications links between the customer and offshore supplier to enable easy and secure access. Second, many US customers opt for redundant lines so that downtime is not an issue. Third, the Indian government has replaced the telecommunications monopoly with competition. According to the former President of MCI, India is in the process of laying fiber optic cables in 100,000 Indian buildings – as compared to 30,000 building wired in the United States. All of these initiatives will serve to increase telecommunications service quality and reduce costs.

The more common problem US customers experienced was mobilizing in-house resources to create the infrastructure, such as setting up a VPN, cubicles, computers, access cards, logonIDs, and access to systems. There was some level of managerial disconnect between the US project managers and their systems administrators. In one company, offshore workers who arrived in the United States could not begin work for two weeks while the US project manager scrambled to establish the infrastructure. In best practice organizations, Program Management Offices bridge the gap by anticipating infrastructure needs.

Lesson 13. Use fixed-price contracts, when possible, to mitigate workforce risks

Several participants complained that some of the suppliers' employees were inexperienced, overworked, and frequently turned over. As one Biotech participant noted, "CMM certification is no substitute for experience." The customer is most affected by workforce risks when using a time and materials contract. Because the customer is billed hourly, the customer subsidizes a new supplier employee's learning curve. Also, supplier employees who are unproductive take more hours to complete tasks, again reflected in the customer's bill. Some customers try to mitigate this risk by demanding to see resumes of supplier employees or by setting minimum years of experience. These practices place the customer in the business of managing the supplier's resources, which can increase transaction costs and create animosity between customer and supplier. A better practice is to incent the supplier by using a fixed-price contract with clearly defined deliverables. The supplier can best decide how to staff the project to meet their contractual obligations while maximizing their own profit margin. The supplier is incented to put their most productive people on the project to increase their margin, or the supplier may make a strategic decision to finance their own employees' learning curves.

The practices to mitigate social and logistical risks are covered in the following section.

Practices to work effectively with offshore suppliers

Managing remote teams with project members from different countries, cultures, time zones, and who speak different languages is one of the most difficult challenges of offshore sourcing. Fortunately, there are many practices that can help customers work effectively with offshore suppliers.[12]

Lesson 14. Design effective organizational interfaces

Our research has uncovered three models of organizational interfaces, each with its own set of benefits and costs. The funnel design, shown in Figure 9.1, is used by both Retail and Manufacturer 1 and provides the greatest constriction of the communication pathways between the customer and their supplier. Since communication from local business units and technical staff is funneled through the project managers and then to the on-site engagement manager, this model places a high degree of importance on the vendor's selection for an on-site engagement manager. This reliance on a specific individual does pose risk to both the parties. Retail, for example, experienced one major failure with a large Indian firm because the engagement manager originally chosen to lead the

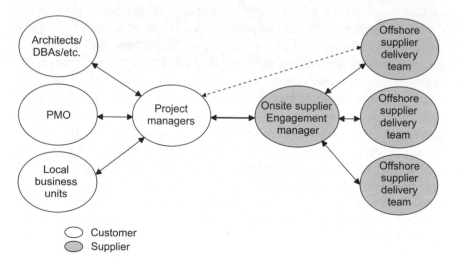

Figure 9.1 The funnel design

engagement did not possess the skills or experience to work with a Fortune 100 company. Once the shortcomings were brought to the attention of the vendor, action was quickly taken and a new, more senior engagement manager was put in place. However, time and confidence in the vendor were lost. Despite the risks associated with this model, the benefits include better control over the engagement, and a single point of contact, which will help to mitigate the cultural, time zone and communication risks. This model also requires the engagement to be large enough to warrant a dedicated on-site employee from the vendor.

The network design (shown in Figure 9.2) offers much greater pathways of communication between the vendor and the supplier. The network design, used by Biotech, shows communication taking place between all stakeholders at both the vendor and the supplier. Particularly interesting is the direct link between local business units and the supplier. This linkage offered mixed results for Biotech. One project that allowed local business units to communicate directly with the supplier to define requirements was successful. The local business unit in this case was very low on the priority list of the internal IT staff and felt neglected. Once connected with the offshore delivery team, their needs were assessed, requirements gathered and the project proceeded with a greater focus on the user. This project came in on time and under budget and with very high customer satisfaction numbers for the offshore vendor.

One project nearly failed due to this linkage. The post mortem showed that when the local business unit (whose needs are often boundless) was

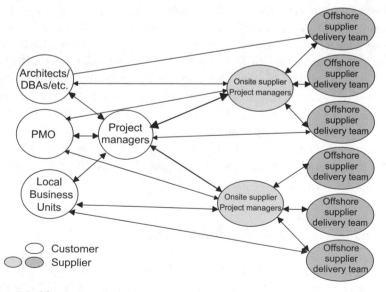

Figure 9.2 The network design

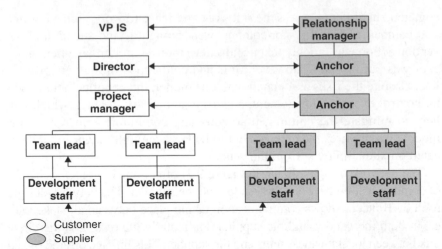

Figure 9.3 The mirror design

Source: Kaiser and Hawk (2004).

allowed to communicate directly with the supplier (whose promises of delivery are often boundless), scope, feature, and budget creep proceeded unchecked. While the project was completed, it was constantly delayed and finished well over budget.

The third model, which we call the mirror design, was actually studied and documented by Kaiser and Hawk[13] (see Figure 9.3). They reported on an eight-year relationship between a US financial insurance company and an India-based supplier that evolved from outsourcing to *co-sourcing*. Co-sourcing describes a close vendor/customer relationship in which the vendor augments or even replaces the customer's IT competencies. The supplier even serves as team lead for some types of work. To effectively manage the supplier's increased responsibility, the two partners realized they needed multiple levels of formalized communication. They designed the Dual Project Management Hierarchy, or the mirror design. This model has a significant onshore supplier presence, including the supplier's systems analysts on the development staff. This increases costs compared to the previous two models, but is warranted by the higher value work provided by the vendor.

Lessons 15–17: Addressing CMM challenges

These lessons address the process gap between US customers and their offshore IT suppliers. Every participant brought up the need to coordinate work processes, particularly with suppliers who are committed to the Software Engineering Institute's Capability Maturity Model. While Indian suppliers were all certified at CMM level 4 or 5, the US customers were usually lower. At higher levels of certification, an immense amount of documentation is required. US project managers had never before been through such a rigorous process to define requirements.

At Biotech, for example, requirements definition is an informal process when done onshore. Project managers speak frequently with users who are usually located on campus headquarters. The user feedback cycle is quick. In contrast, project managers working on the offshore pilots had to engage in many formal and planned communications with suppliers and users to create the required documents. One Biotech Global Team Member said, "the overhead costs of documenting some of the projects exceeded the value of the deliverables."

So what can be done to more effectively coordinate work with the supplier's CMM processes? The following practices were used by participants.

Lesson 15. Elevate your own organization's CMM certification to close the process gap between you and your supplier. Participants suggested that the best way to extract value from the supplier's CMM processes is to become CMM certified yourself:

> A real problem we had was our CMM level 1.5 guys talking to the vendor's level 5 guys. So together, we have worked out a plan with our vendor to help bring our CMM levels up. When we do, it will be a benefit to both of us; our specifications will be better and so they can use them more efficiently. (Director of Application Development, U.S. Transportation Company)

The outstanding issue is the level of certification required to effectively work with suppliers. The Vice President at Financial Services 4 believes that customers only need to approach level 2 to extract value. The Officer of IT Services at Financial Services 3 believes customer organizations need at least a level 3. Still other customer organizations believe higher certification levels (at least CMM 4) are required to interact with suppliers.[14]

Lesson 16. Bring in a CMM expert with no domain expertise to flush out ambiguities in requirements. US customers often complain that the requirements process is long and requires much expensive iteration. This is usually because the US customer doesn't understand how the supplier will interpret the requirements. Some US customers, for example, were surprised that supplier team members did not understand the concept of a mortgage. One US customer was surprised that the suppliers did not allow female name fields in the software to be altered unless recently married (as is the rule in India). In another example, the Indian supplier left-justified numeric data fields, causing the frustrated PMO director to lament: "Is this how ridiculously detailed my requirements are supposed to be?" To reduce the cycles during the requirements definition stage caused by misinterpretations, one Indian supplier sought a unique solution. He brings in a CMM level 5 expert to the client site who purposefully has no domain knowledge. This enables him to identify ambiguities in the requirements documents that the offshore delivery team will likely have, thus reducing the number of iterations.

Lesson 17. Negotiate "flexible CMM." The project manager at Financial Services 1 noted, "You ask for one button to be moved and the supplier has to first do a twenty page impact analysis – we are paying for all this documentation we don't need." He is negotiating for exactly which documents Financial Services 1 will and will not pay. This will enable him to only use the CMM processes he perceives to add significant value. While this practice is unique, a customized interface with each customer could serve to increase the supplier's costs, which may eventually result in higher prices.

Some Indian suppliers are accepting, rather than fighting this practice by actively marketing the idea of "flexible CMM." The managing director of a tier 2 Indian supplier recognized the frustration and reluctance of US customers to wade through the necessary steps for the supplier to maintain CMM certification. He says:

> My clients are telling me, "You do what you have to do to pass your audits, but I can't afford all of this documentation!" So we have developed a flexible CMM model which maintains the processes necessary for high quality but keeps the customer facing documentation and overhead to a minimum. Our customers have reacted favourably and our internal processes are still CMM 5.

Lesson 18. Tactfully cross-examine, or even replace, the supplier's employees to overcome cultural communication barriers[15]

We heard from many participants that Indian employees would not challenge the customer even if they perceived the customer was making a mistake. Indian employees will not readily deliver bad news, and will not express incomprehension. One frustrated participant said, "The place could be on fire and they would say, 'Oh it's great, a little warm, but it is great!' "

While being anxious to satisfy a customer is certainly a sought after supplier quality, it can actually be detrimental to effective communication. One of Biotech's Global Leadership Team members offered the following anecdote:

> You can sometimes be talking with someone and across the table they'll be nodding their head as if they understand and agree with everything you're saying. You find out later that they didn't understand what you were talking about. That's one of the interesting things to learn. Apparently, the culture does not challenge, so there is a "customer is always right" sort of a feel to it. So you have to learn, when you're in the dialog, to ask the questions that ensure that understanding is happening.

One American who works for a major offshore supplier says he learned to cross-examine his Indian counterparts to ensure they tell him bad news. Whereas in America he asks, "How is the project going?" in India he asks much more pointed questions, to the point where he worries about being rude. Another participant solved the issue by complaining to the supplier's senior management that the supplier's project manager was evasive about the project status. The supplier replaced that individual with a woman who was much more forthcoming.

The next lesson is another strategy to address this issue.

Lesson 19. Require the supplier to submit daily status reports

At a financial services company, for example, the customer was getting increasingly frustrated with the supplier's inability to flag problems or report delays in the weekly conference calls. The project manager for the bank designed a status report that would only take the offshore team members a few minutes each day to complete. At first, the supplier employees agreed, but she could not get them to comply. After several iterations with the supplier's management team, she discovered the supplier's delivery team did not understand how to fill in the report and were afraid to ask her. Once the instructions were clear, the delivery team members accurately completed the daily status reports, which now serve as the major tool to identify and solve problems. Manufacturer 2 had almost an identical story – supplier team members would not verbally report bad news in weekly conference calls, but would report items on a daily online status report. It is this level of micro-management that sometimes serves to frustrate US customers. But at the same time, it was the only tool these two customers found to overcome cultural communication barriers.

Lesson 20. Let the project team members meet face-to-face

One project manager at Financial Services 1 said he regretted never being allowed to visit India. He felt he would have been a much more effective project manager if he could have met the people face-to-face to get a better understanding of their work practices. The need for the customer's project manager to visit the supplier site is clearly emerging as a best, albeit expensive, practice to get past cultural communication barriers. It is much easier to switch to lower cost media such as teleconferences and email after meeting people face-to-face. Biotech bore the cost of the team members meeting face-to-face: "Once you get good at specking out what you need face-to-face, then an awful lot of the work happens by e-mail and it's just follow up questions and lots of that happens by e-mail" (Global Leadership Team member).

While this lesson carries considerable expense (a round trip coach ticket from the United States to Bangalore costs approximately US$2000 and a business class ticket is US$6500), the benefits are clear and immediate. After his first trip to see the vendor's offshore delivery team, the manager of Manufacturer 1's Software Center of Excellence reported:

> I can't believe I waited two years to meet the people I have been only emailing and seeing in video conferences! What a difference this trip has made. Now I know my team. I should have done this at the very beginning. I now have faces and more importantly personalities to go with names and titles. This trip was worth every penny.

Lesson 21. Consider innovative techniques, such as real-time dashboards, to improve workflow, synchronization, and management

Project managers noted difficulties with transferring work, keeping track of programming and database versions, and when and how to verify supplier work. At Biotech, most pilot projects required transfer of work every two weeks. At Financial Services 1, the customer takes possession of programming code every 15 days, but needs to check the database architecture daily. Sometimes there are discrepancies in the database schemas.

One possible solution is a real-time dashboard. Dashboards are emerging tools that allow the customer to glimpse at the supplier's work in real-time. Although only one of our participants (Manufacturer 1) has implemented a dashboard, they all saw a need for better workflow management. This dashboard allows for real-time governance of the engagement, with all projects color-coded based on current status.

Lesson 22. Manage bottlenecks to relieve the substantial time zone differences

Time zone differences are often marketed as a bonus of offshore sourcing because operations can occur around the clock. While that may be true of call centers, time zone differences do not typically facilitate IT development projects. For concurrent tasks, like telephone conferences, the US customers have to stay at work very late or the supplier has to get up very early. For sequential tasks, if US customers don't stay late to complete deliverables, the consequence is that the supplier sits idle for an entire day. For example, the project manager at Financial Services 1 said he doesn't have the power to make the database administrator stay late to finish schemas, resulting in a bottleneck as the supplier waits. At Biotech, the project managers' number one complaint about offshore sourcing was the effect on their work hours. While Biotech's Global Leadership Team has the power to enforce "crazy hours," within the IT department, it is more difficult to get business unit managers and end users to cooperate. Biotech learned that a best practice to minimize bottlenecks was to co-locate people: have some Indian supplier employees on site in the United States and some Biotech staff on site in India. The Indian supplier S2tech minimized the problem by setting the work hours in Hyderabad from 1:00pm to 10:00pm to provide a three-hour overlap with US customers. Other practices include flextime for US employees working on offshore projects, even if it is formally against company policy, and giving US employees Indian holidays off to compensate for longer hours worked at other times.

Practices to ensure cost savings while protecting quality

While participants did not expect to lose money during the pilot-testing phase, the main objective was testing the proof of concept. Substantial cost savings can only be achieved after learning has accumulated and the size of projects increase. In this section, we discuss what participants learned about the necessary size of projects and quality assurance practices to ensure cost savings while protecting quality.

Lesson 23. Consider both transaction and production costs to realistically calculate overall savings

For US companies, the initial offshore driver is undoubtedly labor cost savings, a production cost. In the United States, average labor cost per year per IT employee were US$63,331 in 2004/05,[16] compared to less than US$12,000 in India. But even production costs can be difficult to assess. For example, Biotech estimates projects based on an eight-hour workday but the Indian offshore suppliers bill nine-and-a-half hours per day. The management challenge is extracting overall cost savings when both transaction and production costs are considered. Transaction costs are considerably higher with offshore sourcing. According to studies by the Meta Group, Gartner Group, and Renedis, transaction costs of offshore sourcing range from 15 to 57 percent of contract value for vendor selection, transitioning the work, layoffs and retention, lost productivity due to cultural issues, improving development processes, and managing the contract.[17] In contrast, transaction costs of domestic outsourcing range between 4 and 10 percent of contract value.[18]

Most CIOs find it very difficult to calculate the transaction costs of offshore sourcing. At Biotech, the Head of the Offshore Program Management says:

> It is clear that we saved money on a per hour basis, there is no way to argue about that, but did they [offshore provider] save us money? Did they do it as fast as we would do it? The other big complaint came from the project managers: "Managing offshore projects is really hard ... if I had to count up how hard this is, then we lost money."

Lesson 24. Size projects large enough to receive total cost savings

Clearly, some critical mass must be reached so that the transaction costs do not swallow all the production cost savings. But how big do engagements have to be? Our research did not identify a definitive benchmark for the size of IT project required to achieve significant savings. Participants had a range from as low as five FTEs to as high as 1000 FTEs. On the high end, a telecommunications participant reported that overall cost savings of 40 percent did not occur until the size of their engagements reached 1000 people offshore. On the low end, only suppliers claimed five FTEs were enough to create total cost savings for their customers. Participants from Biotech did not achieve total cost savings even when the engagements reach 50 FTEs offshore. However, this was because they divided the work into too many two or three FTE projects. Biotech learned that larger sized projects are the key to getting overall cost savings: "We picked projects that were so small, the overhead crushed any value" (Head of Offshore Program Management Office).

Beyond our customer participants, we asked a senior researcher at the Gartner Group how big an IT software project has to be in order to achieve 15 to 20 percent overall savings. He quoted us between 80 and 100 FTEs, although he admonished that this number was based on his personal experience.

Lesson 25. Establish the ideal in-house/ on-site/offshore ratio only after the relationship has stabilized

The CEO of an offshore intermediary firm stated that the ideal ratio is 15 percent of client staff on site to maintain direction, 15 percent supplier staff on site to serve as liaisons and project managers, and 70 percent of the supplier staff offshore. While customers are in the experimental phase, the ratio is likely to be much higher. For example, when Insurance started offshoring, they had 70 percent people onshore and 30 percent people offshore. They aim to reverse this distribution as the relationship stabilizes.

Similarly, when Financial Services 3 started offshore sourcing in 2001, the onshore/offshore ratio was 50/50. Wipro, the supplier, has a dedicated staff on site, as well as a dedicated offshore delivery team. Up to 2005, the relationship was successful in that Wipro delivered 115 projects with an above average customer rating. As Financial Services 3 conquered the learning curve and established a good supplier relationship, the Officer of IT Services aimed to shift the ratio to 30/70.

In other cases, the customer and supplier relationships have stabilized to such a point that the supplier has no permanent staff on the customer premises. For example, for some of the projects at Retail and Manufacturer 2, no on-site supplier presence is needed because the team members know the context and each other very well.

Lesson 26. Give offshore suppliers domain specific training to protect quality and lower development costs

When managers from Manufacturer 1 began to engage their Indian supplier, they realized they needed to carefully manage the knowledge transfer process. The supplier did not initially possess the domain expertise in the design and maintenance of embedded software, which differs substantially from traditional software development. To bridge this gap, Manufacturer 1 decided to give the supplier's delivery team the same new employee orientation sessions and training that is provided to new internal employees. The content of this training included tools, methodologies, and technologies used at Manufacturer 1, as well as more traditional orientation subjects such as facility tours, introductions to peripheral departments, and human resource issues. The technology and project training, which was conducted by the lead architects and project managers, dramatically increases Manufacturer 1's transaction costs. However, these upfront transaction costs were needed to protect quality and lower development costs in the long run as the supplier became more knowledgeable and productive.

Lesson 27. Overlap onshore presence to facilitate supplier-to-supplier knowledge transfer

This lesson is related to several other lessons. Customers need to transfer domain knowledge (lesson 26) to the supplier primarily by having the supplier's key liaisons, leads, and managers on site (lesson 25), which increases costs (lesson 23). The knowledge transfer process between the customer and these key on-site supplier leads can take weeks or even months. Furthermore, it is very difficult for these on-site supplier leads to manage their remote teams. So some customers, like Insurance, end up bringing over much of the supplier's delivery team. This is how on-site/offshore ratios can swell to a 70/30 percent split.

Manufacturer 1 had a good solution to ensure knowledge transfer without over-inflating the supplier's on-site presence. They staged assignments so that the supplier's next on-site project managers overlapped for three to six months with the previous supplier's on-site project managers. This way, the new on-site project managers were fully prepared to assume charge when their predecessors left. The predecessor then went back in India to train and manage the offshore delivery team, thus further disseminating knowledge. This overlap and ultimate transfer to offshore allowed the supplier to center the delivery effort offshore where rates were typically less than half of the onshore rates. In addition, there were other benefits according to the engagement manager:

> The overlap allows us to help ease the transition. We can share the stories, and the history at a personal level. For example, there are "inside jokes" that only the delivery teams would understand. We can transfer that "soft knowledge" along with technical lessons learned about the creation of embedded software.

Lesson 28. Develop meaningful career paths for subject matter experts, governance, and technical expertise

Participants stressed the need for subject matter experts (SMEs) and good project managers to define and deliver business requirements and governance experts to manage external suppliers. But as US organizations increasingly outsource entry-level positions like programmers, how will future generations of SMEs, project managers, and governance experts be groomed?

> All of the best project managers I have ever worked with all started as coders. If all the hardcore coding is being done offshore, where will we get our good project managers? (Global Leadership Team Member)

At Manufacturer 2, the CIO hopes to swiftly groom future project managers by putting all in-house IT staff through project management training, even for low-level graphics designers. The Vice President of Technologies for Financial Services 6 addressed this worry by partnering with local universities to create Centers of Excellence. The Centers' mission is to develop skill sets aimed at "priming the pump" to ensure the talent pipeline does not dry up. These centers work with Financial Services 6 to understand the changing landscape of IT work and adapt their curriculum to create graduates with the necessary combination of business, project management, and technical skills.

Senior executives looking for an in-depth answer to career paths of the residual staff may refer to the Core Capabilities Model from Chapter 3.[19]

Lesson 29. Create balanced scorecard metrics

All participants identified the need for measures that consider costs, quality, timeliness, and risks, but only participants from one company were fully satisfied with current assessment measures. Manufacturer 1 tracks in-house, domestic, and offshore suppliers' costs, quality, and productivity using a standardized activity measure. The data is captured by an in-house dashboard and analyzed monthly by management to monitor real development costs and trends. They learned that real savings from offshore do not occur until after they have invested significant upfront training of every offshore developer and team leader. They also share this data with vendors so that all parties understand the total cost trends.

Figure 9.4 shows metrics used by PMO managers to track performance of offshore work. The strategy and vision is important because it suggests not only which metrics to track, but suggests the specific targets for those metrics. For example, consider the metric "percentage of supplier business," which measures how much of the supplier's revenues come from the client organization. One US client wanted this number to be high, believing that a high percentage would motivate better service from the supplier. In another company, the client wants the "percentage of supplier business" to be low (less than 30%) because they don't want to be obligated for the supplier's failure if they later choose to terminate the relationship.

Utilization rates are very important metrics to one US customer that uses a retainer model for offshore work. Rather than use time-and-materials or fee-for-service contracts, this company retains a certain number of the supplier employees each month for a fixed fee. If, for example, they pay a

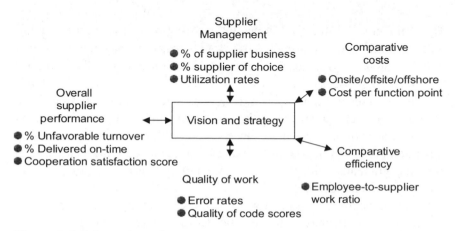

Figure 9.4 Balanced metrics

retainer for five employees for a certain month, they seek to utilize at least 90 percent of the time for which they paid.

The comparative efficiency metric assesses the relative productivity of in-house employees to offshore employees. In most cases, in-house employees could produce more work (as measured in function points) than offshore suppliers in a given time period, but the offshore employees were significantly less expensive. Thus the target metric does not expect equal performance.

But the politics of measurement cannot be ignored. For example, one PMO manager said, "When I go ask our internal IT department to give me an estimate on how long it would take them to do this piece of work they say 'X' but my [offshore] supplier says 'Y,' who do I believe?"

Conclusion

While organizations may initially venture offshore primarily to seek lower costs on short-term projects, if they stay, they stay for more strategic reasons like quality, speed, and agility. Senior executives we interviewed eventually used global sourcing to bring products to market faster and cheaper, financing new product development, accessing new markets, and creating new businesses. In this Chapter, we presented 29 practices to help senior executives accelerate the learning curve. Many of these practices require executives to equip their project managers with the things they need to be successful, such as program management offices, CMM training, offshore site visits, and techniques to monitor the supplier's work. To help prevent panic among internal employees, senior executives must openly communicate the objectives of an offshore initiative to assuage irrational fears. Senior executives also have to rally support from stakeholders outside of the function, such as business unit managers and end users, to prevent bottlenecks, scope creep, and poor quality.

Notes

1. See, for example, the McKinsey Global Institute research report cited in Farrell, D. (2004), "Beyond Offshoring: Assess Your Company's Global Potential," *Harvard Business Review*, Vol. 82, 12, p. 82.
2. McCue, A. (2005), "Outsourcing Flops Blamed on Tunnel Vision," Silicon.com published on ZDNet News, June 22.

3. See Carmel, E. and Agarwal, R. (2002), "The Maturation of Offshore Sourcing of Information Technology Work," *MIS Quarterly Executive*, Vol. 1, 2, June, pp. 65–77.
4. Agarwal, R., and Sambamurthy, V. (2002), "Principles and Models for Organizing IT," *MIS Quarterly Executive*, Vol. 1, 1, March, pp. 1–16.
5. The percentage of ownership is typical in India. Whereas only 51 percent ownership is required in US ventures for complete control over the enterprise, Indian law requires 76 percent ownership for equivalent rights.
6. "TWR and Satyam to Form Strategic Alliance," press release posted on www.satyam.com.
7. Field, T. (2002), "The Man In The Middle," *CIO Magazine*, April.
8. Lacity, M. and Willcocks, L. (2001), *Global IT Outsourcing*, Wiley, Chichester.
9. For spreading risks through multi-country sourcing, see Vestring, T., Rouse, T., and Reinert, U. (2005), "Hedge Your Offshoring Bets," *Sloan Management Review*, Vol. 46, 3, pp. 27–29.
10. Although this arrangement met Biotech's security needs, the supplier's IT staff did not like commuting across town to Biotech's facility. Apparently it was like asking a New York Manhattan resident to commute to Queens.
11. Employees need to hear messages from their managers about offshore outsourcing, rather than relying on public sources that inspire fear, such as Hof, R., and Kerttetter, J. (2004), "Software: Will Outsourcing Hurt America's Supremacy?" *Business Week*, March 1, pp. 84–95; McGee, M. (2003), "Offshore Outsourcing Drags Down U.S. Bonus Pay," *InformationWeek*, August 25.
12. For a good discussion of overcoming distance, time, and cultural issues, see Carmel, E. and Tjia, P. (2005), *Offshoring Information Technology*, Cambridge University Press, Cambridge. For more on controlling outsourced software projects, see Choudhury, V. and Sabherwal, R. (2003), "Portfolios of Control in Outsourced Software Development Projects," *Information Systems Research*, Vol. 14, 3, pp. 291–308.
13. Kaiser, K. and Hawk, S. (2004), "Evolution of Offshore Software Development: From Outsourcing to Cosourcing," *MIS Quarterly Executive*, Vol. 3, 2, June, pp. 69–81.
14. For detailed cases on implementing CMM within an organization, see Jalote, P. (2000), *CMM in Practice*, Addison Wesley, Boston and Adler, P., McGarry, F., Talbot, W. and Binney, D. (2005), "Enabling Process Discipline: Lessons from the Journey to CMM Level 5," *MIS*

Quarterly Executive, Vol. 4, 1; Gopal, A., Mukhopadhyay, T. and Krishnan, M. (2002), "The Role of Software Processes and Communication in Offshore Software Development," *Communications of the ACM*, Vol. 45, 4, pp. 193–200.

15. For more information on managing cross-cultural issues, see Krishna, S., Sahay, S., and Walsham, G. (2004), "Managing Cross-Cultural Issues in Global Software Development," *Communications of the ACM*, Vol. 47, 4, pp. 62–66.

16. Thibodeau, P. and Hoffman, T. (2003), "Surviving Offshore Cutbacks," *Computerworld*, April 28, Vol. 37, 17, pp. 41–42.

17. Overby, S. "The Hidden Costs of Offshore Outsourcing," *CIO Magazine*, September 1, 2004; Amrosio, J. (2003), "Experts Reveal Hidden Costs of Offshore IT Outsourcing," *CIO Magazine*, April.

18. Lacity, M. and Willcocks, P. (2001), *Global IT Outsourcing*, Wiley, Chichester.

19. Feeny, D. and Willcocks, L. (1998), "Core IS Capabilities for Exploiting Information Technology," *Sloan Management Review*, Vol. 39, 3, pp. 9–21.

CHAPTER 10

From application service provision to netsourcing: A risk mitigation framework

*Thomas Kern, Leslie Willcocks,
and Mary Lacity*

Introduction: What ever happened to ASP?

Many organizations were initially excited about the value proposition of renting applications over the Internet, initially called "application service provision," "ASP," or more informally – "apps on tap." This sourcing model promised to deliver best-of-breed business applications to customer desktops for a low monthly fee based on number of users or number of transactions at the customer site. In addition, business managers were promised:

- Minimal or no upfront IT infrastructure costs because the supplier hosts the applications,
- less expensive in-house expertise because the supplier is fully staffed,
- scalable solutions that grow or shrink with the customer's requirements,
- superior cash flow because there are no upfront, lump-sum software license fees
- rapid implementation in days and weeks rather than months and years.

In 2000, some research groups predicted that the application service provision market would be US$25 billion by 2005. Clearly, that never happened. The high estimates for market size in 2004 were under US$4 billion. Many people think ASP failed to meet market projections because of the dot.com bubble burst. After all, most application service providers were start-up companies. But what really happened? We have been studying this space since 2000, carrying out ten in-depth case studies and a customer survey of 274 current and potential ASP customers. We found that the ASP space, as initially defined, was more costly than anticipated because customers needed expensive hand-holding and customized services – not simply logon IDs and passwords. More specifically, customers wanted help integrating their home-grown applications with ISV software, customized services, training, and even the end-to-end delivery of entire business processes.[1] In addition, large companies were not willing to accept the level of risk associated with ASP, such as reliability and security risks of the Internet. Furthermore, many business managers felt that their business requirements were too idiosyncratic for canned, "one-to-many" solutions and did not trust outsiders to supply important systems. Those business managers who did adopt ASP, learned that Internet delivery is not merely a matter of "apps on tap," but like any outsourcing decision, required significant risk mitigation and management oversight.

What we found is that the ASP space rapidly evolved from a "one-to-many" model to a blend of customized service offerings. The most successful uses of "ASP" we studied were actually when ASP was part of a delivery platform for a much more sophisticated customer–supplier relationship. For example, parts of the Hewitt and Xchanging services discussed in previous chapters are delivered to customers in an ASP-like manner. But the characteristic one-to-many business model of the initial ASP concept was blended with one-to-one customization of some aspects of the supplier's products and services.

In this chapter, we fully explore the close relationship between one of Europe's best "ASP" suppliers, Siennax, and its customer, Abz Insurance. Abz Insurance (acquired by ADP in 2004) is a conglomeration of several Dutch insurance companies that created a shared services organization to reduce the cost of automobile claims processing through standardization and centralization. Abz Insurance serves as a single point of contact for all participants involved in automobile insurance claims, including insurance companies, repair shops, and claimants. Since its inception in 1984, Abz Insurance relied on traditional, exchange-based IT suppliers to provide nearly all of its IT needs. By 1999, these cumbersome contracts no longer met Abz's customer demands for web-based applications, such as online car insurance quotes, credit checks, and issuances. Enter Siennax. In 2000, Siennax became Abz's primary IT supplier, supplying nearly all aspects of the "networking service stack" (see Table 10.1), except the business process delivery, which is Abz's primary competitive positioning.

Table 10.1 The netsourcing service stack

Netsourcing Service	Example
Business Process Delivery	Provides business process delivery for transactions, reporting, and services within functional domains like human resources, procurement, accounting, and finance
Customized Application Access and Support	Provides access and support to the customers' homegrown applications or customized software packages
Standard Application Access Level	Provides access and support to independent software vendor packages
Application Operating Infrastructure	Provides middleware for accessing applications from remote locations
Hosting Infrastructure	Provides data center facilities, leases servers, and manages server performance
Network Services	Provides network monitoring and security
Network Connectivity	Provides connectivity options which are matched to customers' bandwidth and data throughput rates

A good way to understand the complexity of the ASP space is to look at it from a service stack perspective (see Table 10.1). To capture the variety of service offerings such as those provided by Siennax, we have ceased to call this space simply "ASP," but adopted the broader nomenclature "netsourcing." *Netsourcing is the set of services delivered to customers over a network. We distinguish "netsourcing" from "web services" in that we view the web services standards and protocols as the technological infrastructure that allows netsourcing.*[2]

As we will see in the Siennax/Abz case, most customer–supplier relationships in netsourcing space are much more complicated than the initial one-to-many "apps on taps" model. A netsourcing supplier may have primary accountability to a customer, but the supplier in turn may subcontract hardware, monitoring, billing, help desk, and support services to many players. This, of course, poses more risk to the customer as well as the netsourcing supplier, who remains accountable for products and services outside their direct control. To help business managers assess and mitigate netsourcing risks of complex netsourcing arrangements, we provide a risk analysis framework, which will be illustrated through a case study of Abz Insurance.

Risk analysis and mitigation framework

In the context of IT outsourcing, customers take risks when they believe suppliers who may oversell their capabilities, when they negotiate incomplete contracts, or when they do not properly manage the relationship. The negative outcomes from these risks include excess costs, poor service, loss of competitiveness, loss of revenues, and loss of customers.

Table 10.2 provides a comprehensive list of IT outsourcing risks and compares these risks for IT traditional outsourcing and netsourcing. We adopted Jurison's recommendation that IT outsourcing risks be qualitatively assessed as low, medium, or high because it is unlikely that the outcomes and their probabilities are known.[3] As Table 10.2 illustrates, the risks of traditional outsourcing are the same as for netsourcing, but the probabilities for occurrence are different.[4]

Of the fifteen risks found in Table 10.2, nine are greater in the netsourcing context. We will focus on these higher risks in our case study. But

Table 10.2 Risks, risk assessment, and risk mitigation in traditional IT outsourcing and netsourcing

Risk	Traditional, exchange-based outsourcing	Netsourcing	Risk mitigation strategies
1. *Unrealistic customer expectations*	Medium	High	Align stakeholder expectations through detailed contract negotiations; disseminate contract highlights to entire user community.
2. *Customer's lack of maturity and experience with IT outsourcing*	Low/Medium	High	Source incrementally – start small to gain experience with capabilities required to successfully outsource.
3. *Power asymmetries favor the supplier*	High/Medium	Low	Source to multiple suppliers; sign short-term, detailed contracts. (This risk is greatest for highly customized services because it is more difficult to switch suppliers.)
4. *Treating IT as an undifferentiated commodity thereby forgoing strategic IT exploitation*	High	Medium	Treat and manage IT as an integrated portfolio, with careful consideration of current and future business, economic, and technical factors.
5. *Inflexible contracting*	High	Low	Negotiate short-term contracts with mechanisms of change; use performance based contracting where possible.
6. *Oversold supplier capability*	Medium/Low	High	Select suppliers with proven track records; demand customer references illustrating turnaround cases.
7. *Supplier goes out of business*	Low	High	Select supplier with sound financial position, stable customers, and stable strategic partners; understand if and how suppliers earn a profit; require notification of premature termination of contract; require transfer clause to facilitate movingthe activity back to customer or to another supplier.

Continued

Table 10.2 Continued

Risk	Traditional, exchange-based outsourcing	Netsourcing	Risk mitigation strategies
8. *Supplier learns and exploits customer expertise*	Low	Low	Include non-compete clauses in contracts.
9. *Incomplete contracting*	Medium/Low	Very high	Detail contracts by including costs, service levels, penalties for non-performance.
10. *Customers' inability to manage the supplier relationship(s)*	High	Low/Medium	Ensure contract monitoring, coordination, and user-supplier liaison capabilities.
11. *Transition failure*	High	Medium	Mitigate risk through transition planning and testing, incremental or parallel implementation.
12. *Supplier subcontracting problems*	Medium/Low	High	Require full disclosure and customer approval of all subcontractors.
13. *Security breach*	Medium/Low	High	Encrypt data; retain access control in-house; consider virtual private networks for highly sensitive data.
14. *Application unavailability*	Low	High	Negotiate service level guarantees with penalties for non-performance for supplier-caused failures. (Suppliers cannot be held accountable for Internet failures.)
15. *Slow response time*	Low/Medium	High	Negotiate service level guarantees for response time variables within the supplier's control; restrict applications to thin-client versions for Internet delivery.

we also note that five risks are actually lower for netsourcing than for traditional, exchange-based outsourcing: treating IT as an undifferentiated commodity, power asymmetries favoring the supplier, inflexible contracting, customer's inability to manage the relationship, and transition failure. These risks are high when the customer cannot readily switch suppliers because the assets, capabilities, and services are highly idiosyncratic to a particular customer. These remain among the greatest risks with traditional IT outsourcing because the transactions are tailored to a customer. In contrast, switching suppliers with netsourcing is usually much easier because customers are typically purchasing standard products and services offered by many suppliers.

Table 10.2 also includes risk mitigation strategies proven to be useful by a large number of our case study and survey respondents. However, business managers will find that best practices cannot be mimicked effectively in every situation. Instead, each company must decide for itself appropriate risk mitigation tactics. The case study of Abz Insurance illustrates this point beautifully – while Abz Insurance encountered most of the risks listed in Table 10.2, some of the best practice risk mitigation strategies were infeasible for its situation. We also chose this case because it encompasses both traditional IT outsourcing as well as netsourcing, providing examples of the different levels of risks for each. The case study also illustrates a netsourcing deal that encountered significant problems and shows how power symmetries served to facilitate problem resolution. And finally, the case shows how close a customer can become to a netsourcing supplier, serving as a trusted partner in the business.

Illustrative case study of risk management: Abz Insurance[5]

Several Dutch insurance companies started Abz Insurance in 1984 to reduce the cost of automobile claims processing through standardization and centralization. They created the company to serve as a single point of contact for all participants involved in automobile insurance claims, including insurance companies, repair shops, and claimants. Corné Paalvast, the Operational Director for Abz discusses the history of the company:

> The company basically started 16 years ago as an initiative in the area of car claims handling. The insurance industry saw that working together to get the process organized and supported by IT was much better handled by all insurers together. So Abz was the result and today that means that every damaged car that is covered by an insurance company in Holland is handled over our IT systems. We provide applications to calculate the damage, to process the damage, to record the damage with photos, etc. So everybody involved in processing the damage is connected to our system – insurance companies, body repair shops, expertise companies, spare parts companies, etc.

Since its inception Abz depended heavily on external providers for information technology solutions, including Getronics, CMG, and Pink Roccade. These suppliers developed and operated IT infrastructure for Abz during the 1980s and early 1990s. The use of multiple suppliers was intentional, as Abz Insurance wanted to mitigate the risk of *power asymmetries favoring suppliers* (risk 3 in Table 10.2) by dividing the contracts among multiple parties.

The initial underlying argument for outsourcing was that IT was a commodity, not core to Abz's business. In accordance with this view, the IT outsourcing contracts were focused on daily operations and operational efficiency. While this initial stance may have been valid early on, by the mid-1990s Abz Insurance experienced the consequences of *treating IT as an undifferentiated commodity,* including the inability to exploit IT for competitive advantage (risk 4 in Table 10.2). At that time, its growing customer base and its key shareholders (i.e., the large European insurance companies) demanded a greater exploitation of IT to enhance existing services and to define new services. For example, Abz's customers wanted Abz to provide functionality that would allow end customers to apply for car insurance, to give accurate rate quotes based on a customer's history and credit rating, and issue car insurance in real-time over the Internet. Thus, Abz was expected to provide more than standardized claims processing; it was expected to also host and manage individual insurer's applications and data. This demand was certainly beyond the scope of Abz's current in-house IT capabilities, but more troubling, the demand was beyond the scope of their current IT suppliers' capabilities. Abz was becoming increasingly frustrated with their service firms because they were not keeping Abz abreast of innovations or responding to customer demands for full-service Internet applications and support.

Abz Insurance's experience is replicated many times in the traditional IT outsourcing arena.[6] *Inflexible contracts* (risk 5 in Table 10.2) typically fail to respond to more strategic initiatives. Supplier account managers are required to deliver on the contracts and may price additional, well-defined requests, but are rarely empowered to completely restructure deals. Abz executives perceived that the only viable way to achieve their goals was for Abz to seek a new partner rather than renegotiate with existing suppliers. Corné Paalvast, the Operational Director from Abz explained:

> We had had an outsourcing arrangement with Getronics at that for about six years. They provided us with most of our IT services for marketing and selling our services to the insurance industry. Their services covered our complete intranet and extranet environment, which included our transaction services. Yet for our current and long-term development we were looking for an IT partner, rather than a commodity type service supplier like Getronics. We sought an IT partner that could help us define new products, services, and generally would be more proactive in its interactions with our customers ... we were looking for a partner who could tell us what was available and help us identify new opportunities.

As a result, in November 1999, when the contract with Getronics was nearing its end, Abz began exploring the market for a new IT partner. Abz envisaged a solution that would give them flexibility, a means to keep on top of innovations, and access to new and ongoing application developments. But how could it do all this without significant capital investment in IT? At the time, the ASP business model was being widely discussed and covered by media, and Abz found it to be a good fit with their requirements. By February 2000 the company had internally decided to opt for an ASP-driven solution. In the words of the decision maker:

> Back then we did not know much about ASPs. Yet we were convinced that this was a way to help us innovate and develop new services faster than we could think of at the time. The in-depth discussions and negotiations with Graddelt and Siennax [two ASPs] confirmed this assumption. Yet when we scanned the market, everybody seemed to be claiming they were an ASP – even our existing service provider, Getronics. But most of them did not provide the kind of service we sought, the scalability and the necessary "Internet hotel" – the environment where we could run our own business applications, and the infrastructure to plug in our own business applications. (Corné Paalvast, the Operational Director from Abz)

Abz Insurance wanted to offer their insurance customers one-stop insurance business services, enabled by both standard and customized applications that would be hosted and technically managed by an ASP. Abz hoped a full suite of services would increase Abz Insurance's customer loyalty as well as generate new revenues.

Abz Insurance was well aware of the risks of *suppliers overselling their capabilities* (risk 6 in Table 10.2). They evaluated suppliers based on their proven ability to provide a portfolio of applications and services: *"Proven results, that was one of the selection criteria"* (Corné Paalvast, the Operational Director from Abz). Another factor that played a role in Abz's evaluation was the threat of *power asymmetries developing in favor of the supplier* (risk 3 in Table 10.2). While Abz had mitigated this risk in the past by sourcing to multiple suppliers, the level of integration and coordination among the new application services required sole sourcing. Their new risk mitigation strategy was to select a small-sized, start-up supplier that had few customers and was not as well known in the industry. Abz managers believed that a start-up IT supplier would pay close attention to their needs, and maintain a balanced relationship that would be slightly in Abz's favor. Underlying this strategy was Abz's experience, which had shown that partnerships with small suppliers led to faster response times, improved communication, and decreased hierarchical interface levels.[7]

A third factor in Abz's selection criteria was the threat of the *supplier utilizing their intellectual capital and entering the market as a competitor* (risk 8 in Table 10.2). Abz was particularly concerned about one supplier that could easily copy Abz's services and activities and then offer them in the same market either directly or indirectly through partnerships. Usually, customers mitigate this risk with non-compete clauses, but Abz Insurance mitigated this risk by restricting their search to ASP start-ups, like Graddelt (now called marviQ) and Siennax. Both of their resource bases are relatively small and thus they were unlikely to enter their own market to steal customers.

The final driving selection criterion in addition to the above objectives was whether the supplier could be trusted:

> But most important, the ASP market being an immature market you need to have trust in people and individual relationships. That was one of the most important triggers for choosing Siennax. (Corné Paalvast, Operational Director Abz)

In March 2000, Abz and Siennax signed an agreement of intent. Because of their accumulated experience in IT outsourcing (thus risks 1 and 2 in Table 10.2 are rated low for Abz), Abz was aware of the risk of signing an *incomplete contract* (risk 9 in Table 10.2). The parties thus took nearly six months to conduct due diligence and to negotiate a detailed contract including service levels and penalties for non-performance for well-defined Siennax services. The contract detailed escalation procedures, responsible managers, uptime guarantees, reaction times, reaction procedures, and change request procedures. (This level of detail was unusual among our net-sourcing case studies – most ASP customers signed supplier-off-the-shelf, three page contracts.)

But for some parts of the contract, Siennax could not commit to details. For example, Siennax did not have any hands-on experience with integrating a customer's legacy systems with their own service solution. This part of the deal required a more *flexible contract* (risk 5 in Table 10.2), and the integration merely defined the intention of the services expected and the wish list of Abz. (Based on our prior study of such mixed contracts in Lacity and Willcocks (2001), 55 percent of such deals were successful, but 36 percent of such deals experienced significant problems with the "to be defined" portions of the contracts a few years into the relationship.)

In addition to attending to the contract, Abz also planned structures and procedures to ensure they could *effectively manage the relationship* (risk 10 in Table 10.2). A steering group comprised of executives from both Abz and Siennax was formed to monitor the costs and service performance, resolve escalated problems, and identify new business opportunities. An operational team was also formed to manage operations and services. Together, the steering group and operational team would also define and fully detail the exact service levels of the deal after transition.

Abz Insurance was worried about the risk of *transition failure* from Getronics to Siennax (risk 11 in Table 10.2). To mitigate this risk, both parties invested time upfront in identifying a project team responsible for transitioning the services. The project team decided to transition incrementally the legacy services from Getronics to the Siennax platform. The migration began with relatively easy parts, such as the html front-end applications and was then expanded in steps to cover the whole Abz extranet. Abz desired an incremental approach because it gave them the possibility to always retreat if problems became serious, and re-contract with easily identifiable alternative suppliers or, if necessary, even go back with Getronics. Although complex in nature, the transition was rolled out as planned:

> We started to discuss the transition of their extranet from their servers to our own environment. This transition was something that had never been done before. So it was something new to both organizations. To my advantage I had, and we formed … . a very good working project team. This cooperation really helped in migrating the services smoothly. Yet there was one exception, which was the implementation of the Verisign certification. On that we were facing a number of problems. (Pieter Bokelaar, Abz Account Manager at Siennax)

The inherent problem was that Abz also acts as a Trusted Third Party agent to its customers, providing them with a crucial digital signature/passport functionality. Abz was delivering this service conjointly with Getronics, but needed to find a new supplier who could work with Siennax. Abz initially took the leadership in selecting a subcontractor for Siennax, fearing that Siennax did not have the specific business knowledge to successfully subcontract this service on their own. Thus, by Abz taking the lead in searching for Verisign Certification service, they hoped to reduce the risk of *subcontracting problems* (see risk 13 in Table 10.2). Having done a survey of the market, Abz identified a supplier they had previously done other business with, Pink Roccade. From Abz's perspective, Siennax only needed to subcontract with Pink Roccade and integrate their service into Abz's existing service package.

However, Siennax did not want to partner with Pink Roccade because they viewed them as competing in the same markets as Siennax. Instead, Siennax wanted to subcontract with a start-up company called BlueX and successfully argued to Abz that Siennax should have control over its own subcontractors, which eventually adversely affected Abz's business:

> We wanted Verisign, which in Holland is re-sold primarily through Roccade. They [Siennax] however could not really live with Roccade because of the competition worries. So Siennax decided to go into business with somebody else which I hadn't heard of before – called BlueX. They said they could arrange the Verisign service before the first of October and it took them till the 22nd of December to do so. Which put us, as a Trusted Third Party, out of Business for seven weeks. During this time I don't think we lost any customers, but we have had to pay back money for services not available and we have had to say sorry for a lot of things. But the image loss is probably the worst thing about it. (Corné Paalvast, Operational Director Abz)

The implementation delay was largely due to BlueX's inexperience with implementing Digital Signature services in an ASP model. Clearly the choice of BlueX was a risky one because of this *supplier's unproven track record* (risk 6 in Table 10.2). But what is more interesting is how Abz responded to the migration failure. Although fully empowered by a sound contract, Abz did not require Siennax to pay the significant cash penalty specified in the contract. They feared that the cash penalty would have *severely hindered the supplier's finances* (risk 7 in Table 10.2) thus focusing attention away from solving the problem:

> Financially we have made agreements in the contract. There is a penalty in the contract, which covers damage. But I say to the ASP – keep the money and help me re-establish my image, because that is much more important. (Corné Paalvast, Operational Director, Abz Insurance)

Instead, Abz used the contractual service levels more for constructive feedback at the operational level. Besides the actual reporting of technical failures and problems, Abz placed a great deal of importance on the perceived performance by the internal end-users and Abz's customers. Here Abz measured Siennax's performance based on how problems were being addressed, whether charges were raised for minor issues, whether logs of problems were kept and whether they could have been planned for and hence prevented these problems. After reestablishing operational performance and customer confidence, Abz and Siennax amicably resolved an equitable payment to partly reimburse Abz for the seven-week revenue loss.

The Abz–Siennax relationship matures

Although there were a number of complexities in the start-up phase of the venture and some difficult discussions concerning losses due to lack of services as a result of delays in services, the relationship had matured. With Siennax's help, Abz successfully integrated key insurance intermediary functions for administering policies, underwriting, calculating damages, processing of claims, and generally simplifying the interaction between insurance companies and insurance representatives and/or brokers. By 2002, Abz was serving over 6000 customers and processing 416 gigabytes of data and 25 million emails per year as part of the sales and claims processing services for the insurance industry. By 2004, Abz's value became abundantly obvious to ADP Services, who acquired it early in the year. This catapulted Abz from a small company with US$29 million in sales to a subsidiary of a US$7 billion company. ADP was pleased to continue support from Siennax, and indeed on June 4, 2005, granted Siennax additional business to support Abz's new streamlined reparation service. Abz's "Herstel Verzekerd" service provides automatic financial exchange between all parties involved in an auto claim. The CEOs of Abz Insurance and Siennax provided the following comments on the relationship[8]:

> The financial world is of constant change and of new developments, so the timely and accurate flow of information is an absolute imperative. Working with Siennax, we can build on the universal nature of the Internet to better provide the mission-critical financial applications our customers rely on. With this deal, we are able to present end-users with a compelling solution to use the Internet to access their information anytime, anywhere. (Gerrit Schipper, CEO and president of Abz)
>
> The co-operation with Abz is an important win not only for Siennax as a company, but for the ASP model. It shows that the added value an ASP offers versus traditional application outsourcing is being recognised in the market. Siennax simplifies the maintenance and deployment of

Abz's applications, which will increase efficiency and reduce cost. (Herb Prooy, CEO of Siennax)

Siennax's success with Abz helped Siennax attract more customers. Siennax saw 70 percent growth rates and by 2006 provided netsourcing services to such giants as ABN AMRO, Deutsche Bank, Commerzbank, and Daimler Chrysler.

Mapping the Siennax/Abz Insurance case to the netsourcing service stack

We mapped the complexity of players to the service stack in Table 10.3. From the perspective of Abz customers, that is, the insurance companies, body repair shops, spare parts companies, and claimants, Abz is the primary point of contact for their insurance applications and services. It is very unlikely that these customers are even aware that many of the

Table 10.3 The Abz Insurance case mapped to the netsourcing service stack

Netsourcing service	Abz Insurance case study
Business Process Delivery	Abz Insurance provides the end-to-end business insurance processes from searching for auto insurance through to claims resolution.
Customized Application Access and Support	Abz Insurance rents Siennax's proprietary Intranet Suite SX (email, scheduling, calendars and document libraries) and in turn offers these to Abz customers. Siennax hosts and supports Abz's customized software.
Standard Application Access Level	Abz Insurance rents independent software vendor applications from Siennax (who serves as a reseller) including Lotus Learning Space and SABA Learning Management Systems, E- Billing facilities, CRM Application, Documentum I-team collaboration tolls, and Microsoft Email solutions.
Application Operating Infrastructure	Siennax uses JAVA, Microsoft.Net (i.e., Terminal Server), Lotus Domino Lotus Domino and Open Source to connect Abz customers to Abz.
Hosting Infrastructure	Siennax operates Sun Solaris, Compaq NT, and Linux hardware in secure data center or cybercenters of KPN. Oracle and SQL Server are used as standard database services, complete with on-line storage services, back-up routines, security and directoryservices.
Network Services Infrastructure	Siennax use the monitoring and maintenance facilities made available from KPN, who provides the complete network services.
Network Infrastructure	Siennax has no networks of its own, but cooperates with network providers such as KPN.

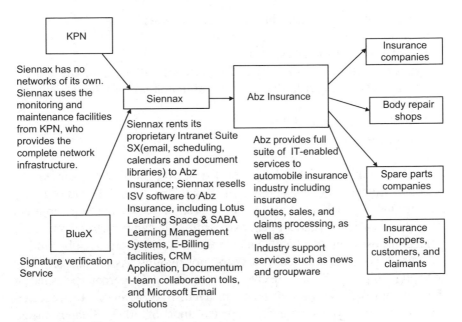

Figure 10.1 Abz's suppliers and customers

underlying Abz services are subcontracted to Siennax and from Siennax to KPN Dutch Telecom and BlueX.

The netsourcing relationships are also depicted in Figure 10.1. Clearly, this is no simple "apps on taps."

Netsourcing risks and case discussion

The purpose of this chapter has been to identify the evolution of the ASP market to netsourcing and to identify, assess, and mitigate risks in this complex environment. What is clear from Table 10.2 is that the risks of netsourcing are the same as for traditional outsourcing, but the probabilities of occurrence for many of these risks are higher in the netsourcing domain. In particular, we identified nine risks that are greater with netsourcing than with traditional IT outsourcing and have grouped them under three categories:

1. Greater netsourcing risks due to start-up suppliers in an immature market
   - supplier oversells capability
   - supplier goes out of business
   - supplier subcontracting problems

2. Greater netsourcing risks due to novice customers:
   - customer signs incomplete contract
   - unrealistic customer expectations
   - customer's lack of maturity and experience with outsourcing
3. Greater netsourcing risks due to technical limitations of Internet delivery:
   - security breach
   - application unavailability
   - slow response time

Immature supplier risks. From the list above, the first three risks are typically higher with netsourcing than with traditional IT outsourcing because the suppliers are mostly start-up ventures. Netsourcing suppliers typically experience years of negative earnings because they invested millions in infrastructure and only collect revenues with monthly subscription fees. Such spend is recovered in years, not months. As such, many netsourcing suppliers did not survive – an estimated 60 percent perished in the dot.com bust. Those that have survived, like Siennax, still required investor support years after start-up. (In June of 2003, Siennax asked investors to provide €2.5 million for a balance sheet reinforcement, which they did on the basis of their belief in Siennax's future.)

Immature customer risks. While traditional outsourcing customers have learned to mitigate risks of poor contracting and unrealistic expectations gained through mounting outsourcing experiences, such risks are being revisited by a new set of inexperienced customers, such as start-up companies and small- to medium-sized enterprises (SMEs), the majority of early adopters of netsourcing. These inexperienced customers are taking risks with netsourcing that we witnessed customers taking back in the late 1980s with traditional IT outsourcing, such as signing flimsy, three-page contracts. These risks may eventually diminish as netsourcing customers gain experience with outsourcing and as customers learn to adopt mitigation strategies proven effective in traditional outsourcing or to develop new strategies for the netsourcing context.

In contrast to this typical netsourcing customer, Abz Insurance was a seasoned outsourcing customer. Due to their earlier experiences with suppliers, they understood the in-house management attention and expertise required to select, negotiate, transition, and manage suppliers. Even when events went wrong, such as the seven-week delay of BlueX's Verisign Certification, Abz Insurance had the maturity to include contract clauses that anticipated such events, and to proactively manage a solution instead of merely assigning blame.

But what about potential netsourcing customers who have no prior outsourcing experience? One risk mitigation strategy is incremental sourcing.

Customers may start small to gain experience and to develop capabilities to effectively manage suppliers. Customers may also wish to start netsourcing with more commodity type applications rather than with more complicated packages like ERP. Indeed, the results of our international ASP customer survey[9] found that the most frequently ASP-sourced and frequently sought ASP applications were email and communication (43%) and desktop and personal productivity products (39%). Testing the waters with well-known applications reduces risks and enables customers to quickly climb the ASP learning curve.

Immature technology risks. The last trio of high netsourcing risks are associated with delivering products and services over the Internet: security breaches, application downtime, and slow response time. Indeed, our International Survey found that the most frequently encountered ASP problems were slow application response time (40% of respondents) and application unavailability (25% of respondents). Suppliers simply cannot control the applications and data point-to-point over the Internet. While savvy netsourcing customers can negotiate detailed service level guarantees for security, uptime, and response time, suppliers sign these agreements knowing they cannot control these items, but simply "hope for the best," as one respondent reported.

One surprise on the survey: current ASP customers reported no incidences of hackers and only 3 percent experienced data security problems. However, security was rated the number one perceived problem by potential ASP customers. Thus, there is a discrepancy in perceived security risks between actual and potential ASP customers. But just because security breaches have not been observed by current ASP customers, it does not mean that the risk is low. Clearly, Internet delivery poses a much higher security risk than private networks. Any ASP customer should consider risk mitigation strategies such as virtual private networks, encryption, and customer managed access control. We do note however, that one Chief Technology Architect from a large financial services firm told us in 2005, "Virtual private networks provide only an expensive delusion of security."

For Abz, senior executives discussed technology risks in terms of broader service issues rather than sporadic application downtime (the typical interpretation of application unavailability) and long delays between hitting a key and the system responding (the typical interpretation of slow response time). Concerning application unavailability, one of Abz's key applications was unavailable for seven weeks because the application was not ASP-ready. This is an example of an extreme consequence resulting from the technical risks of ASP delivery. Application unavailability caused significant loss of goodwill, even though Abz did not lose customers (because few alternatives are available to their customers in the market). On the response time issue, Abz participants focused on the service response of Siennax, that is, how long it takes them to respond to service requests. On this point, Abz believes that Siennax has actually improved response time:

> Our time-to-market with new services has considerably dropped to a number of weeks, compared to months/years. (Corné Paalvast, Operational Director Abz)

Abz mitigated security risks primarily by using different networks for different types of applications. Applications requiring customer subscriptions (such as underwriting), run on virtual private networks. Because VPNs must define the end points, they are not suitable for mobile users or retail customers. Those types of applications, such as searching for auto insurance, CRM, and Email, run on the Internet, with encryption for sensitive data.

Conclusion

One of our main findings in the ASP space is that netsourcing is vastly more fragmented, complex, and risky than many business managers realize. We have proposed the netsourcing service stack as a good way to understand the complexity of supplier-customer relationships in this space.

We also found that the analysis and management of risk in netsourcing environments is immature, but fast developing. As such, it is dangerous to be too wedded to the idea of "best" practices that can be generically applied. Invariably with IT we find that competitive contexts, capabilities of the parties involved, and types of technology being utilized are specific to deals and have big effects on the distinctive nature of the risks experienced. Fortunately, we have at our disposal a bedrock of more general IT outsourcing experiences from which we can draw innumerable lessons. Table 10.2 encapsulates that learning from earlier studies by the present authors and others who have spelled out the detail of better practices in the field of IT outsourcing – all designed to identify, mitigate, and manage risks inherent in utilizing external IT services.

At the same time, the netsourcing research has enabled us to identify where risks are higher and lower in the netsourcing environment. In particular we find that the fluidity and uncertainty of the marketplace, together with the changing capabilities and strategic objectives of many netsourcing suppliers, and the lack of knowledge of these matters on the part of many customers, make us underline that detailed netsourcing risk analysis is an utterly essential pre-requisite for would-be customers. It is also clear that netsourcing risks require the would-be customer to be much more active that many would believe unnecessary from the "apps on tap" slogans. Netsourcing is clearly not a plug and play solution, but requires significant customer oversight from the scoping stage through to the active daily management of the supplier and its performance.

Notes

1. For an excellent study that further examines client expectations and satisfaction with ASP, see Susarla, A., Barua, A., and Whinston, A. (2003), "Understanding the Service Component of ASP: An Empirical Analysis of Satisfaction with ASP Service," *MIS Quarterly*, Vol. 27, 1, pp. 91–123.
2. The web services model uses the Web Services Definition Language (WSDL), Universal Description, Discovery and Integration (UDDI), Simple Object Access Protocol (SOAP), and Extensible Markup Language XML. Thus, the web service is a collection of protocols and standards used to enable netsourcing.
3. Jurison, J. (1995), "The Role of Risk and Return in Information Technology Outsourcing Decisions," *Journal of Information Technology*, Vol. 10, 4, pp. 239–247, 1995.
4. Our risks and ratings are derived from our eighty-six case studies and two surveys in the traditional IT outsourcing context and ten case studies and one international survey in the netsourcing context. For example, one of the greatest risks identified from our netsourcing survey was the likelihood that the netsourcing supplier would go out of business. But for traditional outsourcing, particularly in our case studies, the suppliers were stable and long-lived, such as Accenture, CSC, EDS, and IBM. Their customers were not concerned that these suppliers would go out of business – customers were much more concerned with the supplier having too much power, commoditizing IT to the point of losing any possible strategic advantage, and trying to negotiate flexible contracts.
5. Case sources: Face-to-face interviews with Michiel Steltman (cofounder and CTO Siennax), Pieter Bonkelaar (Account Manager at Siennax dedicated to ABZ) and Corné Paalvast (Operational Director at ABZ), Siennax case study by Jeroen Kreijger, Abz website and websites of partners, internal reports, press releases, and Siennax White Papers. Interviews were tape-recorded and transcribed. Some direct quotes used in the paper were translated from Dutch to English.

6. See Lacity and Willcocks (2001), op. cit. for many examples of inflexible contracting leading to failure to exploit strategic IT initiatives.
7. In selecting a start-up supplier, one risk Abz did not consider was the possibility of the *supplier going out of business* (risk 7 in Table 10.2). Because of the increased risk of supplier failure, we generally do not see the selection of a start-up supplier as a best practice for mitigating power asymmetry risks.
8. "A Portait of Siennax's Client Abz Insurance," on www.siennax.com
9. Kern, T., Lacity, M., and Willcocks, L. (2002), *Netsourcing*. Prentice Hall, New York.

CHAPTER 11

The future of global sourcing: Trends and enduring challenges

Mary Lacity and Leslie Willcocks

Introduction

When we began research in this area in 1989, the IT outsourcing (ITO) market was quite small, only an estimated US$3 billion market. Today, the global ITO market is a US$200 billion market, and, in terms of size the BPO market is rapidly catching up. Ironically, clients have sought the same benefits from outsourcing for the past 17 years. Clients typically seek operational, transformational, or strategic benefits from global sourcing (see Table 11.1). But despite the growth, learning has been painfully slow. And most disturbingly, outcomes rarely meet all the client's and supplier's a priori expectations.

As this book has shown, the key to achieving these expectations lies in the detailed management on both the client and supplier sides to realize expected benefits. We have made a contribution by identifying proven practices to help clients define a sourcing strategy, identify and nurture core in-house capabilities, evaluate sourcing options, and assess supplier capabilities. Once clients have pre-selected suppliers, we identified practices to ensure successful relationship management, including sound – yet flexible – contracts, risk mitigation, post-contract management processes and structures, and roles to ensure continued relationship alignment and cultivation. Our message is clear: a client's practices must be designed to assure that both parties can win. In particular, clients must assure that suppliers earn a reasonable profit to avoid the winner's curse.

In addition to the proven practices described in this book, another vital factor is the people who execute these practices. On the client side, successful global sourcing requires people who can emancipate themselves from the back office silo mentality to envision and enact agile sourcing networks. On the supplier side, successful global sourcing requires people

Table 11.1   Expected benefits from global outsourcing

Operational benefits	Reduced operating costs Improved service and product quality Faster delivery Financial restructuring (e.g., reducing assets, moving from fixed to variable costing)
Transformational benefits	Technology or business process catalyst – strengthening resources, services and flexibility in technologies and/or business processes to underpin business's strategic direction Business transition to facilitate and support major organizational change Business innovation to improve processes, skills and technology, while mediating financial risk to achieve competitive advantage
Strategic benefits	Focus on core competencies Strategic agility (e.g. ramp volumes up and down to adapt to business cycles, provide business continuity in times of crisis) Strategic sourcing (e.g. offshoring or using offshore competition to get better prices and service, best of breed sourcing) Enhance strategic capabilities by partnering with a complementary supplier Rapid penetration of new markets Operate in new geographies Direct profit generation through joint venturing with vendor partner.

who can emancipate themselves from the sales role to become brutally honest about what can realistically be achieved.

In this final chapter, we look ahead to identify the global sourcing trends and to articulate the enduring challenges in global sourcing. The global sourcing trends are reasonable predictions about several sourcing markets based on substantial data. The enduring challenges are widely known, but solutions are still anecdotal and experimental. These challenges represent the areas hungry for innovations in contracting, services, and relationship management.

Trends 2006 to 2011

The following eleven trends are reasonable predictions of the future of global sourcing markets.

1. **Spending will continue to rise in all global sourcing markets despite 2004–05 media attention on backsourcing.** There have been some high

profile backsourcing (returning services in-house) cases in recent years, for example Sears (1997), The Bank of Scotland (2002), JP Morgan Chase (2004) and Sainsbury (2005). Although media-worthy, these cases never have, and never will represent a dominant trend towards backsourcing. *On our figures, the most popular course of action at the end of a contract will continue to be contract renewal with the incumbent supplier.* We also estimate that a quarter will be re-tendered and awarded to new suppliers, and only a tenth back-sourced. *However a frequent occurrence within deals will continue to be "adjustment sourcing."* With adjustment sourcing, clients take back or further outsource specific tasks, people, or processes as a result of learning and changing circumstances.

2. **Developing countries beyond India will become important players in the global business and IT services market.** There will be many shifts in preferred sourcing locales and suppliers. Countries such as the Philippines and China will likely resume the role traditionally held by India – low cost staff augmentation for repetitive or highly defined tasks. India will remain a strong player, but with a different focus. The large Indian suppliers are positioning themselves higher in the value chain, competing on par with IBM, EDS, CSC, and Accenture. As the large Indian suppliers gain experience and build relationships with US customers, they will be able to demand higher prices to reflect higher value. However, the transition is tough because Indian suppliers are coping with significant challenges caused by rapid growth. Already, the large Indian suppliers are subcontracting to lower wage countries like China, and such trends are likely to continue given the rise of Indian salaries. In the United States, the recent passage of CAFTA (Central American Free Trade Agreement), will further open up ITO and BPO opportunities in Costa Rica, El Salvador, Guatemala, Honduras, Nicaragua, and the Dominican Republic. In March 2005, *CIO Insight Magazine* listed Costa Rica as the third best offshore IT destination based on an overall index of costs and risks. Many US clients already use Central American companies for Spanish-speaking business processes like help desks, patient scheduling, and data entry. Synchronous time zones are another favorable factor for US firms looking to source in Central or South America.

In Western Europe, organizations will increasingly source IT and businesses services to providers located in Eastern Europe and North Africa. For example, the Visegrad-Four Countries (Czech Republic, Hungary, Poland, and Slovakia) offer Western European firms closer proximity, less time zone differences, and lower transaction costs than Asian alternatives. Countries like Morocco already service many French firms because of their French language proficiency. Clearly, every continent will offer viable service providers.

3. **Large companies will give application service provision a second look.** When we first published our book on ASP called *Netsourcing* in 2002, we noted that large companies were not interested in ASP because they already had ASP product offerings and expertise in-house, they wanted customized services, and they wanted to source to stable providers, not risky start-up ventures. Many thought that ASP died with the dot.com burst. But there are several reasons to believe that large organizations will reconsider ASP for targeted activities. First, large organizations will want net-native applications (proprietary applications designed and delivered specifically for Internet delivery) that are only available through ASP delivery (e.g., Salesforce.com). Second, large organizations may finally be ready to abandon their expensive proprietary suites, for cheaper ASP alternatives. For example, Stephen Wildstrom of BusinessWeek predicts that corporate America will eventually source their office suites through companies like Google. Third, ASP providers got the message: customers want customized services, even if the products are standardized. The need for customized services actually increases the service providers' viability because they can generate profits by charging for value-added services. Think of companies like Xchanging and Exult (now Hewitt) that have highly customized service contracts but deliver many services in an ASP manner. Which leads us to our next lesson that ASP, and other ITO, will become increasingly bundled with BPO.

4. **BPO will over shadow ITO.** There are many hyped figures on the size of the future BPO market. On our estimates the market for mainstream BPO expenditure is likely to grow worldwide by 10 percent a year from US$140 billion in 2005 to over US$220 billion by 2010. BPO expenditure will be in areas such as the human resource function, procurement, back office administration, call centers, legal, finance and accounting, customer facing operations, and asset management.

Regardless of market size predictions, business logic drives BPO. Organizations recognize that they under-manage their back offices, and do not wish to invest in back office innovations. Suppliers are rapidly building capabilities to reap the benefits from improving inefficient processes and functions. IT provides major underpinning for, and payoff from, reformed business processes. Thus, many of the BPO deals will swallow much of the backoffices IT systems. This is also evidenced by the shift in strategy of traditional IT suppliers like IBM, HP, and EDS to provide more business process services. Suppliers will increasingly replace clients' disparate back office IT systems with web-enabled, self-serve portals.

5. **IT outsourcing will continue to grow, but with new value propositions from the market.** The ITO market has not run its course. An increasing number of organizations are outsourcing nearly all areas, with the exception of strategic planning. As markets become more mature and competitive, we will see this number continue to increase, particularly with the cost advantage from offshore providers. However, suppliers as a whole will need to become increasingly creative in their search for profitable business models. We expect innovative new value propositions from the market to reinvigorate traditional ITO markets. One example may be the consolidation of networks in the same way suppliers consolidated data centers in the 1990s. It is becoming increasingly too expensive for companies to manage private networks. There are still many opportunities to consolidate private networks to a few large suppliers. As one Lead Architect from a Fortune 500 Financial Services company noted, "We are moving towards the uni-network of science fiction. Instead of these private networks, we'll have a uni-network. To provide the illusion of a secure virtual private network is become too expensive for the providers. Even at the exorbitant rates they charge."

6. **Selective sourcing with multiple suppliers will remain the dominant trend.** For back offices, the best practice has been and will continue to be best sourcing, including a mix of in-house staff, domestic contractors, domestic suppliers, near-shore suppliers, cosourcing with strategic partners, and offshore suppliers. Our research shows consistently that, in the developed economies, over 75 percent of organizations outsource 15–50 percent of their IT budgets, typically with multiple suppliers. However, the average percentage of corporate IT budgets is set to rise. By 2007, the figures are on target to be ITO 34 percent, IT-intensive BPO 15 percent and offshoring 9 percent of that IT budget. If we take into account the rising general BPO market, use of external IT/BP services combined is likely to move from a 2005 average of 12 percent to 20 percent of the corporation's total costs by 2008. Our calculations here are conservative.

7. **Clients are taking control in driving and designing deals.** Fifteen years ago, most deals were written up and designed by suppliers. No longer. Clients are recognizing that they need to understand and control the conditions under which their money is spent. Over 80 percent of contracts are already drafted by the client or based on available templates in the industry or other sources. This represents a significant power shift towards clients, in that suppliers must now decide whether they want to earn their revenue under the clients' conditions or not, as opposed to the reverse (giving the client the conditions under which the supplier will take on

the work). One supplier recently noted "We own 80% of the market here, yet clients are now dictating to us, if we want to stay in business, we have to do it on their terms." This trend was reinforced in the 2001–04 semi-recession, but is irreversible and set to continue. We note, however, that client control can backfire if it results in the suppliers winning a "cursed" deal. In Chapter 5, we warned clients that they need to view the tendering process as a relationship building exercise rather than a spot purchase. Competitive tendering should be thought of as a healthy race among worldclass athletes, not a fight-to-the-death among gladiators. In Chapter 1, we warned suppliers to educate their clients during the earliest possible phase about what can reasonably be delivered.

8. **Clients will invest much more in contract management.** On our figures, the cost of getting to contract is between 0.4 percent and 2.5 percent of the contract value. Ongoing management costs fall between 3 percent and 8 percent of contract value. These costs will increase. This is due, first, to the rise of offshoring, where management costs typically fall between 12 percent and 15 percent of total contract value. Second, clients, albeit slowly, will learn to build their internal core capability to levels that give better payoffs from outsourcing. Third, doing the upfront work is a prime determinate of outsourcing success. After some painful experiences, clients will adopt more readily a spend-to-save philosophy for outsourcing.

9. **Outsourcing will help insourcing.** As organizations become smarter at outsourcing, they are also becoming smarter at insourcing. In-house operations are facing real competition in nearly every area and can no longer assume they will retain their monopoly status with the organization. As a result, in-house operations are adopting the techniques of the market. One such example is the use of Service Level Agreements (SLAs). This typically defines the services provided, the metrics used to evaluate the services, as well as the reporting and governance put in over the deal. Prior to outsourcing, few organizations employ the SLA technique internally. After outsourcing, nearly 60 percent have internal SLAs in some fashion.

10. **Outsourcing failures and disappointments will continue.** Outsourcing will continue to be a high risk, hidden cost process in organizations where learning is painfully slow, in deals where suppliers do not make reasonable margins, and when client organizations do not strategize, configure, contact for, monitor, and manage their deals effectively. There will also be those suppliers who over-promise and under-deliver.

Extrapolating past evidence into 2006–11, we estimate some 70 percent of selective sourcing deals will be considered relatively successful. Typically clients will be spending anything between 15 percent and 58 percent of their relevant budgets on outsourcing. In contrast, we estimate that only 50 percent of large-scale deals involving complex processes that represent more than 80 percent of the relevant budgets will be successful. Ironically, the client organizations with the messiest back offices will benefit the most from total outsourcing – if they can successfully manage the outsourcing life cycle (see Chapter 2). In contrast, companies that successfully clean up their back offices prior to outsourcing leave few opportunities for suppliers to add value.

11. **Clients will move en masse from "hype and fear" into maturity.** Underneath these predictions we expect to see from 2006 to 2011 a slow but rising tide of improvement in client's ability to manage ITO, BPO, and offshore outsourcing arrangements. One can posit a learning curve from Chapter 1 at work. From the late 1980s to the present we tracked organizations moving differently through four ITO phases. "Hype and fear" saw clients naively buying the rhetoric or, fearing the worst, avoiding outsourcing. In Phase 2 we saw Early adopters focusing on costs, and best and worst practices emerging. In Phase 3 the Market matured with the focus moving also to quality and richer practices. In Phase 4 outsourcing became institutionalized as a managerial tool, with the focus on value-added. For ITO organizations are still at different points in this model but the mass are in phases 3 and 4.

With offshore and BPO the bulk of organizations are much lower down this learning curve. However, as outsourcing moves in 2006–11 to become a core part of budgets and organizational management, learning and cross-learning in all three areas will increase. But this is only a prediction. The final CEO and senior management imperative is to make sure this happens.

Enduring challenges

In the 17 years we have been studying global sourcing, clients and suppliers have expressed some enduring complaints about themselves, the industry, and each other. In this section, we identify the enduring issues in global sourcing and present some experimental innovations to resolve them. Clearly, more pioneers are needed to validate experimental innovations and to develop and test new ones.

1. **How can back offices become truly aligned with the business?** Before outsourcing can be successful, the client organizations must resolve some of their own enduring challenges. In nearly every large organization we have researched, the back offices are not truly aligned with the

business. While senior executives may use the rhetoric of the "vital role" back offices provide, they still treat back offices as cost burdens. Consider the following example. The CEO of an $8 billion US manufacturing company had to address eroding profit margins due to decreasing prices on their commodity products. Chinese companies were proving to be formidable competitors. One of the CEO's responses was to demand a 10 percent reduction from each back office manager. This is certainly a reasonable response, and one we witnessed at many large companies facing financial crises. Or is it? The CIO at this manufacturing company had an interesting retort for his CEO. He said, "I can give you 10% off of my $80 million budget, or you can give me 10% more money so I can tackle our $800 million cost of goods sold. If you let me reduce that by 10%, I can deliver $80 million in savings." The CIO argued that the manufacturing company was highly inefficient because all 150 plants had disparate information systems. This was acceptable when 80 percent of each plant's business was local. But increasingly, the manufacturer's customers are national accounts, and the information silos impede customer ordering, delivery, and service. The CIO wanted to replace these costly silos of systems with one integrated ERP package. He promised that the ERP system would reduce the costs of goods sold and that sales would increase through better customer relations. The capital budgeting committee approved his request for more money. We note however, that this CIO's status in the organization is high because of his phenomenal record of past achievement. True strategic alignment between business units and back offices cannot occur until the back office managers have proven track records of performance: "It's very difficult to be seen as Mr. or Mrs. Strategy if the trains aren't running on time" (Steve Agnoli, CIO, Kirkpatrick & Lockhart law firm[1]).

Besides the clout of the back office manager, other structural issues must also be addressed before back offices can be aligned with the business. For example, large companies that have grown through mergers and acquisitions have typically neglected the back offices, resulting in a large number of low-stature backoffices within each business unit. Back offices that are structured as centralized shared services for transactional activities and decentralized for strategic activities can help alignment (see Chapter 3).

2. **How can suppliers' incentives be truly aligned with their clients' needs?** Since we first started to interview ITO clients and suppliers in 1989, the issue of strategic alignment between clients and suppliers has been a largely unresolved issue. Incentives are clearly mis-aligned because every dollar out of a client's pocket typically goes into the supplier's

pocket. Clients are incented to demand more services from the supplier without wanting to pay more. Suppliers are incented to squeeze as much profit from existing contracts or to sell additional services to increase revenues.

During the 1990s, clients and suppliers attempted to resolve this issue with strategic partnerships and joint ventures. The idea was that the supplier investor would sell the client's assets or excess capacity to third parties and share the revenues with the client. Examples of these deals included Swiss Bank and Perot Systems, Xerox and EDS, and Delta and AT&T. As we saw in Chapter 1, these deals did not work as planned. The suppliers had their plates full just servicing the client investors' internal needs. In addition, clients frequently oversold the value and portability of their assets. The deals we studied all reverted to fee-for-service relationships or were completely terminated.

The most innovative alignment we found is the enterprise partnership model described in Chapters 6, 7 and 8. With this model, the supplier only earns a profit based on the cost savings it delivers to the client. For example, if the client transfers US$100 million in budget to the supplier and the supplier can deliver the agreed upon services for US$80 million, the supplier earns US$10 million and the client gets rebated US$10 million (assuming a 50/50% gain share). While this is the best model of strategic alignment we have seen, it is most appropriate for clients with messy back offices. The suppliers have to be able to generate immense savings through consolidation, standardization, reduced headcount, better technology, and better processes (see Chapter 6). The model is also appropriate where economies of scale can deliver substantial savings, such as consolidating procurement across many large buyers (see Chapter 7).

3. **How can clients and suppliers manage knowledge transfer while at the same time protect intellectual property?** What happens to knowledge when you outsource? Our research shows that very few organizations have thought about, let alone formulated a knowledge strategy to deal with the consequences of knowledge retention, knowledge transfer, and securing the knowledge potential from supplier relationships. The hidden business value in knowledge leverage is left behind on the bargaining table by both parties. Yet subsequent problems and disappointments invariably have knowledge dimensions. We addressed some of the knowledge management issues in Chapter 8, but many challenges remain.

In the offshore outsourcing market, for example, knowledge transfer has been one of the biggest impediments to success. With offshore outsourcing, clients do not typically transfer knowledgeable employees to the supplier (like they typically do in large-scale domestic outsourcing).

Clients complain that offshore employees have little understanding of their business domains. It is quite expensive to train offshore supplier employees, and the threat of supplier turnover and loss of intellectual property (IP) is high. One US company solved these issues in the following way.

Managers from a US Industrial Equipment Manufacturer were very concerned about knowledge transfer and protection of IP when they outsourced the development of strategic embedded software products offshore.[2] They implemented two practices. First, Industrial Equipment had to give the suppliers domain knowledge training in tools, methodologies, and technologies used at Industrial Equipment. Industrial Equipment made the suppliers ensure that trained supplier employees remained on the account for a certain period of time, or the suppliers had to reimburse training costs. Second, they dispensed work between three offshore suppliers (two large Indian suppliers and one boutique Indian supplier) to effectively distribute the intellectual property. They view their IP as a puzzle. By distributing small pieces among three suppliers, no one supplier can assemble the puzzle on their own. According to the manager of engineering:

> We keep a very tight rein on where our IP is and who has it. We never let any one development team or any one vendor see too much at one time. We feel it would be impossible for our IP to be lost through offshore sourcing.

Utilizing multiple suppliers also helps Industrial Equipment to limit the risk of a dependence on one supplier or losing the advantages of a competitive environment.

---

4. **How can clients retain enough knowledge when engaging in large-scale outsourcing?** Whereas the previous issue focused on knowledge transfer, this issue focuses on the client's knowledge retention. After the first few years of a large outsourcing contract, the client's knowledge retention can dramatically erode through attrition. While all organizations deal with turnover, clients that extensively outsource have a smaller pool of talent to attract, retain, and develop. We have increasingly heard clients say, "Where will the next generation of our project managers come from?" While the core capabilities model addresses what types of talent to nurture, there are unresolved HR management issues associated with its

implementation. These include: How can client organizations pay them enough to compete with service providers? How can client organizations provide them consistently with the level of challenge they look for in the job? How can client organizations provide them with a career path despite the very small numbers? We have not found organizations that have dealt successfully with all these issues.

5. **How can clients and suppliers sustain the early enthusiasm of budding relationships for the long term?** During the past 15 years, a number of pundits have referred to outsourcing relationships as marriages. With that analogy, clients and suppliers perceive each other as seductive partners during the wooing phase, enthusiastic partners during the honeymoon phase, then bored partners during the "seven year itch."

We have called this later phase the "mid-contract sag," and we found that it usually occurs in year three, not seven. The mid-contract sag occurs after the supplier has dispensed all their transformational levers (consolidation, standardization, reduced headcount, better technology, and better processes). The suppliers' transformation leaders typically move on to new challenges on new accounts. The remaining staff on both client and supplier sides are too exhausted or lack ideas for launching new rounds of transformation.

How can the relationship be invigorated? Throughout this book, we have addressed some practices to address this issue, such as the Supplier Development Capability discussed in Chapter 3, and Xchanging's plans for sustainability (Chapters 6 and 7). Beyond our work, there are a few case studies that suggest that outsourcing relationships can evolve from a fee-for-service relationship to a "co-sourcing"[3] or "insourcing"[4] elationship.[5]

But one thing is clear, contract renewal is not indicative of a sustainable relationship. We found that contracts are renewed primarily because of the high switching costs, not because partners are still thrilled with each other. The issue here is not longevity, but sustainability of fresh innovations. Returning to the marriage analogy, the partners in sustainable relationships help each other actualize their potential as individuals and as partners.

Final thoughts

As academics, we have always seen our role in outsourcing as "organizational therapists." Because we are outsiders, both clients and suppliers are able to truthfully share their experiences with us. This allows us to bypass agendas, politics, and "saving face" to illuminate and address real challenges in outsourcing. We do our best to ensure that outsourcing benefits both client and supplier organizations by disseminating the best and proven practices we find in innovative relationships. In addition, we warn of well-intended, yet poisonous practices. We are continually awed by the pioneers in the field who continue to tackle the hard issues, experiment with new contracting and services, and start new enterprises. Not all of them succeed, but the outsourcing industry will prosper only through such persistence, innovation, and sheer hard work. We look forward to working with and learning from the pioneers, and also from those practitioners who make their own contribution daily towards improving the global sourcing of business and IT services.

Notes

1. Levinson, M. (2004), "CIO and CEO: How to Work with Your Boss," *CIO Magazine*, October 1.
2. This case comes from the work of Rottman, J. and Lacity, M., University of Missouri-St.Louis Campus Research award for $12,485, to conduct case studies on Offshore Outsourcing of IT, 2004–05.
3. See for example the eight-year relationship between a US Financial Services Firm and an Indian supplier in Kaiser, K. and Hawk, S. (2004), "Evolution of Offshore Software Development: From Outsourcing to Cosourcing," *MIS Quarterly Executive*, Vol. 3, 2, June, pp. 69–81.
4. See the optimistic examples from Friedman, T. (2005), *The World is Flat*, Farrar, Strauss, and Giroux, New York.
5. Kaiser, K. and Hawk, S. (2004), op. cit.

Authors' publications on global sourcing of business and IT services

Books

Cullen, S. and Willcocks, L. (2003), *Intelligent IT Outsourcing: Eight Building Blocks For Success*, Butterworth-Heinemann, Oxford.

Currie, W. and Willcocks, L. (1998), *New Strategies In IT Outsourcing: Major Trends and Global Best Practices*, Business Intelligence, London.

Kern, T., Lacity, M., and Willcocks, L. (2002), *Netsourcing: Renting Business Applications and Services Over a Network*, Prentice Hall, New York (Chinese translation, 2005).

Kern, T. and Willcocks, L. (2001), *The Relationship Advantage: Information Technologies, Sourcing and Management*, Oxford University Press, Oxford.

Lacity, M. and Willcocks, L. (2001), *Global IT Outsourcing: Search For Business Advantage*, Wiley, Chichester. (Korean translation, 2004; Arabic translation, 2005; Second Edition with Sara Cullen forthcoming, 2007, as *Global IT Outsourcing: 21st Century Search for Business Advantage.*)

Lacity, M. and Hirschheim, R. (1995), *Beyond the Information Systems Bandwagon: The Insourcing Response*, Wiley, Chichester.

Lacity, M. and Hirschheim, R. (1993), *Information Systems Outsourcing: Myths, Metaphors and Realities*, Wiley, Chichester.

Willcocks, L., Olson, N., and Petherbridge, P. (2002), *Making IT Count: Strategy, Delivery Infrastructure*, Butterworth-Heinemann, Oxford.

Willcocks, L. and Sauer, C. (2001), *Moving To E-Business*. Random House, London.

Willcocks, L. and Lacity, M. (eds) (1998), *Strategic Sourcing of Information Systems*, Wiley, Chichester.

Willcocks, L. and Fitzgerald, G. (1994), *A Business Guide to Outsourcing Information Technology: A Study of European Best Practice in the Selection, Management and Use of External IT Services*, Business Intelligence, London.

Refereed journal publications

Cullen, S., Seddon, P., and Willcocks, L. (2005), "ITO Configuration: Research into Defining and Designing Outsourcing Arrangements," *Journal of Strategic Information Systems*, December, Vol. 14, 357–387.

Cullen, S., Seddon, P., and Willcocks, L. (2005), "Managing Outsourcing: The Lifecycle Imperative," *MIS Quarterly Executive*, June, pp. 229–246.

Cullen, S. and Willcocks, L. (2004), "IT Outsourcing: Carving The Right Strategy," *General Management Review*, January–March, pp. 1–6.

Currie, W. and Willcocks, L. (1998), "Analysing IT Outsourcing Decisions in the Context of Size, Interdependency and Risk," *Information Systems Journal*, Vol. 8, 2, pp. 119–143.

Feeny, D., Lacity, M., and Willcocks, L. (2005), "Taking the Measure of Outsourcing Providers," *Sloan Management Review*, Vol. 46, 3, pp. 41–48.

Feeny, D. and Willcocks, L. (1998), "Core IS Capabilities for Exploiting Information Technology," *Sloan Management Review*, Vol. 39, 3, pp. 9–21.

Feeny, D. and Willcocks, L. (1998), "Redesigning the IS Function Around Core Capabilities," *Long Range Planning*, June, Vol. 32, 3, pp. 354–367.

Hindle, J., Willcocks, L., Feeny, D., and Lacity, M. (2003), "Value-added Outsourcing at Lloyds and BAE Systems," *Knowledge Management Review*, Vol. 6, 4, pp. 28–31.

Hirschheim, R. and Lacity, M. (2000), "Information Technology Insourcing: Myths and Realities," *Communications of the ACM*, Vol. 43, 2, pp. 99–108.

Kern, T. and Willcocks, L. (2002), "Exploring Relationships in IT Outsourcing: The Interaction Approach," *European Journal of Information Systems*, Vol.11, 1, pp. 3–19.

Kern, T. and Willcocks, L. (2002), "Exploring ASP as Sourcing Strategy: Theoretical Perspectives Propositions for Practice," *Journal of Strategic Information Systems*, Vol. 11, 2, pp. 153–177.

Kern, T., Willcocks, L., and van Heck, E. (2002), "The Winners Curse in IT Outsourcing: Strategies for Avoiding Relational Trauma," *California Management Review*, Vol. 44, 2, pp. 47–69.

Kern, T., Willcocks, L., and Lacity, M. (2002), "Application Service Provision: Risk Assessment and Mitigation," *MIS Quarterly Executive*, June, Vol. 1, 2, pp.113–126.

Kern, T. and Willcocks, L. (2000), "Contracts, Control, and Presentation in IT Outsourcing: Research in Thirteen UK Organisations," *Journal of Global Information Management*, Vol. 8, 4, pp. 20–35.

Kern, T. and Willcocks, L. (2000), "Exploring IT Outsourcing Relationships: Theory and Practice," *Journal of Strategic Information Systems*, Vol. 9, pp. 321–350.

Lacity, M., Feeny, D., and Willcocks, L. (2004), "Commercializing the Back Office at Lloyd's of London: Outsourcing and Strategic Partnerships Revisited," *European Management Journal*, April, Vol. 22, 2, pp. 127–140.

Lacity, M. and Willcocks, L. (2003), "Information Technology Sourcing Reflections," *Wirtschaftsinformatik*, Special Issue on Outsourcing, Vol. 45, 2, pp. 115–125.

Lacity, M., Feeny, D., and Willcocks, L. (2003), "Transforming a back-Office Function: Lessons from BAE Systems' Experience with an Enterprise Partnership," *MIS Quarterly Executive*, Vol. 2, 2, pp. 86–103.

Lacity, M. (2002), "Global Information Technology Sourcing: More Than a Decade of Learning," *IEEE Computer*, Vol. 35, 8, pp. 26–33.

Lacity, M. and Willcocks, L. (2000), "A Survey of IT Outsourcing Experiences in USA and UK," *Journal of Global Information Management*, March, Vol. 8, 2, pp. 23–39.

Lacity, M. and Willcocks, L. (1998), "An Empirical Investigation of Information Technology Sourcing Practices: Lessons From Experience," *MIS Quarterly*, Vol. 22, 3, pp. 363–408.

Lacity, M. and Willcocks, L. (1997), "IT Outsourcing – Examining the Privatization Option in US Public Administration," *Information Systems Journal*, June, Vol. 7, 2, pp. 1–24.

Lacity, M., Willcocks, L., and Feeny, D. (1996), "The Value of Selective IT Sourcing," *Sloan Management Review*, Vol. 37, 3, pp. 13–25.

Lacity, M. and Willcocks, L. (1996), "Interpreting Information Technology Sourcing Decisions from a Transaction Cost Perspective: Findings and Critique," *Accounting, Management and Information Technology*, Vol. 5, 3/4, pp. 203–244.

Lacity, M., Willcocks, L., and Feeny, D. (1995), "IT Outsourcing: Maximise Flexibility and Control," *Harvard Business Review*, May–June, pp. 84–93.

Lacity, M. and Hirschheim, R. (1995), "Benchmarking as Survival Strategy in Mis-Aligned Organizations," *Journal of Strategic Information Systems*, Vol. 4, 2, pp. 165–185.

Lacity, M., Hirschheim, R., and Willcocks, L. (1994), "Realizing Outsourcing Expectations: Incredible Expectations, Credible Outcomes," *Information Systems Management*, Fall, Vol. 11, 4, pp. 7–18.

Lacity, M. and Hirschheim, R. (1993), "The Information Systems Outsourcing Bandwagon: Look Before You Leap," *Sloan Management Review*, Fall, Vol. 35, 1, pp. 72–86.

Lacity, M. and Hirschheim, R. (1993), "Implementing Information Systems Outsourcing: Key Issues and Experiences of an Early Adopter," *Journal of General Management*, Autumn, Vol. 19, 1, pp. 17–31.

Margetts, H. and Willcocks, L. (1994), "Informatization in Public Sector Organizations: Distinctive or Common Risks?" *Informatization and the Public Sector*, Vol. 3, 1, pp. 1–19.

Rottman, J. and Lacity, M. (2004), "Twenty Practices for Offshore Sourcing," *MIS Quarterly Executive*, Vol. 3, 3, pp. 117–130.

Willcocks, L. and Feeny, D. (2006), "IT Outsourcing and Core IS Capabilities: Challenges and Lessons at DuPont," *Information Systems Management Journal*, December, Vol. 23, 1, pp. 49–56.

Willcocks, L., Feeny, D., and Olson, N. (2006), "IT Outsourcing and Retained Core IS Capabilities: Implementation Challenges and Lessons." *European Management Journal*, March, Vol. 24, 1, pp. 20–33.

Willcocks, L., Hindle, J., Feeny, D., and Lacity, M. (2004), "Information Technology and Business Process Outsourcing: The Knowledge Potential," *Information Systems Management*, Summer, Vol. 21, 3, pp. 7–15.

Willcocks, L. Hindle, J., Feeny, D., and Lacity, M. (2003), "Knowledge in Outsourcing – The Missed Business Opportunity." *Knowledge Management Journal*, Vol. 7, 2, pp. 3–9.

Willcocks, L. and Plant, R. (2003), "How Corporations E-Source: From Business Technology Projects to Value Networks," *Information Systems Frontiers*, Spring. Vol. 5, 2, pp. 175–194.

Willcocks, L. and Lacity, M. (1999), "Information Technology Outsourcing: Practices, Lessons, and Prospects," *Australian Stock Exchange Review*, No. 2, pp. 44–49.

Willcocks, L., Lacity, M., and Kern, T. (1999), "Risk in IT Outsourcing Strategy Revisited: Longitudinal Case Research at LISA," *Journal of Strategic Information Systems*, Vol. 8, pp. 285–314.

Willcocks, L. and Lacity, M. (1999), "IT Outsourcing in Insurance Services: Risk, Creative Contracting, and Business Advantage," *Information Systems Journal*, Vol. 9, 61, pp. 1–18.

Willcocks, L. and Kern, T. (1998), "IT Outsourcing as Strategic Partnering: The Case of the Inland Revenue," *European Journal of Information Systems*, Vol. 7, 29–45.

Willcocks, L., Currie, W., and Jackson, S. (1997), "In Pursuit of the Reengineering Agenda in Public Administration," *Public Administration*, Vol. 75, 4, pp. 617–649. ANBAR EXCELLENCE CITATION, 1998.

Willcocks, L. and Currie, W. (1997), "IT Outsourcing in Public Service Contexts: Towards the Contractual Organization?" *British Journal of Management*, June, Vol. 8, pp. S107–120.

Willcocks, L. and Currie, W. (1996), "Information Technology and Radical Reengineering: Emerging Issues in Major Projects," *European Journal of Work and Organizational Psychology*, Vol. 5, 3, pp. 325–350.

Willcocks, L., Fitzgerald, G., and Lacity, M. (1996), "To Outsource IT Or Not? Recent Research on Economics and Evaluation Practice," *European Journal of Information Systems*, Vol. 5, 3, pp. 143–160.

Willcocks, L., Fitzgerald, G., and Feeny, D. (1995), "IT Outsourcing: The Strategic Implications," *Long Range Planning*, Vol. 28, 5, pp. 59–70.

Willcocks, L., Lacity, M., and Fitzgerald, G. (1995), "Information Technology Outsourcing in Europe and the USA: Assessment Issues," *International Journal of Information Management*, Vol. 15, 5, pp. 333–351.

Willcocks, L. and Choi, C. (1995), "Cooperative Partnership and 'Total' IT Outsourcing: From Contractual Obligation To Strategic Alliance?" *European Management Journal*, Vol. 13, 1, pp. 67–78.

Willcocks, L. (1994), "Managing Information Systems in UK Public Administration – Trends and Future Prospects," *Public Administration*, Vol. 72, 2, pp.13–32.

Willcocks, L. and Fitzgerald, G. (1993), "Market as Opportunity? Outsourcing IT and Services in the United Kingdom," *Journal of Strategic Information Systems*, Vol. 2, 3, pp. 92–108.

Refereed conference proceedings

Cullen, S., Seddon, P., and Willcocks, L. (2006), "What is IT Outsourcing Success?: A Multi-Dimensional Perspective," *Proceedings of the Thirty-Eighth Hawaii International Conference on Systems Sciences*, Hawaii, January.

Currie, W. and Willcocks, L. (1998), "Large-Scale IT Outsourcing: The Case of British Aerospace," *Proceedings of the Third UK Association for Information Systems Conference*, Lincoln, April.

Currie, W. and Willcocks, L. (1997), "Analysing IT Outsourcing Decisions in the Context of Size, Interdependency and Risk," *Proceedings of the Second UK Association for Information Systems Conference*, Cranfield, June.

Currie, W. and Willcocks, L. (1996), "The Impact of Compulsive Competitive Tendering of IT Services in Local Government," *Proceedings of the Third Financial Information Systems Conference*, Sheffield, September 9–10th.

Fitzgerald, G. and Willcocks, L. (1993), "IT Outsourcing in The United Kingdom and Europe – Recent Research Evidence," *Proceedings of the Fourteenth International Conference in Information Systems*, Orlando, FL, December 11–14.

Hirschheim, R. and Lacity, M. (1998), "Reducing Information Systems Costs Through Insourcing: Experiences from the Field", *Proceedings of the Thirty-first Annual Hawaii International Conference on System Sciences*, Kona, Hawaii, January 6–9.

Kern, T., Willcocks, L., and Heck, E. (2000), "Evidence of a Winners Curse in ICT Outsourcing and Its Effects on the Outsourcing Relationship," *Academy of Management Conference*, Toronto, August 7–9.

Kern, T. and Willcocks, L. (1999), "Presentation in Contracting for IT Outsourcing. A Study of Thirteen Organizations," *Proceedings of the Seventh European Conference in Information Systems*, Copenhagen, June 23–25.

Kern, T. and Willcocks, L. (1998), "Cooperative Relationship Strategy in Global Information Technology Outsourcing: The Case of Xerox Corporation," *Proceedings of the Fifth International Conference on Multi-Organizational Partnerships and Cooperative Strategy*, Balliol College, Oxford, July.

Kern, T. and Willcocks, L. (1996), "The Enabling and Determining Environment: Neglected Issues in IT Outsourcing Strategy," *Proceedings of the Fourth European Conference in Information Systems*, Lisbon, July 2–4.

Kumar, K. and Willcocks, L. (1996), "Offshore Outsourcing: A Country Too Far?" *Proceedings of the Fourth European Conference in Information Systems*, Lisbon, July 2–4.

Lacity, M. and Hirschheim, R. (1994), "Information Systems Outsourcing Evaluations: Lessons from the Field," *Proceedings of the IFIP TC8 Open Conference on Business Process Re-engineering*, Queensland Gold Coast, Australia, May 8–11.

Lacity, M. and Hirschheim, R. (1994), "The Role of Benchmarking Services in Demonstrating I.S. Effectiveness," *Proceedings of the Second European Conference on Information Systems,* Nijenrode, The Netherlands, May 30–31.

Lacity, M. and Hirschheim, R. (1993), "The Information Systems Outsourcing Bandwagon," *Proceedings of the Management of*

Change: Market Testing and Outsourcing of IT Services, London, May 19.

Oshri, I., Kotlarsky, J., and Willcocks, L. (2005), "Before, During, and After Face-To-Face Meetings: Lifecycle of Social Ties in Globally Distributed Teams," *Proceedings of the International Conference in Information Systems*, Las Vegas, NV, December 11–14.

Plant, R. and Willcocks, L. (2004), "The Sourcing of eBusiness Projects: Research into Practice," *Proceedings of the Thirty-Seventh Hawaii International Conference on Systems Sciences*, Hawaii, January.

Seddon, P., Cullen, S., and Willcocks, L. (2002), "Does Domberger's General Theory of the Contracting Organization Explain Satisfaction with IT Outsourcing?" *Proceedings of the International Conference in Information Systems*, Barcelona, December.

Willcocks, L. (2003), "IT and Business Process Outsourcing in Europe, USA and Australia: Recent Research," *Proceedings of the CRIC Conference on Knowledge Intensive Services and Changing Organizational Forms*, Manchester, November 26–27.

Willcocks, L. and Feeny, D. (2003), "Implementing Core IT Capabilities," *Society For Information Management Conference*, Seattle, December 13.

Willcocks, L. and Lacity, M. (1999), "IT Sourcing at Polaris: Risk, Creative Contracting and Business Advantage," *Proceedings of the Seventh European Conference in Information Systems*, Copenhagen, June 23–25. WINNER OF BEST CASE STUDY PAPER.

Willcocks, L., Lacity, M., and Kern, T. (1999), "IT Outsourcing and Risk Mitigation: Recent Case Research," *Proceedings of the Fifth Decision Sciences Conference*, Athens, July 5–7.

Willcocks, L. and Currie, W. (1997), "IT Outsourcing and Risk Mitigation at the Logistic Information System Agency: A Case Research Study," *Proceedings of the 1997 British Academy of Management Conference*, London, September.

Willcocks, L. and Kern, T. (1997), "IT Outsourcing as Strategic Partnering: The Case of the UK Inland Revenue," *Proceedings of the Fifth European Conference in Information Systems*, Cork, June. WINNER OF OFFICERS' PRIZE FOR EXCELLENCE.

Willcocks, L. and Feeny, D. (1996), "Reconfiguring the Information Systems Function: A Core Capabilities Approach," *Proceedings of the Australasian Conference in Information Systems*, Hobart, December 12–14.

Willcocks, L. and Currie, C. (1996), "Information Technology in Public Services: Towards the Contractual Organization?" *Proceedings of the Tenth Annual Conference of the British Academy of Management*, Aston Business School, Birmingham, September 15–18.

Willcocks, L., Lacity, M., and Fitzgerald, G. (1995), "IT Outsourcing in Europe and the USA: Assessment Issues," *Proceedings of the Third European Conference on Information Systems*, Athens, Greece, June 1–3. BEST CASE STUDY PAPER.

Willcocks, L., Fitzgerald, G., and Feeny, D. (1994), "Information Technology Outsourcing: From Incrementalism to Strategic Intent," *Proceedings of the Second SISNET Conference*, Barcelona, September 26–28.

Willcocks, L. and Fitzgerald, G. (1994), "Towards the Residual IS Organization? Research on IT Outsourcing Experiences in the United Kingdom," *Proceedings of IFIP WG8.2 Transactions on Computer Science and Technology*, University of Michigan, USA, June 12–14.

Willcocks, L. and Fitzgerald, G. (1994), "Relationships in Outsourcing: Contracts and Partnerships," *Proceedings of the Second European Conference on Information Systems*, Nijenrode, The Netherlands, May 30–31.

Willcocks, L. and Fitzgerald, G. (1994), "The Outsourcing of Information Technology," *Proceedings of the British Academy of Management Conference*, University of Lancaster, September 12–14.

Willcocks, L. and Fitzgerald, G. (1994), Contracting for IT Outsourcing: Recent Research Evidence," *Proceedings of the Fifteenth Annual International Conference in Information Systems*, Vancouver, December 13–16, pp. 91–98.

Willcocks, L. and Fitzgerald, G. (1994), "To Outsource IT or Not? Recent Research on Economics and Evaluation Practice," *Proceedings of the Evaluation of IT Investments Conference*, Henley Management College, September 13–14.

Other publications

Cullen, S., Willcocks, L., and Seddon, P. (2001), *IT Outsourcing Practices In Australia*, Joint Deloitte-Touche Tohmatsu and University of Melbourne.

Feeny, D., Willcocks, L., and Lacity, M. (2006), "Business Process Outsourcing, Knowledge, and Innovation," in R. Hirschheim, A. Heinzl, and J. Dibbern (eds), *Information Systems Outsourcing in the New Economy*, Springer-Verlag, Berlin-Heidelberg-New York.

Feeny, D., Willcocks, L., and Lacity, M. (2003), *Business Process Outsourcing: The Promise of Enterprise Partnership*, Xchanging sponsored research published as an Executive Research Briefing for Templeton College, Oxford in March.

Feeny, D. and Willcocks, L. (2000), "Core Capabilities and Selective Sourcing. Leadership Strategies," in T. Davenport and R. Marchand (eds), *Mastering Information Management*, FT/Pitman, London.

Feeny, D. and Willcocks, L. (1999), "The Emerging IT Function – Changing Capabilities and Skills," in W. Currie and R. Galliers (eds), *Rethinking MIS*, Oxford University Press, Oxford.

Hirschheim. R. and Lacity, M. (2002), "Four Stories of Information Systems Insourcing," in R. Hirschheim, A. Heinzl, and J. Dibbern (eds), *Information Systems Outsourcing in the New Economy*, Springer-Verlag, Berlin-Heidelberg-New York, pp. 348–391.

Kern, T., Lacity, M., and Willcocks, L. (2002), "Customer Decision Drivers for Netsourcing," *Montgomery Research Europe*, pp. 82–89.

Kern, T. and Willcocks, L. (2002), "Contract, Control and 'Presentation' in IT Outsourcing: Research in Thirteen Organizations," in Tan, F. (ed.), *Advanced Topics In Global Information Management*, Idea Group Publishing, Hershey, PA, pp. 227–249.

Kern, T., Lacity, M., Willcocks, L., Zuiderwijk, R., and Teunissen, W. (2001), *ASP Market-Space Report 2001: Mastering the Customers' Expectations*, CMG Report, pp. 1–57.

Kern, T. and Willcocks, L. (1999), "Cooperative Relationship Strategy in Global IT Outsourcing: The Case of Xerox Corporation's Relationship Locally," in D. Faulkner, J. Child and M. Le Rond (eds), *Cooperative Strategies*, Oxford University Press, Oxford.

Lacity, M., Willcocks, L, and Feeny, D. (2005), "BPO as Enterprise Partnership: The BAE-Xchanging Transformation Strategy For HR Procurement," in P. Brudenall (ed.), *Technology and Offshore Outsourcing Strategies*, Palgrave, Great Britain, pp. 133–160.

Lacity, M., Willcocks, L., and Feeny, D. (2004), "Transforming Indirect Procurement Spend: The Case of BAE Systems and Xchanging's Enterprise Partnership," in P. Brudenall (ed.), *IT and Business Process Outsourcing Strategies*. Heidelberg Press, London.

Lacity, M., Willcocks, L., and Feeny, D. (2004), "Transforming Indirect Procurement Spend: A Case Study," *Cutter Consortium*, Vol. 5, 2, pp. 1–25.

Lacity, M. (2002), "Twenty Customer and Supplier Lessons on IT Sourcing," *Cutter Consortium*, Vol. 3, 3, pp. 1–23.

Lacity, M. and Willcocks, L. (2002), "Survey of IT Outsourcing Experiences In US and UK Organizations," in F. Tan (ed.), *Advanced*

Topics In Global Information Management, Idea Group Publishing, Hershey, PA, pp. 160–189.

Lacity, M. and Willcocks, L. (2000), "IT Outsourcing Relationships: A Stakeholder Perspective," in R. Zmud (ed.), *Framing the Domains of IT Management Research: Glimpsing The Future Through The Past*, Jossey Bass, New York, pp. 355–384.

Lacity, M. and Willcocks, L. (2000), *Inside IT Outsourcing: A State-of-the-Art Report. Executive Report*, Templeton College, Oxford, May.

Lacity, M., Willcocks, L., and Feeny, D. (1999),: IT Outsourcing: Maximizing Flexibility and Control," in Harvard Business Review (ed.), *Business Value From IT*, Harvard Business Press, Cambridge, MA.

Lacity, M., Hirschheim, R., and Willcocks, L. (1997), "Realizing Outsourcing Expectations," in R. Umbaugh (ed.), *Handbook of IS Management*, Auerbach, Boston.

Lacity, M., Willcocks, L., and Feeny, D. (1997), "The Value of Selective IT Sourcing," in L. Willcocks, D. Feeny, and G. Islei (eds), *Managing IT as a Strategic Resource*, McGraw Hill, pp. 277–303.

Lacity, M. (1997), "IT Outsourcing in the US: Experiences, Trends, and Lessons," in W. Currie, and L. Willcocks (eds), *New Strategies in IT Outsourcing: Major Trends and Global Best Practices*, Business Intelligence, London, pp. 39–58.

Lacity, M., and Hirschheim, R. (1997), "Information Systems Outsourcing: What Problems are We Really Trying to Solve?" in R. Galliers and W. Curry (eds), *Re-thinking Management Information Systems*, Oxford University Press, pp. 326–360.

Lacity, M., Willcocks, L., and Feeny, D. (1996), "Sourcing Information Technology Capability. A Decision-Making Framework," in M. Earl (ed.), *Information Management: The Organizational Dimension*, Oxford University Press, Oxford, pp. 399–425.

Lacity, M. and Willcocks, L. (1996), "Best Practices in Information Technology Sourcing," *The Oxford Executive Research Briefings*, No. 2. Templeton College, Oxford, June.

Lacity, M. and Hirschheim, R. (1996), "Information Systems Benchmarking Practices," in L. Willcocks (ed.), *Investing in Information Systems*, Chapman and Hall, London, pp. 313–331.

Poppo, L. and Lacity, M. (2002), "The Normative Value of Transaction Cost Economics: What Managers Have Learned About TCE Principles in the IT Context," in R. Hirschheim, A. Heinzl, and J. Dibbern (eds), *Information Systems Outsourcing in the New Economy*, Springer-Verlag, Berlin-Heidelberg-New York, pp. 235–276.

Rottman, J. and Lacity, M. (2004), "Proven Practices for IT Offshore Outsourcing," *Cutter Consortium*, Vol. 5, 12, pp. 1–27.

Willcocks, L., Feeny, D., and Lacity, M. (2006), "Outsourcing, Knowledge, and Organizational Innovation: A Study of Enterprise Partnership," *Business Process Transformation*, Idea Group Publishing, Hershey, PA.

Willcocks, L. and Cullen, S. (2005), *The Outsourcing Enterprise 1: The CEO Role in Creating Strategic Advantage*, Logicacmg, London.

Willcocks, L. and Cullen, S. (2005), *The Outsourcing Enterprise 2: The Power of Relationships*, Logicacmg, London.

Willcocks, L. and Cullen, S. (2005), *The Outsourcing Enterprise 3: Selecting Suppliers and their Capabilities*, Logicacmg, London.

Willcocks, L., Hindle, J., Feeny, D., and Lacity, M. (2004), "Leveraging Knowledge Through Outsourcing: Enterprise Partnering in the London Insurance Market," in R. Lawson (ed.), *Achieving Competitive Advantage Through Collaborative Partnerships*. CO, London.

Willcocks, L., Lacity, M., and Cullen, S. (2006). "Information Technology Sourcing: Fifteen Years of Learning," in C. Avgerou, Robin Mansell, Danny Quah and Roger Silverstone (eds), *Oxford Handbook of ICTs*, Oxford University Press, Oxford.

Willcocks, L. and Plant, R. (2004), "E-Sourcing: From Projects to ASPs and Value Networks," in W. Currie (ed.), *Value Creation For E-Business Models*, Butterworth-Heinemann, Oxford.

Willcocks, L. (2002), "Outsourcing IT and E-Business," in D. Remenyi and A. Brown (eds), *Make or Break Issues in IT Management*, Butterworth, Oxford.

Willcocks, L. and Lacity, M. (2000), "Strategic Dimensions of IT Outsourcing," in D. Marchand and T. Davenport (eds), *Mastering Information Management* FT/Pitman, London.

Willcocks, L. and Lacity, M. (1999), "Experience of Information Technology Outsourcing," in J. Angel (ed.), *The Outsourcing Practice Manual*, Sweet and Maxwell, London.

Willcocks, L., Graeser, V., and Lester, S. (1999), "Cybernomics and IT Productivity: Not Business as Usual," in R. Galliers, D. Leidner, and B. Baker (eds), *Strategic Information Management*, Butterworth Heinemann, London.

Willcocks, L. and Currie, W. (1998), "IT Outsourcing in Public Service Contexts: Towards the Contractual Organization?" in M. Mische (ed.), *The High Performance IT Organization*, Auerbach Publications, Oxford.

Willcocks, L., Lacity, M., and Fitzgerald, G. (1997), "IT Outsourcing In Europe and the USA," in L. Willcocks, D. Feeny, and G. Islei (eds),

Managing IT as a Strategic Resource, McGraw Hill, Maidenhead, pp. 306–337.

Willcocks, L. and Fitzgerald, G. (1996), "The Changing Shape of the Information Systems Function," in M. Earl (ed.), *Information Management: The Organizational Dimension*, Oxford University Press: Oxford, pp. 270–294.

Willcocks, L., Lacity, M., and Fitzgerald, G. (1995), "Information Technology Outsourcing: Economics, Contracting and Measurement," in B. Farbey, F. Land, and D. Targett (eds), *Hard Money, Soft Outcomes: Evaluating and Managing the IT Investment*, Alfred Waller, Henley, pp. 149–172.

Willcocks, L., Fitzgerald, G., and Feeny, D. (1993), "Effective IT Outsourcing – The Evidence in Europe," in Elite/BCS (eds), *The Management of Change: Market Testing and Outsourcing of IT Services*, Elite/ British Computer Society, London.

INDEX

Aberdeen Group, 179
Abz Insurance, case study of risk
    management, 5
  Abz–Siennax relationship, 267–8
  company background, 261
  customer development, 263, 269
  IT outsourcing of, 262–3
  mapping to netsourcing service stack, 268
  supplier management, 263–4, 269
  transition process, 265
Accenture, 19, 28, 77, 104, 107, 147, 149, 214,
    229, 233, 277
ACS, 104, 147
adversarial interactions, *see* client and supplier
    relationships, types of
agency theory, 13
Amoco, 89
AMS, 200
analysis strategy, 46
Andersen Consulting, 146
AON, 147
application service provision, 5, 256–7
  netsourcing risks and risk management,
    269–272
architect phase, 38, 40, 58
Arco, 89
ASP, *see* application service provision
AT&T, 6
auction theory, 13

back office services, 1
  approaches to, *see* back office
    transformations, approaches to
  assessment of, *see* back portfolio,
    assessment of
  challenges and issues in, 74–6
  contracts for, *see* contract models
  feedback in, 11
  learning curve for, 9–11
  market options, evaluating, *see* market
    options, for sourcing process
  nine core capabilities for, 71–4
  other, 9

sourcing options, *see* sourcing options
back office transformations, approaches to,
    98–101, *see also* core back office
    capabilities, for client interests; provider
    competencies, critical areas of; supplier
    capabilities, potential
  benefits of, 3
  capabilities to performance, 111–12
  do-it-yourself model, 4
  enterprise partnership model, 6–8
  fee-for-service outsourcing model, 5–6, 229
  joint venture model, 6, 229
  hire management consultants, 4–5
  netsourcing model, 5
  other models of, 4
back portfolio, assessment of
  core portfolio selection, 13–15
  noncore capabilities, identification of, 15–16
  as portfolio capabilities, 11–13
  theories of, 13
BAE Systems, 102–3, 104, 108
  case study of transformational HRO, *see* BAE
    systems/Xchanging, case study of
    transformational HRO
  enterprise partnership implementation at, *see*
    BAE Systems/Xchanging, enterprise
    partnership implementation at
  transformational procurement outsourcing,
    see BAE systems, transformational
    procurement outsourcing
BAE systems, transformational procurement
    outsourcing, *see also* XPS competencies
  business development, 192–202
  customer perspective of, 187
  enterprise partnership, 188–9
  lessons for customers, 203–4
  partnership issues, negotiation of, 191–2
  transition phase, 190–1
  XPS organization, 189
BAE Systems/Xchanging, case study of
    transformational HRO, 149; *see also* BAE
    Systems/Xchanging, enterprise partnership
    implementation at